GUNS ON THE
WESTERN WATERS

The U. S. S. *Carondelet,* possibly the most famous of all the river gunboats of the Civil War.

Guns on the Western Waters

The Story of River Gunboats in the Civil War

~ ~ ~ ~ ~

H. ALLEN GOSNELL

Louisiana State University Press

Baton Rouge and London

LIBRARY OF CONGRESS CATALOGING-IN-PUBLICATION DATA

Gosnell, Harpur Allen, b. 1890
    Guns on the western waters : the story of river gunboats in the
Civil War / H. Allen Gosnell. — Louisiana pbk. ed.
        p. cm.
    ISBN 0-8071-1890-7 (pbk. : alk. paper)
    1. United States—History—Civil War, 1861–1865—Naval operations.
I. Title.
E591.G67 1993
973.7'5—dc20   93-28435
                                                                    CIP

The paper in this book meets the guidelines for permanence and durability of the Committee on Production Guidelines for Book Longevity of the Council on Library Re-
sources. ⊚

Louisiana Paperback Edition, 1993

02 01 00 99 98 97 96 95 94 93   1 2 3 4 5

CONTENTS

ILLUSTRATIONS

INTRODUCTION

VERY LITTLE history of distant events can be much more than a rehash of material which has already been told or written before. Accordingly, no apologies will be made for reprinting without change the several eye-witness contributions which constitute the heart of this volume. As has so often been done, I might have taken these selections and transformed the narratives into my own words; by so doing I might perhaps receive more acclaim as a "writer of history" than will come to me under the present arrangement. I am satisfied, however, that the stories would lose a good deal through the transformation; therefore I am presenting them unchanged for that reason if for no other. If this scheme proves acceptable to the reader it should furnish him with a method of absorbing history painlessly. With the same aim in view, the "scholarly approach" is deliberately avoided in this volume. At the same time the greatest effort has been made to give every fact and judgment with the utmost accuracy.

A sufficient number of firsthand tales are included herein to provide a pretty good picture of the gunboat operations on western waters during the Civil War. Selections have been made with the aim of furnishing examples of the various phases of the fighting. However, there were a couple of events of which I have been unable to discover any suitable narratives written by participants—events which were too dramatic to omit. Accordingly I have, myself, reconstructed those happenings as well as I was able to do it from the records. I hope that the quality of that work will not seem to fall too noticeably below the standards of the rest. The other new work included herein is of two kinds. To begin with, the several firsthand contributions are tied together to form a more continuous story of the four years of war in the West. And secondly, at the start and finish, sketches are provided of the more important affairs which took place on each of the other naval "fronts." Thus it is hoped that the reader may obtain an adequate view of the whole naval war from 1861 to 1865, even though all the emphasis is on the western rivers.

Everything that appears in quotation marks is exactly as originally printed, the sole exception being a negligible number of slips of a typographical or similar nature; there has been no "editing to improve." The closest approach to any alteration of a text has been made in a couple of instances where the order of paragraphs has been changed; this was done only to bring the recorded events into chronological order and to make the story clearer to the reader. Of course a great deal has been omitted from many of the narratives, and each point of omission is indicated. In almost every case the material was deleted because it was either not interesting or not pertinent. In a few places certain sentences or phrases, if left in, would tell "how the story comes out." In one or two of the pages that follow, one may think that some of the gruesomeness should be omitted. One cannot obtain a true picture of any fighting, however, unless the fact be impressed upon him that war is not solely thrills and high adventure. Even so, I have cut out some lines which were just a bit *too* gruesome. Occasionally the gunboats suffered frightful casualties to personnel; but in this connection it is both interesting and significant to note that the flimsiest wooden vessels often could be terribly shattered by gunfire without being put out of commission.

The question of errors in the quoted material is of course a very important one. All specific errors on concrete facts are corrected in bracketed interpolations or in contiguous new paragraphs. No correction is made where the writer says something which merely *may* be wrong, provided the statement is not connected with the matter in hand and is of no consequence anyhow. Nor is issue taken with any statement where the true facts are practically unobtainable and in great controversy. In this connection in general, the reader must always bear in mind the source of the contribution, and judge its exactness, its reliability, and its value according to the position and standing of its author. This, of course, is of special importance where partisan feeling influences a writer's judgment.

Some of the tales included in this volume are told by nonnaval and nontechnical men. Accordingly, it should be remembered that their terminology is often incorrect from a naval standpoint. There is one fortunate item in this connection, however. Most of the vessels encountered in the western rivers are "boats"; they are not "ships" because they are not seagoing. Therefore the great majority—writers and readers—who call everything a "boat" up to and including the *Normandie* will unwittingly be correct more frequently in these pages than is ordinarily the case.

The reader should bear in mind three other points in order to avoid confusion. A naval officer is of course called "Captain" when he has the rank of captain. A more frequent case, however, is where an officer is called "Captain" because he is in command of some kind of a vessel; he may not even hold commissioned rank.

Formerly steering gears were so rigged that movement of the wheel to starboard, for instance, moved the *tiller* to starboard and the ship to *port*. Nowadays if the wheel is moved to starboard, the *rudder* and the ship go to starboard. Thus wheel and ship go together now; but it is well to remember, when reading the following pages, that if a steersman "ports his helm," for instance, the vessel is going to swing to the *right*.

Another confusing item is the matter of "torpedoes." We now think of torpedoes only as those missiles which travel through the water under their own power (automobile torpedoes). We speak of the anchored or floating explosive charges as "mines." Throughout the Civil War there were no automobile torpedoes. They called mines "torpedoes." In these days, the only method of moving a torpedo to its target was to fasten it onto the end of a spar projecting from the bow of a steam launch. An explosive charge so placed was called a "spar torpedo." This term is still in use though the era of the spar torpedo was a brief one. The main point to remember is that our "mines" were then known as "torpedoes."

For those who wish to delve more deeply into naval science and gunboat construction, a discussion of these subjects is provided in Chapter I. For the reader who prefers to turn immediately to the story in hand, let him proceed from this Introduction directly to Chapter II.

Finally, a word particularly to those who know part or all of the Mississippi River as it exists at the present time. It must be pointed out that this great stream changes its course to a very great degree as the years go by. Parts of it may be altered very much in the span of a few years, or even in a week. Towns disappear completely. Accordingly, few stretches of the river viewed in the following pages can even be recognized now as being the same places they were in 1861–65. The river simply has moved, and in some cases is an appreciable distance from its former channel. This is notably true at Vicksburg, for instance. Describing the topography of the various places would be awkward if the past tense were to be used continually—such as pointing out that the lay of the land "used to be" so-and-so "though it is now" something else. Therefore, a variation of the "editorial present tense" will be employed in most instances where consideration is being given to the actual setting for a battle or the like. The changes at each spot in the last eighty-five years, together with the actual and hypothetical effects of such changes, would provide a long and interesting study. For our present purpose, however, we may as well forget about such things. For the sake of smooth reading and graphic perception, let us try to picture the river in our minds only as it was while the fighting was going on.

H. ALLEN GOSNELL

Princeton, New Jersey

GUNS ON THE
WESTERN WATERS

CHAPTER I

THE GUNBOATS AND HOW THEY FOUGHT

NAVAL SCIENCE AND TACTICS

Obviously it is a highly desirable object in warfare to bring as many guns as possible to bear upon the enemy. Since the length of a ship is much greater than its breadth, more guns can be installed to fire abeam than in any other direction. Under ordinary circumstances, therefore, two hostile ships or fleets will oppose each other on roughly the same (or reverse) courses. Thus for centuries the classical engagement has taken place with the opponents arranged in two approximately parallel lines. This is equally true for sail and steam. However, as will be seen later, cases are altered considerably under conditions of constricted movement such as exist on rivers and in harbors. By 1861 the steam engine had very definitely supplanted sails as the prime mover of men-of-war, even though auxiliary sail power continued to be provided as late as the nineties. Although there were many large sailing vessels in all the navies at the outbreak of the Civil War, they were of no value in narrow waters except as stationary floating batteries.

In this war there were few fleet actions and few formal unrestricted contests between single ships or other small units. Due to the disparity of the two forces, the naval war was almost wholly one of blockade and counterblockade. The former often developed into contests between ships and forts. The latter brought attacks upon the individually weaker but seagoing blockaders by special types of vessels which, though very powerful, were able to operate only in smooth water. These new types possessed armor or rams or both. Torpedo boats, both surface and submarine, also appeared on the scene, but these will be considered later.

It was steam that brought the ram back to naval warfare from which it had been absent since the days of the oar. It is obviously impracticable to maneuver a sailing vessel in a manner sufficiently effective to ram a moving opponent. In a great many respects the days of steam men-of-war are quite analogous to the days of the galleys. The ability to control the speed and course of both types of vessels brings about a close similarity between the naval tactics of the ancients and the moderns.

Armor came in not long after steam. In these early days it was commonly built up of iron plates. It is generally thought that the *Monitor* and the *Merrimac* were the first ironclads. This is not correct. In the Crimean War, the French employed armored steam warships against the Russian fortress of Kinburn at the mouth of the Dnieper River (1855). They were perfectly good ironclad men-of-war. Possibly their popular name of "Kinburn *batteries*" has been the chief cause for the mistaken belief that they were merely immobile barges. Even some of the western river ironclads were in action before the *Monitor* and *Merrimac*. The famous duel in Hampton Roads was the first fight *between* ironclads.

The U. S. S. *Merrimac* was a wooden screw-propelled frigate sunk by her own people just before capture by the Confederates. Her captors raised her and renamed her the C. S. S. *Virginia*. As the first step in her reconstruction she was cut down almost to the water line. On the highest remaining deck was built an armored gun-house, and to her forefoot was secured an iron ram. She constituted the first counterblockade measure of any consequence. On March 8, 1862, she came out of Norfolk and rammed and sank the frigate *Congress* and the sloop-of-war *Cumberland,* both anchored sailing vessels. Her sloping armored sides proved impervious to the heavy shot which struck them. Though the reconstructed *Merrimac* was slow, the system of ramming was an effective as well as an inexpensive method of destruction. Although the victims were built of wood, their hulls would have been little, if any, less vulnerable had they been made of iron. With such a setup, the *Merrimac*'s guns were devastating but superfluous.   •

The next morning the *Merrimac* came out again for the purpose of completing the destruction of the Union squadron in the Roads. But the U. S. S. *Monitor* had arrived during the intervening night from the hands of her New York builders, thus finishing one of the most amazingly close races in naval history. A drawn battle ensued and the *Merrimac* withdrew once more. She did not again attempt to break the blockade of those waters, and her own crew blew her up two months later to prevent capture. Her slow speed, deep draft, unseaworthiness, and general unhandiness were not generally realized at the time. Accordingly, the consternation that her appearance created in Washington and throughout the North was immense—impossible to exaggerate.

"Monitor" was the christened name of this first one of a brand-new type of vessel, consisting primarily of a very low raft-like deck with practically nothing on it but a cylindrical armored turret rotated by a steam engine and enclosing two heavy guns. She possessed no ram. All subsequent men-of-war having a very low freeboard have been called "monitors." They can cross the ocean but cannot fight effectively in a seaway. The *Monitor* was the first "all-big-guns-on-the-center-line" ship. She was soon followed by double-turreted monitors mounting guns as large as 15-inch. And in 1863 the eight-year-old U. S. steam frigate *Roanoke* (a seagoing ship) appeared in reconstructed form; she had *three* centerline turrets, each with its usual pair of big guns. Her armament was that of a real battleship; she was far ahead of her time, and it is amazing that more than forty years passed before the idea caught on again. The centerline emplacement of the battery of course makes it possible to aim through the widest possible angles the greatest proportion of guns installed.

The *Merrimac* was successful on her first sally because she selected stationary targets for her ram. A stationary target is not absolutely essential, but obviously it is of immense assistance to an attacking ram. This and other important angles of the blockade-breaking problem were demonstrated early in 1863 off Charleston, South Carolina, a port often successfully used by blockade-runners. An attack was made by two Confederate ironclads upon the blockading ships in waters which were much more open than Hampton Roads. The blockaders were not at anchor but were for the most part hove to—i. e., stationary, and necessarily with fires low. The two attackers issued from the river in the darkness, damaged very seriously two steam gunboats by ramming, and caused the rest of the squadron to haul out of their reach. Here the injuries inflicted on the Federal naval forces weakened them to a negligible degree. But the moral effect was great. The blockade was "raised" for a few hours only, because the scattered blockaders returned as soon as the vicinity was clear of the enemy. The rams were not sufficiently seaworthy to venture into anything but smooth water, nor were they sufficiently speedy to engage an unwilling adversary except by surprise. Nevertheless, to everyone in the North, this kind of affair was very annoying—to put it mildly.

Three months later, in the same spot, was provided a demonstration on a grand scale of "ships *vs.* forts." A plan had been brewing for a gigantic naval attack upon the strong defenses of Charleston, the aim being the capture from seaward of the harbor and the city itself. Not only was Charleston the most important port still in the hands of the Confederates, but, together with Fort Sumter, it was the very living symbol of "Rebellion." Its occupation was mightily desired by the North. The harbor defenses of Charleston were very strong indeed; but a great fleet of ironclads was advancing to completion, and to them was assigned the mission of reducing the forts. The backbone of the ironclad squadron consisted of powerful turreted monitors, then unsurpassed in strength for smooth-water fighting. With Fort Henry and other victories of the naval forces a matter of record, it was felt that again the historic superiority of forts over ships could be disproved. The venture against Charleston included no orthodox army expedition from the land side. A considerable number of troops were employed, but wholly in conjunction with the ships in that they worked their way onto the islands and shores from seaward.

The big day was April 7, 1863. The monitors moved carefully in to the attack and commenced the slow firing of their great guns. As they advanced farther up the narrow channel, they reached points for which the exact range had been previously plotted for the hundred guns of the fortifications. The ships were harried by a strong ebb tide; they were halted by obstructions and mine fields; some never got far enough even to make their strength felt. In brief, those which succeeded in pushing on for any distance received a fearful hammering, got nowhere, and accomplished nothing. The repulse which the fleet suffered was complete. Considering the strength of the opposing forces, this was by far the biggest fight in which the Navy was engaged during the entire war. Although pushed into it against the better judgment of the commanding admiral (Samuel Francis DuPont), the fleet caused great disappointment to its many partisans in the North and to the Department in Washington which had forced the action. Forts still retained their domination over ships, and the blockade of Charleston had to be continued from off-shore for nearly two years more.

Having examined the several phases of naval warfare as conducted in the more customary locale of sea and harbor, we come now to river fighting. Here the principal factors are smooth water and shallow water. Cruising radius becomes less important. The fact that smooth water is assured helps to balance the problems arising from shallow water. Because, when a vessel does not have to be seaworthy, its bottom can be flat. And if the bottom is flat the vessel will draw less water than a vessel of equal weight and size with a more V-shaped hull (bearing in mind that the weight of a vessel determines the volume of the water displaced by it, i. e., the size of the part of the ship which is below the water line).

Further as to river fighting: although many streams are very wide at frequent points, there are not many places, even in the Mississippi, where deep water exists to any great width of channel. Hence no classic engagements on parallel courses are likely to develop. Again, because there is no need for seaworthiness or for speed in a seaway, the boats can be much wider in proportion to their length— 1:3½ for some river gunboats as against 1:11 for some early transatlantic fliers. These two factors combine in such a manner that the reader will find as many as four guns in the bow of a gunboat as compared with one or none in the case of a seagoing man-of-war. In the great majority of instances involving gun and ram, the fighting is likely to be all over before two opponents can draw abreast of one another in narrow waters. Nor are the side armor and guns of river gunboats made particularly heavy for the purpose of engaging fortifications. There is too great an advantage in favor of the latter, especially if they are established on elevated ground as is usually the case. Accordingly, a boat will not attack a fortification broadside on, from the river directly opposite it; the range will be too extremely short. Of necessity this will be the relationship when a boat attempts to run past a river fortification. That, however, is a short-term defensive operation, and the entire design of a vessel must not be influenced by such a prospect alone.

MARINE ENGINEERING

When it comes to the propulsion of these river gunboats there are several special angles which prevail. It has already been pointed out that sailing vessels are "out" so far as river fighting is concerned, except possibly to the extent of their use as floating batteries, with towboats to move them from point to point. So, we shall confine our considerations to steamboats. In this study we shall find a very heterogeneous miscellany because all of them were converted makeshifts except one group of seven. In fact, it is the exception to find any two of them similar in many respects.

As between paddle wheels and screw propellers the latter were comparative newcomers in naval engineering. Many seagoing ships were screw-propelled in 1860, but the shallow water of the rivers called for paddle wheels. It is only in very recent years that design of propeller installations has advanced to the point where adequate plants have been perfected for shallow-draft vessels. Accordingly, we shall find our river craft made up of paddle steamers almost exclusively.

There was—and is—a fairly wide variety of paddle wheels, speaking of general location alone. They may be either side wheels or stern wheels. The side wheels may be amidships or pretty well aft. The stern wheels may be all the way aft in their better-known positions; or they may be forward of the extreme stern, set in a recess between the two sides of the hull. This arrangement will be given a little further attention later on, in the description of a class of gunboats so constructed. The stern wheel is usually a single unit, but may actually be two separate wheels side by side. If the side wheels of a boat are on a divided line of shafting, each half driven by a separate engine, all maneuvering is of course facilitated immensely. Similar advantage is provided by the use of a double stern wheel, in which installations there is of course one engine for each wheel section. Maneuverability with separated side wheels is considerably greater than with a double stern wheel because of the fact that the side wheels are so much farther out from the center line of the vessel. Ability to turn quickly and in a small circle is of great advantage when fighting in narrow waters, especially when employing or avoiding ramming tactics. It was a very common thing for boats to have more than one rudder, one on each side of the stern, for instance. Some of the boats with side wheels amidships are built with such symmetrical construction of hull and arrangement of steering gear that they can be operated almost equally effectively in either direction. These are known as "double-enders"; each one carries a rudder in the bow as well as at the stern. There will be no close meeting with any such craft in this volume, however.

The reciprocating steam engine was of course the universal prime mover in self-propelled craft of the day. The steam turbine and the internal-combustion engine were still far in the future. Compound engines had scarcely been seen afloat at the time discussed here. So all our units are "simple" engines, i. e., single-expansion, even though some of them had two cylinders. The different types of engines met with herein varied in label according to the position in which their cylinder or cylinders were installed—horizontal, inclined, or vertical. If vertical, the engine might drive the side-wheel shaft directly through its piston rod, connecting rod, and crank; or, in addition to this linkage, via an overhead "walking beam" (working beam). A side wheel might be driven by either a vertical or an inclined engine. A stern wheel might be driven by a horizontal or an inclined engine, the latter being easily the most desirable for a man-of-war, in order to have the engine below the water line. The connecting rod on a stern-wheel engine is usually very long; it is known locally as a "pitman." (Except for paddle-wheel drive, all modern steam and internal-combustion engines are vertical inverted.)

Some of these steamboat engines operated condensing and some noncondensing, i. e., exhausting to the atmosphere. The exhaust was often directed up the stack, as in a locomotive, in order to assist the boiler fires with an induced draft. Some of the condensing engines exhausted into a surface condenser as is the universal modern practice. In steamers operating in fresh water, however, almost every condensing engine of the sixties exhausted into a jet condenser.

The steam pressures in use varied from a bare positive gauge pressure up to a figure occasionally exceeding a hundred pounds per square inch. It is possible to discover the operating pressures of very few of the river gunboats, but it is safe to say that even the so-called "high-pressure" engines used steam at a pressure far less than 100. The chief determining factor was boiler construction. Few manufacturers of the time could build a boiler that would be tight and safe when under any pressure appreciably above atmosphere.

Water-tube boilers had not yet advanced much beyond experimental installations. Horizontal fire-tube boilers were the thing —"return-*flue*" rather than "return-*tube*"—with the smoke pipe rising approximately above the furnace doors. A few large flues, rather than many small tubes, returned the hot gases of combustion through the boiler water to the front of the boiler from the rear where the gases had been delivered by the furnace or furnaces. Thus in a fire-tube boiler these passages inside are subjected to external pressure which is much more difficult to withstand than the internal pressure to which the tubes of a water-tube boiler are subjected. Furthermore, the return-flue boiler contained such a great quantity of water at steaming temperature compared with a water-tube boiler of equal capacity that the results of accident or shell hit were far more devastating in the former type. It is true that the modern fire-tube or "Scotch" boiler, operating at a pressure of two or three hundred pounds per square inch, is subject to the same risk of disaster. Modern manufacturing skill, however, has reduced to a minimum the principal danger, that of furnace collapse.

As will be seen later, many of the boilers of the river steamboats were long cylinders of very small diameter as compared with more modern proportions. The newer ones and those built for regularly designed gunboats burned coal. Many of the converted steamboats burned wood under their boilers. A few boats had fans to assist the draft through the fires for the purpose of generating steam more rapidly when higher speed was desired. Usually, however, natural draft was relied upon, as evidenced by the tall smokestacks on almost every vessel. Assisted or forced draft was less unusual on the ocean. However, as was the case with the other innovations such as the screw propeller, compound engine, water-tube boiler, etc., the fireroom blower had not yet reached the rivers noticeably.

ORDNANCE AND GUNNERY

In this period there were at least as many features of ordnance in a transitional stage as we have found with other things which go to make up a navy. Steel was just beginning to replace iron as the material for guns. There had been more progress abroad than in the United States, however, in the use of steel and also wrought iron, to displace the more orthodox cast iron. The breech-loading gun was making its appearance; but practically every gun we shall encounter in this volume will prove to be a muzzle-loader.

Rifled guns had commenced to supersede the smoothbores, and with them came the elongated, pointed projectiles displacing the spherical shot and shell. The rifling in the barrels, giving a spin to the streamlined projectiles, greatly increased the range and accuracy. Some rifled Civil War cannon had a range of several miles, but not an effective range at such distances. They were crude affairs by modern standards. Especially with muzzle-loaders, it was simply a matter of pushing in a loosely fitting projectile with small protuberances on its sides which engaged the grooves of the rifled barrel. A rotating motion was imparted successfully, but, as with the spherical missiles fired from smoothbore guns, there was still a great loss of pressure when the gun was fired, due to the loose fit. For the same reason, the projectile did not progress along the exact center line of the barrel. However, compared with the smoothbore, even the crude rifled ordnance showed a decrease in the "balloting," i. e., the motion of the missile from side to side as it advanced along the length of the barrel. These matters were corrected much later when breech-loading rifles, provided with finely machined lands (rifling ridges), fired projectiles with soft copper rifling bands around their bases. Upon firing, when the band reaches the start of the rifled bore, it fills the grooves in the barrel while the lands bite through the band and impart the desired rotation to the whole projectile. These refinements, however, merely increase the effectiveness of a rifle. The crude Civil War rifled ordnance achieved the correct fundamental principles of rifle fire.

There are other factors affecting range and accuracy, in addition to those just mentioned. A very important one is the length of a gun; the longer the gun the longer the time during which the projectile is being accelerated by the expanding gases from the burning propulsive powder. The diameter of a gun is called its caliber. The length of a gun is measured in diameters. Thus a 30-caliber gun has a barrel with a length 30 times its inside diameter. Often the "caliber" of a gun is used loosely to designate its length in calibers. The proportionate lengths of modern guns are far greater than those of 1861. The principal reason for this is the improvement in manufacturing methods and material. In past days, safe and accurate guns could not be built with so great a length in calibers. Even the very best guns of appreciable length today will "droop" when heated—their own weight measurably bends the barrel down out of a straight line. In one respect, however, the lack of length was not so detrimental then as now. The propelling charge then was fast-burning black powder, whereas now it is smokeless powder which burns more slowly. Thus, formerly a much higher percentage of the energy of the powder was imparted to the projectile during the early part of its travel from the breech. This in turn accounts for the "bottle-shaped" appearance of some Civil War ordnance; the black powder builds up a high pressure very quickly as compared with the smokeless variety.

Perhaps the most important of all the factors determining the range of a projectile is the energy that has been imparted to it by the time it leaves the muzzle of a gun, i. e., the muzzle energy. This in turn is determined by the weight of the charge of propelling powder, in addition of course to its characteristics. This weight was strictly limited by the safety factor. Imperfections of heavy ordnance manufacture, and the uncertainty about these imperfections, combined to restrict the weight of powder used. Thus when the *Monitor* fought the *Merrimac* she used only 15-pound charges in her guns (11-inch smoothbore). It was later demonstrated that 30-pound charges were safe; and with these she might very well have crushed in the armored side of the *Merrimac*.

Trajectory enters into the matter of accuracy. The greater the muzzle energy, the flatter the trajectory for an equal range. The flatter the trajectory the greater the chance of hitting the target when the aim in range is not perfect, as is almost always the case. Lack of range finders and of any but the crudest of sights for elevating made for highly inaccurate shooting at any appreciable distance. In most of the gunboat fighting to be considered, however, the ranges were extremely short, sometimes point-blank. Under such circumstances a clever trick was often employed. When a gunboat was firing at another gunboat or at a water battery it was found effective to aim slightly too low so that the projectile would surely hit the water, after which it would ricochet one or more times on its way to the target. In this way could be avoided the chance of a miss by aiming too high, the most common cause of bad shooting at short ranges. Incidentally, it must be remembered that most fighting, *generally speaking*, takes place at ranges where weapons of the era are effective, and this has been true through the ages. Where either party is mobile, it is likely that he will not use up his ammunition at ranges at which it will be wasted. Nor will he, out of choice, move in so close that his losses will be inordinate. Thus battle losses do not increase from century to century as the range of weapons increases, but probably the contrary.

There are a few other varieties of ordnance to be mentioned. A projectile may be either a solid shot or an explosive shell, depending upon the kind of damage it is designed to inflict. For instance, a solid shot is best for the purpose of crushing an armored shield; a shell, for causing casualties to personnel. An effective missile for the latter purpose was shrapnel—shell from which the explosive charge scattered many bullets in addition to the fragments of the shell itself. Contrariwise, however, solid shot have caused much damage, over centuries, both to wooden ship and to crew, through flying splinters; and a "splinter" might be an 8-by-8-inch piece of timber 15 feet long! A solid shot is somewhat heavier than an equivalent shell. Civil War projectiles were not "armor-piercing" and were prone to shatter upon impact. Shells were ordinarily exploded by crude fuses rather than by impact; the fuse was ignited by the firing of the propelling charge. The length of the fuse was first cut in accordance with the estimated time of flight to the target, or to a point just short of it. A special type of projectile, met here only briefly, was the hot shot—a cannon ball heated to a red or white heat in a furnace and fired into a ship or other structure of wood for the purpose of setting it on fire.

One special type of gun was the mortar, which was large in diameter and very short in length, having thick walls for heavy propelling charges. Mortars were used for high-angle fire. Their proportions were often so exaggerated that they approached a hemisphere in shape. When fired at angles of elevation for near-maximum distances, their range was very great. Though usually employed only for the bombardment (with shell) of large targets such as fortifications, their accuracy at a matter of miles was very surprising.

The vast majority of naval guns and many fortress guns were fired through an opening which did not permit a very wide angle of train (horizontal movement). Accordingly, it was necessary for them to wait for their own ship or their target to come into position by the relative movement of one or both. Some horizontal movement of the gun could be effected by hauling on the carriage with block and tackle. A "pivot gun" was sometimes installed, usually on the forward deck. It could be trained to fire through an arc of maybe 300 degrees, limited only by the danger of hitting the superstructure on its own vessel. Hand power was required here also, together with a complicated network of circular tracks on which to roll the wheels of the gun carriage. Crude, nontelescopic sights on the gun barrel were available for aiming in deflection (horizontally). Although sights for pointing (vertical movement) were almost nonexistent, the gear for elevating the gun had been improving. A screw gear on the breech was now in general use for pointing, this constituting the latest step in an advance over the use of wedges under the rear of the gun barrel. This new device could set and hold the gun at the desired vertical angle with an accuracy easily within the accuracies of the gun and projectile and powder themselves. At least the grave inaccuracies resulting from the motion of a ship in a seaway were almost entirely absent on inland waters. Thus the lack of sights for the gun pointers was not so serious.

The ammunition was largely of the "semifixed" variety—i. e., the projectile was one piece, and the charge of propelling powder was in a cartridge constituting a second piece. After the cartridge was rammed home through the muzzle (with the projectile next), the paper or cloth bagging of the cartridge was pricked and pierced, through a hole above it in the top of the gun's breech. In this hole was inserted a "primer" containing fine powder plus a small amount of very fast-burning explosive such as fulminate of mercury on top of it. When the gun captain desired to fire the gun, he would pull a lanyard (light rope) which would fire the fulminate by either percussion or friction, according to the method provided. In this way an igniting flame would reach the main powder charge much more rapidly than with the old method of applying a burning "match" directly to some coarse powder in the touchhole. There was no roll of the ship to be taken care of in the river fighting, and the sequence just described was *almost* instantaneous. Nevertheless, the deflection of the target might be changing rapidly and this rate had to be estimated by pure guesswork. So it was well to reduce to an absolute minimum the time elapsing between the pull on the lanyard and the departure of the projectile from the muzzle.

The methods in use for absorbing and checking the recoil had advanced little in centuries. No such things as springs or hydraulic cylinders were to appear for some time, apart from a rare spring used as a bumper. The recoil was simply checked by ropes leading from breech and carriage to the bulwarks or other fixed points toward the muzzle. Or, in the case of some fortress pieces, the recoiling gun rode uphill on a slide on the carriage. With the crudeness of this and other gear already described, it is not surprising to find that the length of time required to fire each round was a matter of minutes rather than seconds. It might run as high as six or seven minutes for the largest pieces. In addition to the manhandling with block and tackle required for getting the gun back into loading position, all remnants of burning powder-bagging had to be swabbed out; heavy powder and projectile lifted by hand, perhaps requiring a mechanical hoist for assistance; wads inserted if for no other reason than to prevent a ball from rolling out if the barrel dipped through a roll of the ship or from depressed aim; finally, the whole mass had to be hauled forward again into firing position and then pointed and trained. A thick wet mass of wadding had to be inserted between powder and shot if the latter was to be "hot shot."

THE GUNBOATS THEMSELVES

It is rather difficult to get a completely accurate idea of the river gunboats in general as they were such a very heterogeneous lot. All but one group of seven were makeshift conversion jobs, and the Confederate boats were a particularly variegated collection, scarcely a one of them built after the war began. Probably the best way for the reader to obtain a picture of them is to study descriptions of four different groups which are prominent in this volume. The boats in each unit operated together at least for a time and were more or less similar in some respects; therefore, the average characteristics of each squadron will be given.

It will not be easy to do even that much for the guns. They were perhaps the most diverse of all the items involved in the river fighting. The guns installed in almost every naval vessel were changed one or more times during the course of the war. Those listed in the following pages will be the ones that were in place during the most important incidents recorded herein. Both sides being wholly unprepared for any gigantic struggle, all guns of every type, size, and age were gathered up and installed. The Confederates had virtually no ordnance foundries at the start, and few later. A vast windfall accrued to them, however, when the Federals botched the defense of the Norfolk Navy Yard and surrendered it together with hundreds of guns of all calibers. So these U. S. Navy cannon were to be found shortly all over the Confederacy, in their forces afloat and in their western river defenses. On each side the most notable example of this diversity of ordnance matériel was the variety of types of guns to be found even on one ship in two or more spots where the same duty was to be performed. This made for great complications in ammunition supply if nothing else. Many of the monitors had two different types of guns in the same turret!

When it comes to designating the sizes of the various guns it will not always be possible to state the diameter and length. In that day a gun was often rated by the weight of the whole gun itself and by the weight (nominal) of its standard projectile. This was almost always the method of designating smoothbore guns designed for the firing of solid shot. And in this general connection it might be mentioned here that the exigencies of a situation occasionally brought about the use of projectiles different from those for which the gun was designed. This ordinarily meant a clearance between the projectile and the gun barrel that was greater than usual, and even the normal clearance was serious.

The question of ship tonnage is always a great problem, as there are a half a dozen ways of measuring it. The desired method for naval vessels is to measure the weight or the displacement (these being the same); for, this figure is a measure of the vessel's machinery, armor, and guns which are the cardinal factors of fighting strength. The displacement figure may be the "normal" or the "full-load" tonnage, depending on whether the normal or full allotment of fuel, stores, and ammunition is aboard. The records are complicated by the fact that so many of the gunboats were built as commercial vessels. Thus the tonnage figures may have been determined by some other method of measurement. Furthermore, even the official figures for some boats vary greatly in different places. For instance, both 355 and 614 tons can be found for one of them. The best that can be done under such circumstances is to deduce from the dimensions which figure is more likely to be correct.

We shall consider the four groups of boats in the chronological order in which they appear.

THE FIRST THREE UNION GUNBOATS

The first ones on the western rivers were three wooden boats, the *Tyler, Conestoga,* and *Lexington.* Their general appearance may be noted by reference to the accompanying photograph showing the *Conestoga* after her conversion. They were former freight-passenger steamers averaging roughly 535 tons displacement, 180 feet length, 42 feet breadth, 6 feet draft at full load, and 7 feet depth of hold. The last two figures demonstrate that the main deck forming the top of the hold was little above the water line, and likewise that the bottom of the boat was the only deck below it. From the photograph it will be observed that there were two decks or partial decks built up above the main deck.

On the three boats, each side wheel was driven by one single-cylinder, high-pressure steam engine, the three pairs of engines averaging approximately 21 inches in diameter by 7-foot stroke. The boilers were three or four in number. This plant gave a speed of 7 to 10 knots through the water. In the matter of armament we encounter a mixture right away. At the beginning—the important period for them—there were only two types of guns on the three boats put together: guns weighing 4,300 pounds (43 hundredweight, or "43 cwt.") and throwing a ball of 32 pounds nominal weight ("32-pounders"); and guns of the Dahlgren design weighing 63 cwt. and having a bore of 8 inches ("8-inch" guns). But the mixture was typically extreme. The *Lexington* had two 32-pounders and four 8-inch; the *Tyler,* one 32-pounder and six 8-inch; and the *Conestoga,* four 32-pounders and no 8-inch. (All guns mentioned herein may be considered as smoothbores unless specifically listed as rifles.)

In these craft is found one of the standard varieties of protection —just plain wood. Oak bulwarks, five inches thick, were installed when the boats were converted. These were proof against musket balls only. Everyone and everything had to take their chances when anything heavier came along. When practicable it was intended that barges be lashed alongside to protect the hull and paddle wheels.

THE IRONCLADS

The U. S. S. *Benton* was one of the two odd numbers among the nine Union ironclads; she was not one of the seven sister ships. Nevertheless, an inspection of the accompanying drawings of her will provide a good insight into the general features of these craft, as well as into some of their details. She was the largest but had only the same three decks as the eight smaller boats. The topmost or "hurricane" deck was not sufficiently strong to carry any weight of guns or the like. For instance, in the case of the Confederates' Mobile Bay ironclad *Tennessee,* the top was only a grating, so the sides were called the "shield." Worthy of note are the inclined engines, recessed double stern wheel, return-flue boilers, and armored casemate sloping at a 45-degree angle. The hull extended beyond the stern wheel on either side; the two sections were joined and covered by a deck ("fantail") abaft the wheel, but were not connected across the bottom or across the stern.

The seven sister ironclads had the following characteristics: 512 tons and 6 feet draft at full load; two horizontal high-pressure engines, each with one cylinder 22 inches in diameter and 6-foot stroke, driving a 22-foot wheel which operated in a 60-by-18-foot horizontal opening in the deck aft; five horizontal, cylindrical return-flue boilers 24 feet in length and 3 feet in diameter, necessarily having only one furnace per boiler; speed, 6 to 7 knots "through the water"; six 32-pounder 43-cwt. guns, three 8-inch 64-pounder Dahlgrens, four 42-pounder 84-cwt. Army rifles, and one 12-pounder rifled (small-)boat gun. The front of the casemate was protected by 2½ inches of iron backed by 20 inches of oak; the sides abreast of the engines and boilers were covered with 2½ inches of iron, the steam plant not being below the water line. The remainder, including the wheel, was unprotected.

It may be of interest to point out here the rarely realized fact that as much protection can be obtained by building the *same weight* of iron into a vertical wall as into a sloping one; and by doing so a much greater space is provided behind the armor for working the guns and carrying on ordinary daily existence. The reason for this seeming paradox is the fact that a vertical wall of the same height as the sloping one is much shorter. Thus a vertical wall weighing the same as the 2½-inch, 45-degree wall would be more than 3½ inches thick. Vertical oak backing more than 28 inches in thickness would weigh no more than the 20-inch backing on a 45-degree slope. Vertical armor would have been especially preferable to the sloping variety when engaging the enemy at long range, at which his high-trajectory projectiles would be falling at an appreciable angle; the same is true for projectiles plunging from a high emplacement, even at short range. The great advantage of sloping armor (*of equal thickness*) is against projectiles with the flat trajectories which they have at short to point-blank ranges.

A civilian engineer named James B. Eads did a splendid job in building these seven craft. They were completed in one hundred days from the date of the contract, nor was it any slipshod performance. Thus the first of these, the *St. Louis*, became the first U. S. ironclad, antedating the *Monitor* by several months. She was later renamed the *Baron de Kalb* as there was another U. S. S. *St. Louis*.

The first river gunboats had an even more variegated crew than the average Union ship in the first part of the war. The commanding officers were Regular Navy and the others were Volunteer Officers recruited chiefly from the river steamers. The crews were a little of everything: man-of-war's-men from the Atlantic Coast, men formerly of Great Lakes and river craft, and, on occasion, soldiers borrowed from neighboring Army units to fill out the crews. This last was not always a happy solution. The soldiers were not used to the discipline and other requirements of a naval vessel, and sometimes did not take to their new duties readily. On one occasion David D. Porter got 250 of them for his fleet. The major of the 250 and his adjutant arrived with their horses, but Porter decided that they had better remain unmounted while serving afloat. On the soldiers' very first night aboard, a large part of the flagship *Benton*'s crew got hold of half a barrel of whiskey with not unexpected consequences. An important secondary result was that a company of the soldiers mutinied and refused duty. Admiral Porter handled the situation smartly. He arrested the entire company and sent them back to Grant in irons, noncommissioned officers as well as men.

The commissioning of the two groups of gunboats just described marked the start of an anomalous arrangement which was not finally cleaned up for nearly a year. The boats had been procured by the War Department for use in joint operations with the Army. As has been noted, they were manned by the Navy; but they remained under the War Department even after commissioning. This means that they came under the orders of Army officers in the field who were senior to the squadron commanders. This seniority was the rule rather than the exception and, to say the least, was often annoying to the Navy people in the flotilla. Fortunately no serious trouble resulted. This was because of the happy circumstance that, in the real fighting, Navy officers like Porter and Foote were dealing with Army officers like Grant. The top Army offices in Washington appear not to have interfered very much with these gunboats directly. In addition, Foote co-operated with General Pope in an important operation and this relationship also seems to have been maintained fairly well. Although the leader of the land forces became impatient for a time, he made little or no attempt to exercise any Army-over-Navy authority; and all was well at the end of the operation anyway.

THE CONFEDERATE GUNBOATS

The data on the Confederate gunboats are distressingly meager. Of the two groups which fought in any respect as fleets we at least find a little more information on the one which interests us here than on the other. Half of the eight-boat flotilla which is prominent in this volume were captured by the enemy. From Union sources, therefore, we are able to obtain several characteristics of those vessels and their equipment which are missing on the other four. A doubly unfortunate situation lies in the fact that the eight boats had very diverse characteristics. Accordingly, wherever some dimension or feature is given here as average, it should be borne in mind that many of the eight may have departed considerably from the factor given. The boats were taken over for their speed and size, primarily, as the objective was ramming; after that their respective commanding officers decided upon their conversion and equipment!—of which more later.

It can be safely said that, in general, these boats were of a type distinctly different from that of either group of Union craft already described. They were more of the typical "river-steamer" type—

larger and higher and deeper. Most of them had two at least partial decks above the main deck; and several were of such deep draft (12 feet and more), and such a depth of hold (below the main deck), that there was space for two decks below also. Only the bottom would be a complete deck, however; due to space requirements of the machinery, the deck between the main deck and the bottom of the boat would be only a partial or "platform" deck. Most of the boats had side wheels well aft, with one vertical, 1-cylinder, low-pressure engine on each wheel. The average number of boilers was two but it should not be forgotten that the size of the boilers (unknown to us) was all-important. Such an engineering plant gave them an average speed of nearly 12 knots, which was high speed. It is scarcely worth averaging the tonnages as they ran almost from 100 to 1,000. But rarely did the length of any of them approach 200 feet. At a rough guess we can say that typical armament for a boat was one 32-pounder 42-cwt. smoothbore gun, and one 30-pounder rifle, one mounted forward and one aft. The bows of each boat were cased in iron to increase the damage inflicted by ramming, as well as to decrease the damage to itself incurred by the impact.

Here we have several instances of makeshift armor other than iron or tough wood. Bales of cotton and hay were favorite articles of protection for the crew on some of the flimsy Civil War craft. Boats "armored" in such ways were described respectively as "cotton-clad" and "hay-plated." The so-called "tinclads" were protected by thin iron; they were safe against musketry where covered by their plates of, say, ¼-inch thickness. Heavy ropes were often wound around the pilothouse. Anchor chains were frequently hung along the sides of the seagoing ships when about to fight in smooth water, as was usually the case in this war.

In view of its novelty in these waters it will be mentioned that one of the boats (the *Little Rebel*) was screw-propelled, and had one horizontal engine with one cylinder 18 inches in diameter and 24-inch stroke. She drew 12 feet when displacing 150 tons. All in all, she was undoubtedly a seagoing craft, though pretty definitely the smallest of the eight.

The organization of this fleet was of a most amazing character. All of the ships' companies were civilians from beginning to end! President Jefferson Davis appointed two river steamboatmen to start the ball rolling. They appointed others to the commands of the remainder of the boats, making a total of fourteen at first, and the appointments were approved. "Commodore" Montgomery and his outfit reported theoretically to the general commanding the area. The latter had plenty of misgivings about the setup: ". . . fourteen Mississippi captains and pilots would never agree about anything after they had once gotten under way." As has already been mentioned, each captain planned and supervised the equipping and fitting out of his own boat. Naturally this did not tend to decrease the lack of standardization already existing among the requisitioned steamers. "There is little or no discipline or subordination, too much 'steamboat' and too little of the 'man-of-war' to be very effective." This could hardly have been otherwise. It is no surprise to learn that the commanders of the regular forces ashore and afloat became somewhat exasperated at times. This River Defense Fleet did not do well in its try to block the way to New Orleans from the south. Foreseeing their failure, an attempt was made to provide Navy supervision and control over them to bolster their efficiency. But they "had entered the service with the distinct understanding or condition that they were not to be placed under the orders of naval officers." So there was never any connection between the Navy and the River Defense Fleet. The later performances of these river men were much improved but, in the eyes of their countrymen, their reputation remained low, except in bravery and spirit. They were judged "unable to govern themselves and unwilling to be governed by others." But it will be noted in these pages how this bravery and spirit achieved some splendid results.

As in the North, they too had a strange and unfortunate experience with their mixed crews. They needed soldiers to complete their complements at the last, to man the guns particularly, and several Army units volunteered. The result was continuous friction between the soldiers and the civilians serving together—naturally. Finally, just before the last battle—as it happened—the Army men (six companies) walked off in a body, and that was that.

THE U. S. ARMY RAM FLEET

Everything considered, this was perhaps the strangest outfit of all. Having many similarities to the picture just studied, this collection of Union rams was better conceived, constructed, and operated. A civilian engineer named Charles Ellet, Jr., not to be confused with any of his several related namesakes, had long been sold on the idea of sinking enemy vessels by ramming them with strong, swift craft carrying little or no armament. If they were as fast as they should be for ramming they would also be too fast for the enemy to hit with gunfire, and so would require no protection either. Surprise, speed, structural strength, and aggressive tactics formed the backbone of Ellet's theory of fighting in narrow waters. He was right. However, for a long time he could persuade no one in Washington of the merits of the idea. Finally the performance of the *Merrimac,* in addition to other factors, convinced the War Department. It and not the Navy told him to go ahead and put together a fleet according to his specifications. This relationship pleased him; he feared, and rightly, that his novel and extreme tactics would be hampered by the orthodox and conservative minds of the Navy leaders that he would meet even at the front. He was given a commission of colonel.

He knew just what he wanted and he carried out his project expeditiously. He had a wider choice of better boats than did Commodore Montgomery down the river and he selected nine good ones. He did not demand boats of any great length but did get ones which were well built and in good condition. Their average displacement was probably under 500 tons. He wanted boats that could make "18 to 20 knots downstream"—say over 15 through the water. However, it is doubtful if he procured many that could greatly exceed 12. Nevertheless, 13 knots was a good speed and it made little difference what the rate of the current might be unless he should catch an enemy tied up. The average dimensions of the seven largest ones were approximately 175 foot length, 35 foot breadth, 5 foot draft, and 7 foot depth of hold. Four of the seven were side-wheelers and three were stern-wheelers. The other two boats, which also were stern-wheelers, were much smaller than the rest. They were small towboats procured for use as tenders, but they were strengthened the same as the rest so that they could be used effectively as rams if the occasion should arise. Ellet understood correctly that the speed of the ram was much more important than its weight—force is proportional to the square of the velocity but only to the first power of the mass ($f = m \, v^2$).

It is interesting to note the protection which he provided for his boats. He joined to his fleet three coal barges with high oak bulwarks. He proposed to lash these alongside on the engaged beam, if it should become necessary between pitched battles to run past shore batteries. Also the coal itself under these circumstances would of course provide a strong protection to his hulls.

In constructing or converting a boat for ramming, it was of prime importance to be able to deliver a blow without putting oneself out of commission while so doing. Thus Ellet not only strengthened the bows of his craft, he made the whole of each boat very strong all the way from stem to stern. He accomplished this by running three parallel bulkheads the whole length of the boat, each from 12 to 16 inches thick—which is very, very thick for such small boats, or for any vessels. These main bulkheads were strongly braced against each other and against the decks and sides of the boat; and the two sides were stayed together all the way across by iron rods and screw bolts. This not only made the hull almost immune to longitudinal shock; it also made it so stiff that the impact of the boat's entire weight would strike the target vessel at the same instant, which was of vast assistance. The boilers and engines were stayed as strongly as possible in all directions, as they were the units most vulnerable to shock. We shall see in the early pages of this volume how that single factor put out of commission the first Confederate ram to see action.

As sole deference to defensive strength, an oak shield 2 feet thick was built around the boilers and engines. The pilothouse was made proof against musketry. Armament: none—until later.

Ellet did not quite equal Eads's remarkable job for expedition. Flooded sawmills at a critical period did not help. But, from the time he received the word to go ahead, to the time he was on hand with his fleet ready for action, it was only two months.

So much for the boats themselves.

With an Army officer in command of a flotilla of fighting craft we might expect many queer mix-ups. There were some, but things worked out a great deal better than expected. With the exception of a few more Ellets and others commissioned like himself from civil life, Charles Ellet, Jr., manned his boats by hiring civilian river personnel—captains, pilots, engineers, and some deck hands. They were not sworn into the Service. He preferred "daring and skillful river men" to naval officers. The crew of each boat was supplemented by a military guard of twelve to twenty men. These soldiers served as a sort of Marine guard—they were there to handle the small arms aboard if the fighting should ever become that close. On one occasion Commodore Foote asked the Secretary of the Navy for men with which to man the "steam rams." This, however, was before he had been advised of the setup. Colonel Ellet took his orders from Secretary of War Edwin M. Stanton.

These crews on the whole performed very well. The chief blot on their record developed aboard the flagship itself, the *Queen of the West*. Ellet was doubtful of his men and decided to try them out. He ordered the *Queen* (and the *Monarch*) into probable danger whereupon the captain, two of the three pilots, the first mate, and nearly all the crew quit. Ellet put them ashore (for good) and hastily got together a volunteer crew, including two good engineers from his military guard. The operation was carried out successfully, whereupon the reputation and integrity of all of the crews were much enhanced.

By this time Davis had relieved Foote in command of the iron-clad gunboats so that it was with him that Ellet had to carry on the necessarily difficult relationship. Secretary Stanton had ordered Ellet, in each of his planned operations, to have the "concur-rence" of the senior Navy officer present; and the ambiguity of that term caused a good deal of trouble. Ellet wanted Davis' help on his first big proposed venture. Davis would not give it but he "concurred" in Ellet's going ahead with his plan. The two sides of the question are too long to cover at this point. Just about the time it was settled that Davis would not co-operate and that Stan-ton would not require Ellet to have Davis' co-operation, the Con-federates withdrew. So the controversy ended, for a few days at least. By the rarest coincidence, *at almost the exact minute* that the same Ellet-Davis argument was about to resume farther down the river, the Confederate River Defense Fleet chose to put in an appear-ance. As a result there *was* no further argument—everybody simply pitched in.

There was one amusing aftermath of the ensuing fight, though apparently not too amusing to Ellet. One of the Confederate boats which had been captured ashore (the flag boat *Little Rebel*) was being held by some of Ellet's men as a prize crew. Davis' people came along and chased these fellows off and absorbed the prize into the gunboat fleet. Nor could Ellet's extensive correspondence on the matter pry the boat away from Davis. There was a verbal memo to the effect that "the *Little Rebel* was a special pet of his [Davis], and that he could by no means think of giving her up, but gave no reason to explain why he should hold her because she was his pet. Though she was Commodore Davis' pet, she was Colonel Ellet's prize."!

Shortly after the last combat controversy, Congress attempted to straighten out the main trouble by transferring the river craft to the Navy. They made matters temporarily worse, however, by the stupidly ambiguous wording of their Act. The key clause read "That the Western Gunboat Fleet constructed by the War Department for operations on the Western waters shall be transferred to the Navy Department." The intent was clear as to all the boats *except* the Ram Fleet—the very ones about which the greatest controversy raged. As they carried no guns it could be argued very plausibly that they were not gunboats. There was no question in the minds of those in the lower brackets on both sides. Each group was sure the rams belonged to them. Simultaneously in Washington, on the other hand, there was a strange Alphonse-Gaston act between the Secretary of War and the Secretary of the Navy, the former asking the latter what he thought, and the latter replying that the decision was up to the former. At long last Lincoln himself had to step in. Nearly four months after the Act was passed, and over five weeks after the gunboats were transferred, the President specifically ordered that the rams be put under the authority of the Navy Department. Thus ended a unique episode in U. S. naval history.

CHAPTER II

PREWAR STUFF

As EVERYONE knows well, the first open hostilities of the Civil War comprised the firing upon Fort Sumter in Charleston Harbor by Southern armed forces. This act took place on April 12, 1861, and the fort fell the next day. Prior to this event, however, a good deal of informal scuffling had been going on for some time. This took the form, in most instances, of Southern attempts to get possession of Northern property lying within or on the borders of seceded States. Many of the incidents occurred in seaports and on rivers, and they involved attacks upon either government-owned or privately owned vessels. One of these affairs will be described in this chapter. Throughout the South the several groups of attackers varied over a wide range as to legal authentication. Some were regular armed forces of the newly formed Confederacy; at the opposite end of the scale were others who were no more than self-organized "vigilantes." Owing to the circumstances in which some Northern vessels were caught, they were easy game for any well-organized undertaking.

South Carolina, it will be remembered, led the seceding States out of the Union by passing an Ordinance of Secession even before the end of 1860. At intervals other States followed. But when April, 1861, rolled around, several of the States which were eventually to secede were still in the Union. Among these was Arkansas. In March that State had voted by a close margin not to secede, and had further voted to leave the question of secession to a popular referendum to be held on the first day of the following August. Our first little scene is laid in the town of Napoleon, Arkansas, located at the entrance of the Arkansas River into the Mississippi. Though no longer in existence, it was a fairly important community in its heyday. Just across the Father of Waters was the State of Mississippi which had been one of the first to secede. Thus a wholly anomalous situation existed here as in so many other localities. Almost anything could happen and frequently did. As might be expected, Napoleon had its active and armed anti-Northern element, and it was this group that furnished our present story.

Our narrator was a quaint and unique sort of individual as will be observed from his writings. Bearing the name of A. Clarke Denson, he had lived his whole life in the South. On the other hand, in his background and sympathies he was a born-and-bred Unionist and antisecessionist. Nor did he often hesitate to let his feelings be known, sometimes with considerable vigor and little caution. Naturally his words show plainly his strong partisan bias. However, any original contemporary material which one may read here or elsewhere is going to prove more or less prejudiced—sometimes strongly so. Therefore, the reader may as well commence at once to learn to discount each writer's bias to the best of his ability in order to obtain the greatest amount of truth from what he reads.

Without further introduction, then, an extract will be presented from a little booklet written by Denson and published in 1865. Its title is *Westmoreland*. The subtitle gives fair warning of the bias of the work, for it reads *Secession Ferocity at the Breaking out of the Rebellion*. And that is strong enough for the most rabid. At any rate this is a typical prehostilities instance of the use of armed force on the western rivers, the event taking place in early April, 1861.

"Reader, I will now give you some account of the scenes and excitement of the ever-to-be lamented night on which an unarmed steamboat, plying the Mississippi in a time of peace, crowded with passengers from nearly every State in the Union, was unhumanly fired into by a maddened multitude.

"The citizens of Napoleon, Arkansas, had hoisted the Secession Flag, and were greatly excited about some powder and lead which had been taken by the United States' authorities at Cincinnati, while bound for ports of Memphis and New Orleans. A few days before this these citizens had captured the Ohio Belle, taken her loading, and driven the passengers off without refunding any of their fare. They, however, a few days after, left on a St. Louis boat, which was allowed to pass unmolested. These enterprising Secessionists had formed a military company, and had planted two six-pound brass cannon on the bank of the river, about two hundred yards apart, for the charitable purpose of compelling all boats belonging to the Free States to 'call in' and see them before they passed up.

"The exciting news of the capture of the Ohio Belle spread like lightning up and down the river, and no boat would pass for several days, for fear of meeting the same fate. At last, early one night, when Queen Cynthia had escaped up high amongst the stars, and was upsetting hogheads of moonshine on land and water, making it just light enough for owls, albino negroes and loafers, and too light for thieves and political polecutters; when the small fish in the river jumped out of the water, for the two-fold purpose of escaping the hungry big ones and at the same time to catch the tune of the concert at the neighboring frog pond; when the feathered and solitary chicken-stealer, in the dense bottoms across the river, hooted with delight at the thought of refreshing himself with a young pullet; while the stealthy cats around the corner of a stable lot were earnestly exercising their voices, claws and teeth amongst each other promiscuously, to the great joy of all the dogs in the vicinity, that barked applause; 'when the sweet wind did gently kiss the trees,' the steamboat Westmoreland, bound for Pittsburgh from New Orleans, hove in sight. She hugged the opposite shore as closely as possible, evidently showing that she meant to run by. But when the party on the wharf perceived her intentions, slam-bang went the savage contents of a six-pounder across her prow. Instantaneously, (as though in anticipation of some event of that sort, the pilot had kept his hand on the throttle valve,) she blew her whistle, soon landed, and tied her head-line to the wharfboat, on the guards of which were the chivalrous infantry with loaded muskets and revolvers—the lower cannon being on a coal-boat adjoining.

"Everybody and his wife and children hastened on board to get an orange, a paper, a drink of iced water or 'tanglefoot,' some one thing and some another. As for *myself,* all I desired was to *get to the bottom of a glass of brandy.* The cabin, the guards, and the space forward, were all crowded with men, women and children, from the town, it being quite early.

"About the time the citizens and passengers got comfortably mixed up, the bellicose captain of the infantry went abroad and demanded the papers of the commander of the boat. When he received them and saw 'Pittsburgh' written upon them, he immediately ordered the surrender of the steamer—the captain of which, on hearing that order, without making any reply, that I heard, quickly ascended to the hurricane roof and commanded a deck hand to take an axe and cut the line, which was done in less than no time; at the same moment the pilot was ordered to back her out.

"When these things were known, sudden confusion grabbed the whole crowd of 'land-lubbers' and dragged them in a hurry scurry, heels-over-head, half-overboard manner off the Westmoreland, and piled them promiscuously on the wharfboat. When this interesting performance was completed, and while the boat was backing out, the aforesaid infantry and belligerent citizens, poured an unceremonious broadside upon the unfortunate passengers, from their muskets and revolvers; repeating the same as fast as they could load. When the steamer had got about two hundred yards, they induced cannon No. 1 to howl after her with a voice of thunder, and a tongue of fire. More ammunition was shouted for by the cannoniers, but in the excitement no one could find it hence, as no time was to be lost, the crowd made a simultaneous rush for the shore, in order to run to cannon No. 2, about two hundred yards up the river.

"Now there was a space of water eighty feet wide between the wharf-boat and the bank, and across this was temporary scaffolding for passengers. On this the frenzied multitude impetuously dashed, when down came the rickety passway, precipitating them miscellaneously into the river, provokingly abstracting, for several moments, their eager attention from its favorite object. All, however, after some wadling, splashing and swimming, arrived on shore, and struck for cannon No. 2—everybody and his family followed the tumult, uttering rapidly all sorts of maledictions in behalf of the 'abolition captain,' and the negligent boys who misplaced the powder and balls.

"Finally belcher No. 2 was reached. The steamer was by this time almost on the opposite side of the river, 'heading up,' and, I thought, running very slowly for a frightened boat. After the frequent repetition of some bulky oaths, and the ranging of the cannon at the proper angle, the match was applied.

"When the match was applied to cannon No. 2, she declined sending her deadly messenger after the fleeing boat, rendering as an excuse that her *charge*, like the individual's that fell into the river, was *damp.* The Westmoreland moved very slowly in consequence of some mishaps to her machinery, as we supposed, judging from the rapid movement to and fro of lights on the boiler deck. The excited crowds now became furious, for the steamer, although ploughing along slowly, was evidently about to make her escape from the barbarous rabble of Napoleon.

"Suddenly some one sung out: 'Fire up the *Charm,* and place the cannon on her, and let us overtake the d—d abolition boat.' 'Fire up the Charm!' was taken up, echoed and reechoed, until all at once the tumultuous mass unanimously made a rush for the Charm, five hundred yards further up the river. Now the Charm was the smallest boat in those waters, and had been laid up some months before, when the water happened to be low. But the river had risen so much that the water was two hundred yards wide from the boat to the levee, and from knee to neck deep. When the crazy multitude arrived opposite the boat, most of them plunged right in for the purpose of wading to her, shouting and yelling to those on shore to bring up the cannon, and prepare them for action before being placed on board the Charm, the suddenly manufactured *man-of-war.*

"Hence, part of the crowd on the bank started after the flying artillery, and another part after the powder and ball, buckshot, or anything else that would slay Yankees. I was particularly amused at one jolly old codger, who ran off and procured a two gallon jug full of 'tangle-foot' for his part in the mighty campaign just about to commence. To this he hung with wonderful tenacity, not unfrequently introducing a quantity of the contents into his pastoral stew-pan, the result of which created in his cerebrum a confusion of ideas which soon became contagious.

"The Westmoreland got her machinery repaired and was out of danger, so far as Napoleon was concerned; but she had still to pass Helena, one hundred miles above. In her cabin lay one man shot dead, and another wounded. Thus she moved on, with her outraged and brutally treated passengers, who knew not how many more times they were to be shot at, or how many more were to be thus inhumanly murdered and crippled. Their situation can be better imagined than described.

"By this time the cannon were brought up, the gentleman who waded to the Charm returned to the shore with the mortifying intelligence that not a stick of wood was aboard, the manheads were out of the boilers, and the fixtures, generally, out of kelter, and that it was impossible to immediately make a man-of-war of her under such embarassing circumstances.

"Every sort of plan to get revenge on the Westmoreland was proposed and discussed. They would have telegraphed to Helena, but no telegraph was near, running in that direction. Finally they gave up the pursuit of the 'd—d abolition boat,' but swore they would be prepared for the next Pittsburgh or Cincinnati tub.

.   .   .   .

"As to the steamer, she passed Helena and reached Memphis, with one man killed, whose name was Harmon, of Tennessee. Several were wounded, among whom, as I was informed, was a lady and child. The secessionists, as an apology for their cowardly act, said that Harmon was a gambler, and ought to have been killed. If this be a good rule, and were it carried out, nearly every one of their leaders would get the treatment they have long deserved. Thus ended the affair of firing into the Westmoreland."

And what happened to Denson himself? Plenty—almost. For he allowed his opinions about the *Westmoreland* incident to be heard that evening within a wide radius and in no uncertain terms. As a result, he was haled to "court" for "trial" by the local "Vigilent Committee." But he certainly was no pussyfooter. His testimony as to his beliefs and feelings was expressed so strongly that his judges were practically forced to choose as their sentence either hanging or acquittal. As a result of his complete frankness and courage the court gave him his freedom, plus twenty-four hours to get out of town—for his own good.

Denson did a small bit of traveling in the South after leaving Napoleon, and wound up in Memphis. There he was located, happily for him, when the city was evacuated by the Confederate forces in June, 1862. He soon joined the Union army as a private, though at the time he was nearly fifty years of age. By the end of his service he had reached the rank of captain.

As to the State of Arkansas, she soon overturned her referendum intention, and voted to secede immediately after hearing of the attack on Fort Sumter. In any case the war was really on, beginning with the hostilities of April 12, nor did much more time elapse before the last one of the seceding States cast its die.

CHAPTER III

THE STORY OF "POPE'S RUN"

OPEN HOSTILITIES having been instituted by armed forces of a seceded State, the long period of uncertainty and irregularity came to an end. It became the duty of the Federal Government to suppress the rebellion with all the forces at its command—forces very limited at that time. The first mission of the Navy was blockade. There were few vessels available for this or any other duty. At the start the Confederates had no men-of-war at all, but the length of their coast line and the number of their ports made the problem of blockade a gigantic one. Of necessity almost anything that would float and carry a gun was pressed into service, especially at the very beginning. Sailing vessels had to be used; and, when it came to steamers, even ferryboats were armed and given active assignments. Needless to say, service in some of these improvised "warships" was a severe ordeal.

The first practicable blockade move was to lie off the Southern ports and endeavor to intercept as many ships as possible of those attempting to slip through. This at best is always the hardest way. And under the circumstances just outlined it was extremely difficult to do the job even passably well until toward the end of 1861. It should be mentioned on this early page that searchlights were nonexistent at this date; and even at the end of the war those that were in service were of the crudest type. The next step in perfecting any blockade is to seize, where possible, the harbor entrance which leads to a port or ports. If this can be accomplished it is possible for perhaps only one ship to prevent absolutely all outside intercourse with the harbor concerned. Furthermore, the greatly reduced numbers of blockading vessels can lie securely in sheltered waters. Although, of course, the final solution is to capture the coast cities themselves and occupy them with troops, the capture of the harbor mouths attains an equally perfect stoppage of sea trade with the outside world.

The first important institution of this secondary blockading step took place on the East Coast. Late in August, 1861, a combined sea and land force bombarded and captured the Confederate forts guarding the Hatteras Inlet entrance to Pamlico Sound, North Carolina. The fort at Ocracoke Inlet on the same Sound was abandoned soon after. Thus were barred from the sea not only Pamlico Sound but also Albemarle Sound, the lower reaches of the Neuse and Pamlico rivers, and many lesser waterways which feed the great Sounds. So the use of almost every North Carolina port was denied to the South at one fell swoop, and the immense importance of the operation became increasingly evident as time went on.

In order to expedite similar movements and in fact to forward the whole Atlantic blockade, one more very important step was necessary. Pamlico Sound could not handle heavy ships so there was no place below Chesapeake Bay in Northern hands that could be used as a fleet base. It soon became desirable to have such a base, i. e., a large, favorably located area of deep, sheltered water having good holding ground for the anchors and which could be defended satisfactorily after capture. It is scarcely necessary to go into the reasons for these needs. After four possible places had been considered, Port Royal, South Carolina, was selected as the objective of another large joint land and sea expedition. Port Royal is about halfway between the Chesapeake and Key West. The fleet employed was the largest ever to have been gathered together under the U. S. flag. It was commanded by DuPont; the army was headed by William T. Sherman.

The attack, November 7, 1861, was almost an exact replica of the one on Hatteras Inlet; the only difference was that the fleet had sufficient water to enable it to countermarch back and forth into and out of the harbor entrance rather than parallel to the coast. The occupants of one of the two forts were blasted out of it, and the evacuation of the fort on the other side of the entrance followed. As in the earlier expedition, there was a small fleet of Confederate gunboats which could not even attempt to offer opposition to the overwhelming force of the enemy. Under the command of Josiah Tattnall they escaped through a small creek in the back area. This marked the first important appearance in Confederate uniform of Commodore Tattnall of "Blood is thicker than water!" fame. Since his Anglo-American entente before the Pei Ho forts only two years earlier, the hemal fluid had apparently thinned out a bit. As a result of the Port Royal movement the Union ships acquired a splendid base, especially fine for operations against Charleston. They also blocked off with finality the city of Beaufort and others on the extensive network of inland waterways in that region.

The seizure of Hatteras Inlet and Pamlico Sound had barred from enemy use practically every North Carolina port but Wilmington. However, the advantage that had been gained had not been pushed. Finally after more than five months' delay the possession of Pamlico Sound was exploited in order to deny to Confederate use the immense maze of rivers, creeks, etc., in the area. To accomplish this, the first step was to capture the forts on Roanoke Island which separates Albemarle Sound from Pamlico Sound. This was done on February 8, 1862, by another joint expedition carried out in sufficient force to assure success. Again the improvised Confederate gunboats had to retreat. This time, however, two days later, a superior collection of Union vessels under Rowan went after them and annihilated the lot off Elizabeth City, North Carolina. Thus all the waters for miles around were exposed to Northern domination. This was the first of the very small number of naval engagements of the Civil War which can possibly be termed fleet actions. A Confederate land battery figured in the conflict, but there were more than half a dozen boats engaged on each side and this time they really "went to it."

Before reaching this point a number of readers have no doubt wondered what has happened to the theory that with "ships vs. forts" it is almost a foregone conclusion that victory will rest with the forts. This theory applies when the fighting strengths of the two opposing forces are at all comparable. If the ships are overwhelmingly superior in offensive or defensive strength or both, they will conquer the forts nevertheless. A fortification mounting only a few small guns is no match for a battleship. So, disparity of force should be borne in mind in all cases.

A mission quite similar to the North Carolina operations was undertaken in the Gulf of Mexico as the opening act in the war of the western waters. There the Mississippi River provides a sea connection to many, many cities, some with a large foreign trade; and this trade would become heavy indeed in wartime if allowed to go unmolested. New Orleans, of course, was the greatest Southern port of the many served by this vast river system.

The Mississippi empties into the Gulf through a number of mouths, at least four of which were important; and it is thirty miles by sea between the two most widely separated mouths. Thus it can be seen that the blockaders on this station had a difficult task on their hands when they tried to stop traffic in and out of the river by watching all the different outlets. On June 30, 1861, Raphael Semmes had slipped out to sea from New Orleans in the raider *Sumter,* and the result was an immense disorganization of Northern commerce. He followed that venture with his exploits in the *Alabama* which were even more devastating. Therefore, a break through the blockade could be a very serious matter.

It so happens that the "passes" to all these mouths of the Mississippi River branch off at one point, each pass being roughly fifteen miles in length, measured to its ever-present bar. At the point of common branching there is a body of deep water measuring about two miles both upstream and across. That is a lot of water if we are going to consider a small number of vessels, especially if most of them are themselves small. This spot is entitled the Head of the Passes. The current is very considerable even though the river widens at that point. For a ship desiring to slip out it was possible to anchor at the Head of the Passes, keep tab directly or indirectly on the situation at each mouth, and dash down any pass whose mouth might be temporarily unguarded. This is how Semmes effected his escape.

All in all, the possession of the Head of the Passes was of considerable value to whichever side held it. Accordingly, it was desirable from the beginning for the Gulf Blockading Squadron to seize this strategic location. Lack of the proper ships and lack of initiative, however, delayed serious consideration for a long time, and no action was taken for still longer. Two suitable ships would have sufficed—or even one—with an able commander who was both aggressive and watchful. But almost six months went by before the Head of the Passes was occupied by U. S. naval forces.

Early in October the first ships went up, and before long there was a heterogeneous collection of four vessels present under the command of Captain J. ("Honest John") Pope of the *Richmond.* This latter vessel was a big, powerful steam sloop-of-war, sister of the *Hartford* and others. (Her rating of "sloop" signifies that she carried guns on one deck only.) Her chief drawback was that she was not sufficiently "handy" for the service to be performed. Of the four ships there, the best one for the job was the side-wheel gunboat *Water Witch,* even though she did not carry a large battery. The other two were the *Preble* and the *Vincennes,* the latter having been the first U. S. naval vessel ever to circumnavigate the globe (1826–30). Although these two also were sloops-of-war, they were sailing ships; so there is no need for elaboration in saying that they were even less suited for blockade duty at the heads of the passes than at the mouths. They were included because of the large number of heavy guns which they added to the total. It was necessary to tow them up the river to the junction point. The *Water Witch* was able to get the *Preble* up but not the larger *Vincennes.* Another steamer had to be brought from another station to stem the current with the heavier vessel in tow. This quartet of ships totaled an armament so superior to anything on the river flying the Confederate flag that it is idle to make a comparison. Suffice it to say they they mounted at least twenty-six guns of 8-inch caliber and above, to say nothing of as many more smaller ones. It is true that there were none of any great range. At any rate there the ships were, quite idle apart from taking preliminary steps toward installing a land battery on the point between the South and the Southwest Passes.

Meanwhile, what was going on up river? At New Orleans a most strange collection of men-of-war was assembling. The key vessel was a Boston-built seagoing tug, the *Enoch Train,* which had been taken over as a private venture, rebuilt, and renamed *Manassas* in honor of the First Battle of Bull Run. None of her old friends could ever have recognized her. All that now appeared above water was a timber and ironclad turtleback that looked like the upper half of a watermelon, if indeed it resembled anything ever seen before. Twin smokepipes rose close together from its top; and peering through a trapdoor forward was a single unpointable and untrainable 32-pounder. The *Manassas* was strengthened and fitted with an underwater ram. Rumors of this forbidding monster had been drifting down the river for some weeks. Upon the completion of the transformation, her enterprising owners endeavored to make a deal with the local naval authorities whereby said civilian owners would receive a certain percentage of the value of all Northern vessels destroyed by the *Manassas*. This proposition was not received favorably nor was any other agreement reached. Whereupon the deadlock was broken through the simple expedient of a boat's crew from the C. S. S. *McRae* taking possession after driving out helter-skelter her complement composed of rather tough customers.

The *McRae* was the flagship of Commodore George N. Hollins, and her immediately past history was interesting too. Before war broke out, and while she was technically a Mexican revenue steamer, she was seized and brought in on the suspicion that she was a pirate. The courts, however, did not bring in the piracy verdict for which her captors had hoped. But before anything further was done about her, hostilities began and she was taken into the force defending the river and New Orleans. It was hoped that she might follow the *Sumter* to sea and serve as another raider. She mounted a 9-inch gun and six 32-pounders, the only Confederate ship present possessing even a halfway respectable battery.

The other Confederate "men-of-war" consisted of four converted side-wheel tugs or towboats, the *Ivy, Tuscarora, Jackson,* and *Calhoun*. There can be no absolute certainty of the guns that each of these boats carried at this time. We do know, however, that the batteries were quite inconsiderable; each vessel mounted either two 32-pounders or their approximate equivalents; at least a few of the guns definitely were rifles. Further additions to the local forces afloat included three fire ships and their two escorting tugs. The theory of fire-ship attack is for tugs to tow the fire vessels close enough to the enemy to ensure contact; for purposes of concealment the ignition of the fires is postponed as long as possible. The "fire ships" in this case were simply river flatboats piled high with combustibles of all sorts. The name of one of the tugs handling the fire rafts seems to have been *Watson*. Another may have been *Music* or *Mosher;* possibly there were three tugs; possibly one boat bore one of the above names before "joining the Navy" and a different name after.

Such was the constitution of the opposing forces. As soon as the Federal vessels had advanced to the Head of the Passes, the Confederates commenced to keep them under observation. And Captain Pope knew it (October 3). This is very important, actually and psychologically. The *Ivy* was the most active and bothersome. She came down on October 9 and proceeded to take pot shots at the *Richmond* and *Preble* with her small but long-range guns. This worried Pope no end; the shots did no damage but he could not reach the *Ivy* at all. At least he thought he could not. (He was wrong about this on a similar occasion later.) He wrote immediately for rifles with a range greater than that of the smoothbores which he had. A rather remarkable feature of this request was that it brought the desired guns to him from Pensacola three days after he had written his letter! But that is merely a side light. The preliminary operations of the *Ivy* constituted a splendid build-up to work upon the Yankees' minds for what was soon to follow. The energetic commander of the *Ivy*, Joseph Fry, was none other than he who was to become "Captain Fry of the *Virginius*" in 1873. In that year he and many members of his crew were executed by the Spanish authorities in Santiago de Cuba after being captured while on an unsuccessful filibustering expedition.

Commodore Hollins determined to make a night attack with his flotilla upon the enemy. The *Manassas* was to lead the way and ram the most suitable target. She was then to send up a rocket immediately as a signal to the others that the first step was complete; whereupon the fire ships were to swing into action. The night of October 11–12 was selected for the undertaking. There was no moon and the sky was overcast. The night was not inky black but it was very dark when the little squadron got under way from its rendezvous off the forts thirty miles up the river. There was a 5-knot current running, so that no time was lost once the vessels were unmoored. Quiet was ordered and maintained. First in the procession steamed the twin-screw ram *Manassas*. Next in order were the three fire rafts held abreast of each other by long cables and towed by two tugs on the wings of the trio; thus this section of the fleet extended an appreciable way across the river. The tow was unhandy and the visibility very bad. It was barely possible to see the distant banks slipping by. The river was high and the current swift. At least there was plenty of water for navigational purposes.

Next after the fire rafts came the flagship *McRae*, the one attacking vessel with any gun power. Astern of the *McRae* followed the four armed towboats in column, first the *Ivy* and next the *Tuscarora*. The *Calhoun* and the *Jackson* were relegated to positions far in the rear, the former because her machinery was deemed to be too vulnerably located for battle risks, and the *Jackson* because her exhaust was too noisy. In those days the engines of nearly all small vessels exhausted into the atmosphere rather than into condensers. If the engine operated on low-pressure steam the sound was not very appreciable. The *Jackson,* however, had high-pressure engines and her puffing was very loud indeed, especially for a stealthy expedition on a dark night. So she had to remain a good distance back, and even there it seemed as if her sharp puffing must surely be heard by the enemy many miles below at the Head of the Passes.

The diminutive procession swept silently on, the ram, the fire rafts, the flagship, and finally the gunboats. Not a light showed; not a sound was audible above the rapid slap-slap of the side paddles. While this advance was in progress, what was the situation among the "abolition" ships? The big sailing vessel *Vincennes* was anchored over on the west side of the Head of the Passes, near the entrance to the Southwest Pass. The rest were over near the east bank, all anchored and all of course heading upstream. The flagship *Richmond* had a coal schooner, the *Joseph H. Toone,* on her port side and from her the "watch on deck" were coaling ship, i. e., those members of the crew who were on watch—it was not an "all hands" affair this time. The sailing ship *Preble* was inshore on the *Richmond's* bow, and the side-wheeler *Water Witch* was on the *Richmond's* starboard quarter. A small prize schooner, the *Frolic,* was just ahead of the *Water Witch* and accordingly was inshore of the *Richmond. Not one picket boat was out to guard against surprise from up river or any other direction.* It was so dark that one ship could scarcely be seen from another except where lights were showing—and most of these should not have been showing. There were dim lanterns on the *Richmond's* spar deck for the coaling detail. No special lookout was stationed. Not only were there no picket boats out; but, it will have been noted, the four ships were not even disposed to any advantage with respect either to each other or to the waters in which they were anchored.

The meager anchor watches were carrying out their dull routine; an occasional clash of a shovel could be heard over on the *Richmond;* the faint lights showing through her gun ports were obscured and reappeared again as the coaling detail went about its business. Everything proceeded as if no ram or any other kind of an enemy was within five hundred miles. The commanding officer of the *Preble*, the most advanced ship, had turned in with his clothes on, about three o'clock in the morning. Suddenly, about 3:40, a midshipman dashed down the ladder and into his cabin exclaiming, "Captain, there is a steamer right alongside of us!" The skipper leaped from his bunk and ran out of his stateroom en route to the topside; as he passed a gun port he saw "an indescribable object" headed for the *Richmond* and it suddenly emitted a dense cloud of smoke. Immediately the *Preble* beat to quarters. At the same instant those on the deck of the flagship saw the same strange apparition loom out of the darkness on the port beam, very close aboard and headed right for them. Of course it was the *Manassas,* and her ram crashed only a few seconds later. By chance the point of attack was just where the coal schooner was tied up. In the smash her lines carried away. The ram passed off onto the quarter where those on the *Water Witch* heard her puffing. Deafening but harmless broadsides began to blaze into the darkness. All was confusion in the surprised fleet. The *Manassas* disappeared from view and again darkness clamped down, with the deadly threat still lurking out there somewhere. Only the gun flashes and the light from the battle lanterns served to illumine the scene of indecision. The firing died away when not even an imaginary target could any longer be seen in the blackness.

Meanwhile up went the signals and out ran the slipped anchor cables. Red light hoisted: "Enemy present." "Get under way." "Act at discretion." Up went a rocket from out on the waters. It was the much delayed signal from the *Manassas* to her consorts. Soon three little sparks appeared up the river. As the National vessels started to move, the sparks not only drew closer but grew larger very rapidly. Fire ships! When the *Richmond* got moving through the water she failed to keep her bow upstream until she obtained sufficient steerageway. Her head fell off to port and she was soon broadside on to the current. The fire rafts were blazing higher and brighter, faintly disclosing the steamers coming along astern of them. *Richmond* to *Vincennes* and *Preble:* "Proceed down Southwest Pass!" The flagship stood across in the same direction "to cover the retreat"! The commanding officer of the *Water Witch* received a report of this precipitate flight and at first could not believe it. After getting under way he steamed around to size up the situation as well as he could in the darkness. The blazes on the fire ships mounted higher and higher and drew closer and closer, making some objects more plain, others more obscure. Meanwhile the *Richmond* continued to drift sideways until she was on her way down the Southwest Pass astern of the sailing ships. Neglecting to make use of an anchor to swing herself around, she went all the way to the mouth, broadside to, having no success with her screw and rudder.

The *Water Witch* dodged the fire rafts without difficulty, wandered around the area for some time looking for anything she might find. About all she ever did see in the vicinity were the rafts and the coal schooner; they finally drifted ashore on the west bank. She waited for daylight and then spied the smoke of five enemy steamers several miles up the river bound north, and saw her own ships, including the prize schooner, several miles down the Southwest Pass. Feeling unable to hold the position alone against possible attack by the whole enemy force, she joined in the withdrawal, giving a tow to the *Frolic* which was trailing the others. *Both* fleets were in full retreat.

We left the *Manassas* as she rammed the *Richmond*. Let us follow her. The crash damaged her ram; that was nothing. The collision, however, also knocked the boilers and both engines loose and completely disabled one of the engines for a time. Either the shock, the coal schooner's hawser, or a projectile carried away the smokestacks flush with the armored shell. The lower parts of one or both pipes were driven out of place, and smoke entered the interior of the vessel almost driving everyone out. Thus, she was no further threat to the enemy although the latter did not know it. She drifted ashore but some little while later was able to get back upstream under her own power. The precipitate retreat of the enemy saved her from capture. The damage she inflicted on herself while ramming the *Richmond* was the cause of the delay in firing the signal rocket. Thus, the fire rafts were lit off too late to be effective. It developed that their tugs did not have sufficient power to handle them properly anyway; it was an unwieldy tow and the current was strong; nor was the breeze entirely negligible. The Confederate gunboats simply did not come into action—that is, until later.

At last mention, the Federal ships were sailing and drifting down the Southwest Pass en route to the open sea. The *Richmond* had given up trying to swing her head around while in the stream. But before the open sea could be reached, the inevitable bar at the river mouth had to be crossed. It was very doubtful that this could be done successfully without a certain amount of preparation and timing. But semipanic still gripped the flagship. The order to all was: "Cross the bar!" The commander of the *Water Witch* pleaded for an about-face and the reoccupation of the Head of the Passes. To no avail. The order stood and the ships continued out toward the bar. First in the procession came the *Preble*. She cleared it. Next came the larger *Vincennes*. She stuck fast, stern up river. Next came the still larger *Richmond*. She stuck, broadside on. The *Water Witch* and *Frolic* got over without difficulty as was to be expected.

It was not long before the Confederates, victors in this game of bluff, came scouting around again. First they noted that the Head of the Passes was entirely clear of the enemy. They made the following captures: the coal schooner and fifteen tons of coal; the *Richmond*'s cutter containing small arms; and, on shore, some lumber for the abortive fort, which they burned. Scouting farther, they observed that all the U. S. ships had deserted the river entirely. And, what was even more interesting, the *Richmond* and *Vincennes* were seen to be aground, the latter in such a position that not one of her guns would bear on the river mouth. Cautiously the Confederate gunboats ventured downstream and commenced a long-range bombardment of the stranded vessels. Bulkheads were removed by the *Vincennes'* people and two guns were mounted aft so as to fire astern. The *McRae*, the *Tuscarora,* and the ubiquitous *Ivy* took part in the action as their guns had the longest range. The rear guards *Jackson* and *Calhoun* tied up at Pilot Town and served as spectators. The Confederates were firing small guns only and they did virtually no damage, but their projectiles did reach their targets and beyond. This was immensely annoying to the enemy, to say the least, especially since the latter incorrectly believed that their own missiles were not reaching. Under such circumstances, when the Federals were having no success in pulling off the stranded ships, things began to look serious even if the Rebel projectiles *were* small.

About this time several boatloads of men were observed pulling away from the *Vincennes*. One bearing her captain came alongside the *Richmond*. That dignitary mounted to the deck and, when received by Captain Pope, was observed to have a large American flag wound about him! When asked the meaning of this strange performance he replied that he had obeyed the senior officer's signal, had abandoned ship, and had lighted a "slow match" to the magazine! Of course, no such signal had been made. However there was nothing to be done about it now. While the banging of the "battle" continued, the large group on the *Richmond's* deck stood watching the *Vincennes,* figuratively holding their ears; they were waiting for the grand explosion which might rain a shower of 1½-ton guns through the decks and bottom of almost any near-by ship. The waiting continued and nothing happened. More waiting and still no cataclysm. Finally it became evident that the *Vincennes* was not going to blow up after all. Her captain was ordered back to her to defend her against whatever attacks might be made upon her; and meanwhile get her afloat.

The Confederate flotilla withdrew around 10 A. M. About the only projectile that struck the hull of any ship on either side during the whole episode was a small one which Captain Pope found in his bureau drawer! In order to get the *Vincennes* off the bar it was necessary to lighten her considerably. In accordance with permission received from Captain Pope, most of her guns and ammunition were thrown overboard. Both she and the *Richmond* were hauled off the following day, and in any case they were not molested after the attack already described. As for the main night attack, thanks to the presence of the coal schooner alongside, the damage done to the *Richmond* by the ram was almost negligible.

The Southerners had really done an extremely creditable job when they drove all the blockading ships entirely out of the river, because they did it with a greatly inferior force. The Head of the Passes was revisited but was not again reoccupied by the enemy until months later, just prior to Farragut's "big push" up the river to New Orleans and beyond. All through the winter the blockade was maintained off all of the unsheltered river mouths separately, and that is the perfect measure of the success of Commodore Hollins. Unfortunately, however, some armchair strategists in newspaper offices at New Orleans and elsewhere began to criticize him for not accomplishing more than he did. This criticism was aggravated moreover by Hollins' report of the operation which made incorrect claims and employed an unfortunate tone. So, not even did the successful participants fare very well. Another incidental disappointment was that the *McRae*'s engines showed themselves to be insufficiently reliable to take the ship to sea on any extensive raid such as had been planned.

On the Union side none fared well except possibly the captain of the *Water Witch*. The commanding officer of the *Vincennes* was relieved of his command very quickly after his exhibition following the grand flight. Pope had to be replaced, of course—condemned out of his own mouth. He was consumed by fears of the unknown and unseen, and he fled because "the whole affair came upon me so suddenly that no time was left for reflection"—this being just one of several unconscious admissions of his shortcomings. Mahan, in his mild way, says that Pope's Run was "to some extent humiliating to the service." Admiral of the Navy David D. Porter does not hesitate to say: "Put this matter in any light you may, it is the most ridiculous affair that ever took place in the American Navy." Captain Pope came out of it beautifully, however. Twelve days after the event he was relieved of his command "at his own request on account of ill health." Amazingly enough he was retired as Commodore the following year, and later had a torpedo-boat destroyer named after him.

Is there no one in all this to whom we may "point with pride"? Yes, there is indeed one—a certain quarter gunner of the *Vincennes*. He is the one who had been ordered to light the slow match which was to send his ship skyward. During the subsequent inquiry he was asked if he had obeyed orders. Yes, he had obeyed orders and lighted the match all right. However, suspecting that his captain might later regret his decision, he had cut off the lighted end before it had burned very far, and thrown it overboard!

CHAPTER IV

BLOOD AND SAND AND STEAM

WITH "Pope's Run" behind us we need no longer
be concerned with matters on which our information is scanty. Of that episode there is a serious lack
of reliable accounts from the Confederate side, in
fact almost no accounts at all. Accordingly many questions of detail are either contradictory or wholly unanswered. From here one
can proceed with confidence. For the next action in the West we
pass on from the extreme south to the extreme north of the battle
front.

The beginning of this story centers approximately around Cairo,
Illinois, where the Ohio flows into the Mississippi. There a "navy
yard" had been established. In those waters the Navy had bought
three side-wheel river steamers for want of anything better. They
were converted into gunboats by lowering their engineering plant,
raising wooden bulwarks, and mounting a varied collection of guns
on the main deck. Their names were *A. O. Tyler, Lexington,* and
Conestoga. The purchases were made by a "three-striper" who
was one of a long line in the U. S. Navy to bear the distinguished
name of John Rodgers. Now, former President John Tyler was a
secessionist, so Rodgers wrote to the Secretary of the Navy: "The
name of the first of these [*A. O. Tyler*] I will, with your permission,
change to *Taylor,* a name of better augury than *Tyler."* Officially,
however, the name was changed only from *A. O. Tyler* to *Tyler.*
But, since the unofficial change to *Taylor* stuck for some time,
an immense amount of confusion resulted and still exists. Yet
there was only one vessel, *Tyler* or *Taylor.* The three were far
from being a formidable flotilla but they "commanded the sea" because the opposition was zero. One boat with one gun is infinitely
superior to nothing.

The first considerable service required of the river gunboats
was in support of army forces. And the first noteworthy undertak-

ing in that part of the country took place on November 7, 1861, less than a month after the Head of the Passes fiasco. As one of the early steps in the southwestward advance of the slowly organizing National armies, General Ulysses S. Grant with 2,500 men undertook an attack upon a Confederate force at Belmont, Missouri. This place is just a short way below Cairo on the right bank of the Mississippi River. The Rebels were driven from the field, whereupon success went to the heads of the verdant victors. While both officers and men were unduly engaged in souvenir hunting instead of pressing their advantage to complete victory, Confederate reinforcements started to cross the river. Although still in commanding position the Northerners withdrew to their transports closely pursued by the enemy. Here the supporting gunboats *Lexington* and *Tyler* entered the picture, inflicting such severe losses that the balance for the day remained heavily with the initial victors. It should be emphasized that in all the engagements which took place during the first year or so of the war, the vast majority of the participants were under fire for the first time in their lives.

The next phase of warfare for the river flotilla consisted of close bombardment of fortifications in conjunction with attacks by the army from the land side. For this purpose armored vessels were required; and they were constructed. Their characteristics can be learned by examining accompanying photographs better than by reading any lengthy description. In general they were flat-bottomed, light-draft, low-freeboard stern-wheelers, each having a sloping, rectangular, armored casemate covering almost the entire deck and enclosing almost everything but the smokestacks. The paddle wheel was several feet forward of the extreme stern. The casemate was of heavy timber faced with iron on the forward end and on the sides abreast of the machinery. This latter was placed as low in the boat as possible. The heaviest iron plating was in the bow. The speeds of the several boats ranged as low as 5 to 8 knots through the water. However, mounting guns as large as 8- and 9-inch, they were formidable customers, all things considered. And they were built expeditiously too; in fact, they came out of the builders' hands more rapidly than crews could be provided for them. There were many, many river men-of-war of various styles built during the course of the war, but the first nine to have the above general characteristics are worth remembering. We shall hear much of them in succeeding pages, so all their names will be given here: *Cairo, Carondelet, Cincinnati, Louisville, Mound City, Pittsburg*, and *St. Louis,* each displacing about 500 tons; and the *Essex* and *Benton,* each of about 1,000 tons. The last-named vessel was a converted wrecking steamer or snag boat; she eventually became the flagship and was a very powerful vessel indeed.

A short distance east of Cairo the Tennessee and Cumberland rivers empty into the Ohio after flowing northward on parallel courses not widely separated. Near the Kentucky-Tennessee border where the streams are little more than ten miles apart, the Confederates had built fortifications in commanding natural positions —Fort Henry on the Tennessee and Fort Donelson on the Cumberland. Henry was on the right or east bank of the more westerly Tennessee River and Donelson was on the left or west bank of the Cumberland. These strongholds were most important strategically for they barred all Federal advance to the south in this region either by land or water; and also protected the eastern flanks of the Confederate positions on the Mississippi River. Henry and Donelson and many other strong points were armed with ordnance captured in the too hurriedly surrendered Norfolk Navy Yard. This great number of guns, *at least 1,200,* constituted an incalculable asset to the South on many fronts throughout the entire war.

In view of the over-all situation General Grant determined to march his army against Fort Henry, the gunboats to ascend the river and attack the fortifications from the water side. Andrew Hull Foote was then in command of the naval force. A youngster named Eliot Callender, who had been working in a tanyard, called upon Foote and endeavored to persuade him that he was qualified for commissioned rank. Unsuccessful in his attempt but not chagrined, he shipped with the rating of ordinary seaman in the *Cincinnati* which was then the flagship. He was a discerning youngster, as will be noted here and in another chapter. In later years he read a paper before the Commandery of the State of Illinois, Military Order of the Loyal Legion of the U. S.; he called his paper "What a Boy Saw on the Mississippi River." It was published in Volume I of the Commandery's *Military Essays and Recollections.* In it he recounts the following event which took place on board his ship:

"An interesting incident, and one that has never seen print, occurred the evening before the battle. Generals Grant, McClernand, [C. F.] Smith, and another officer whose name escapes me, came aboard the 'Cincinnati' about dusk, to hold a conference with the Admiral and arrange a program for the assault on the fort the next day. While they were in the cabin, the wooden gunboat 'Conestoga,' under the command of Lieutenant (now Captain) Selfridge [Phelps], which had been ordered on a reconnoitering expedition up the river to ascertain if the channel was clear of obstructions, dropped alongside the flag-ship and unloaded a huge torpedo, which she had pulled out of the river above, on the 'Cincinnati's' fantail. The fantail of these iron-clads was a clear space at the stern of the boat, near the water's edge, running the width of the boat and about fifteen feet deep, across which worked the steering apparatus connected with the rudders. From the extreme end of the fantail arose the iron end of the gun-deck, about ten feet high on an inclined plane, which was ascended by an ordinary ship's ladder. The conference being over, the army officers, accompanied by the Admiral, came down this ladder to the fantail, and were about embarking on the row-boat with which they had reached the flag-ship, when their attention was attracted to the torpedo, which lay at their feet. They gathered about it with expressions of interest and curiosity, as it was the first seen in the war. It was a formidable affair, being an iron cylinder about five feet long and eighteen inches in diameter, pointed at both ends, with a long iron rod projecting upward, terminating at one end in three iron prongs to catch the bottom of the boat passing over it, and connected at the other end with any ordinary musket-lock which was fixed to explode a cap. General Grant having expressed a wish to see the mechanism of the affair, the ship's armorer was sent for, who soon appeared with monkey-wrench, hammer, and chisels. The iron end was soon loosened and removed, disclosing another ending in a cap with a screw head. The thing was now getting interesting, and the assembled officers bent closely over it in order to get a better view of the infernal contrivance. As this cap was unscrewed, it allowed vent to a quantity of gas inside, probably generated from the wet powder, which rushed out with a loud sizzing noise. Believing that the hour for evening prayer had arrived, two of the army officers threw themselves face downward upon the deck. Admiral Foote, with the agility of a cat, sprang up the ship's ladder, followed with commendable enthusiasm by General Grant. Reaching the top, and realizing that the danger, if any, had passed, the Admiral turned around to General Grant, who was displaying more energy than grace in his first efforts on a ship's ladder, and said, with his quiet smile, 'General, why this haste?' 'That the navy may not get ahead of us,' as quietly responded the General as he turned around to come down. A hearty laugh was now in order, and was indulged in by all hands. The armorer proceeded with his work, and the dissection was completed. The thought has come to me more than once in these later years, how the explosion of that torpedo that evening might have changed the entire history of the war."

To anyone who gave more than a cursory glance at the names of the new ironclads it is evident that all but one were named for cities and towns close by the waters upon which we are now operating. The exception was the *Essex*. Before she was christened, her commanding officer was already scheduled to be William D. ("Bill") Porter, son of the noted Commodore David Porter of older *Essex* fame. So in honor of the father the new vessel was called *Essex* too. William D. was a brother of David Dixon Porter, of whom much more later. The second master of the *Essex* at this time was one James Laning, and fortunately he left to posterity an account of the attack on Fort Henry (quoted in Walke's *Naval Scenes and Reminiscences*). Most of it is reprinted here:

"On February 1st, 1862, the iron-clad gunboat 'Essex,' whilst lying off Fort Holt, received orders from Flag-Officer A. H. Foote, commanding the Western flotilla, to proceed up the Tennessee river, and anchor some five miles below Fort Henry, which was blockading the river at that point. The iron-clads 'Carondelet,' Commander Henry Walke; the 'Cincinnati,' Commander Stembel, and the 'St. Louis,' Lieutenant Commanding Leonard Paulding, were completed and put into commission a few days previous, making, with the 'Essex,' four iron-clads, besides the wooden gunboats 'Taylor,' 'Lexington' and 'Conestoga,' now ready for offensive operations.

"On the 5th of February, after reconnoitering up the Tennessee to Fort Henry, we fired a few shots at the fort and returned towards our anchorage. The enemy made no reply, and apparently took no notice of our shots, until we were well on our way back. When about two, or two and a half miles distant, the fort fired a rifle shot, which passed over our boat to the right and cut down a number of saplings on shore. In a few moments another shot, fired with more precision, passed over the spar-deck amongst the officers; through the officers' quarters, visiting in its flight the steerage, commander's pantry and cabin; passing through the stern; doing, however, no damage except breaking some of the captain's dishes, and cutting the feet from a pair of his socks, which happened to be hanging over the back of a chair in his cabin. These shots reaching us at so great a distance, rather astonished us, as the enemy intended they should.

"After this reconnoissance it was decided to remove the torpedoes from the island chute, and instead of going up the main channel, to steam up the chute, and forming line of battle under cover of the timber on the island, advance towards the fort and open fire as we reached the head of the island at the distance of a mile to a mile and a half and continue advancing. The wooden gunboats 'Taylor' and 'Lexington' were therefore ordered to remove the torpedoes, which they did without difficulty. The army, which was encamped on both sides of the river, were to move at daylight on the morning of the 6th, so as to make a land attack, and prevent the escape of the garrison, whilst the gunboats were to attack as before mentioned.

"On the afternoon of the 5th, Flag-Officer Foote came on board the 'Essex,' and our crew were called to quarters for drill and inspection. After putting them through the evolutions he addressed the crew, and admonished them to be brave and courageous, and above all to place their trust in Divine Providence. The writer, who was in command of the battery, was especially charged with the importance of wasting no shots. 'Remember,' said he, 'that your greatest efforts should be to disable the enemy's guns, and be sure you do not throw any ammunition away. Every charge you fire from one of these guns cost the government about eight dollars. If your shots fall short you encourage the enemy. If they reach home you demoralize him, and get the worth of your money.' After commending all to the care of Divine Providence he left us, and repaired on board the 'Cincinnati,' which was his flag ship at that time.

"During the night of the 5th, or morning of the 6th, a heavy rain fell, which very much retarded the movements of the army. . . . The naval forces, after waiting until 11 o'clock, A. M., got under way and steamed up the river. Arriving at the island chute, the line of battle was formed, the 'Essex' on the extreme right, the 'Cincinnati,' with Flag-Officer Foote on board, on our left, the 'Carondelet' on her left, and the 'St. Louis' on the extreme left— the wooden boats taking position in our rear under cover of the island, and firing over us at long range.

"As we could only use the bow batteries on each boat, we could only bring, on the four iron-clads, eleven guns to bear. The fort, although mounting seventeen guns, could only bring eleven of them to bear on the island chute, so it was a fair and square fight, and the problem was about to be solved whether iron-clad gun-boats could compete with mud fortifications. Under the old system of warfare, I believe, it was conceded that one gun on land was about equal to three on water.

"Upon arriving at the head of the island, the flag ship 'Cincinnati' opened fire, which was the signal to commence the general engagement. The writer had, however, received orders from Captain Porter not to fire until he had particularly noted the effect of the 'Cincinnati' shots, so as to profit by their mistakes, if they made any, in elevation. The first three shots from the flag ship fell short, so there was twenty-four dollars' worth of ammunition expended. A lesson, however, had been learned on board the 'Essex,' and orders were at once given to increase elevation. At that moment the captain's aid appeared on the gun-deck with orders to fire high, and blaze away; and before I could repeat the order, the No. 2 port bow gun belched forth her fiery flame, and sent a 9-inch shell plump into the breastworks, which, exploding handsomely, caused a considerable scattering of earth, and called forth a cheer from the fleet, whilst it produced great consternation in the fort. The 'Essex' had therefore won the honor of putting the first shot into the enemy's breastworks.

"And here I must record the fact, in justice to the memory of a brave man, who lost his life in that engagement, that the honor of that shot belonged to Jack Matthews, captain of the No. 2 gun.

Jack was an 'old tar,' who had seen much service on men-of-war in both the English and American navies, and was always restive under the command of a volunteer officer. Jack, ever on the alert to put in the first licks, and feeling, no doubt, jealous and insubordinate, had increased the elevation of his gun, and just as I was in the act of repeating the captain's order, pulled his lock string, and blazed away.

"The fort seemed a blaze of fire, whilst the boom of the cannon's roar was almost deafening. The wind was blowing across our bows, carrying the smoke away so rapidly as to prevent any obstruction to the view. Our fleet kept slowly approaching the fort, and gradually shortening the distance. Our shells, which were fused at fifteen seconds, were reduced to ten, and then to five seconds. The elevation of the guns was depressed from seven degrees to six, five, and four, and then three degrees, and every shot went straight home, none from the 'Essex' falling short.

"Twenty or thirty minutes after the action had began, some one of the officers ventured to call the attention of Captain Porter to the fact that the officers on the other vessels were leaving the spardecks and going below. 'Oh, yes,' says Porter, 'I see; we will go too, directly.' Just then a shot struck the pilot-house, making the splinters fly terribly, as no plating had as yet been put on the pilot-house. At this the order was given for all to go below, and soon all joined us on the gun-deck. Captain Porter, on coming below, addressed the officers and crew, and complimented the first division for their splendid execution, asking us if we did not want to rest, and give three cheers, and they were given with a will.

"By orders I turned over the command of the battery to the third master, and ordered the first division to give way to the second. Captain Porter then ordered the first division to the stern battery. This was a precautionary measure the importance of which could scarcely be estimated at that time, but became dreadfully apparent a few moments after. A few of my men, however, reluctant to quit the scene of action, lingered by their guns on the forward gun-deck; amongst the number was Jack Matthews. In the twinkling of an eye the scene was changed from a blaze of glory to a carnival of death and destruction. A shot from the enemy pierced the casemate just above the port-hole on the port side, then through the middle boiler, killing Acting Master's Mate S. B. Brittan, Jr., in its flight, and opening a chasm for the escape of the scalding steam and water. The scene which followed was almost indescribable. The writer, who had gone aft in obedience to orders only a few moments before (thus providentially saved) was met by Fourth Master Walker, followed by a crowd of men rushing aft. Walker called to me to go back; that a shot from the enemy had carried away the steam pipe. I at once ran to the stern of the vessel, and looking out of the stern port, saw a number of our brave fellows struggling in the water. The steam and hot water in the forward gun-deck had driven all who were able to get out of the ports overboard, except a few who were fortunate enough to cling to the casemate outside. On seeing the men in the water, I ordered Mr. Walker to man the boats and pick them up; Captain Porter, who was badly scalded, being assisted through the port from outside the casemate by the surgeon, Dr. Thomas Rice, and one of the men.

"When the explosion took place Captain Porter was standing directly in front of the boilers, with his aid, Mr. Brittan, at his side. He at once rushed for the port-hole on the starboard side, and threw himself out, expecting to go into the river. A seaman (John Walker) seeing his danger, caught him around the waist, and supporting him with one hand, clung to the vessel with the other, until, with the assistance of another seaman, who came to the rescue, they succeeded in getting the captain onto a narrow guard or projection, which ran around the vessel, and thus enabled him to make his way outside, to the after port, where I met him. Upon speaking to him, he told me that he was badly hurt; and that I must hunt for Mr. Riley, and if he was disabled I must take command of the vessel, and man the battery again. Mr. Riley was unharmed, and already in the discharge of his duties as Captain Porter's successor. He had been saved by a sailor (John W. Eagle) from going overboard in much the same manner that Captain Porter had been. This man Eagle was captain of the No. 1 gun, and like Jack Matthews, would not leave his gun, and although badly wounded, with his right hand in a sling, he begged me, with tears in his eyes, not to remove him, but to let him fight his gun. I reported the case to Captain Porter, who decided to let him remain; and this brave fellow fought his gun most admirably through the action, and then 'capped the climax' of his bravery and heroism by grasping the casemate with his wounded hand, and clasping Executive Officer Riley with the other

one as he was falling overboard, sustaining him until both regained a footing on the projection before mentioned.

"In a very few minutes after the explosion our gallant ship
(which had, in the language of Flag-Officer Foote, fought most effectually through two-thirds of the engagement), was drifting slowly
away from the field of glory; her commander badly wounded, a
number of her officers and crew dead at their post, whilst many
others were writhing in their last agony. As soon as the scalding
steam would admit, the forward gun-deck was explored. The pilots,
who were both in the pilot-house, were scalded to death. Marshall
Ford, who was steering when the explosion took place, was found
at his post at the wheel, standing erect, his left hand holding the
spoke, and his right hand grasping the signal bell-rope. Pilot James
McBride had fallen through the open hatchway to the deck below;
he was still living, but died soon after. The captain's aid, Mr. S. B.
Brittan, Jr., had fallen by the shot as it passed through the gun-
deck before entering the boiler. A seaman named James Coffey,
who was shot-man to the No. 2 gun, was on his knees in the act of
taking a shell from the box to be passed to the loader. The escaping
steam and hot water had struck him square in the face, and he met
death in that position. Jack Matthews had gone overboard badly
scalded. He was picked up by the boats. Third Master Theo. P.
Terry was severely scalded, and died in a few days. He was a brave
officer.

"Our loss in killed, wounded and missing amounted to 32. Of
these 3 were killed instantly, 4 died that night, several were
drowned (the number not definitely known), and about half the
wounded recovered.

"The flag-officer continued approaching nearer and nearer to the
fort, pouring shot and shell from the boats at still shorter range . . .
until they showed the white flag to surrender. When I told Captain
Porter that we were victorious, he immediately rallied, and raising himself on his elbow, called for three cheers, and gave two
himself, falling exhausted on the mattress in his effort to make the
third. A seaman named Jasper P. Breas, who was badly scalded,
sprang to his feet, naked to the waist, his jacket and shirt having
been removed to dress his wounds, exclaiming: 'Surrendered! I
must see that with my own eyes before I die.' Before any one could
interfere, he clambered up two short flights of stairs to the spar-

deck, where he was gladdened with the sight of his own flag proudly
and victoriously floating in the breeze. He shouted, 'Glory to God!'
and sank exhausted on the deck. Poor Jasper died that night, that
his country might live.

"The 'Essex' fired seventy-two shots from two 9-inch guns during the battle. In obedience to battle orders, I had instructed the
powder boys to keep count of the number of charges served to
each gun. Job Phillips, a boy fourteen years old, was powder boy
of No. 1 gun. After the action, I asked Job how many shots his gun
had fired. He referred me to a memorandum on the whitewashed
casemate; where with a rusty nail he had carefully and accurately
marked every shot his gun had fired; and his account was corrobo-
rated by the gunner in the magazine. This may be considered as a
striking example of coolness and bravery in a boy of fourteen, who
had never before been under fire."

The story of Fort Henry is completed by Commander Walke
in his *Naval Scenes and Reminiscences;* he commanded the *Carondelet* at this time, it will be remembered.

"In approaching to take possession of Fort Henry, the 'St. Louis'
ran ahead, and with frantic cheers some of her crew landed at the
fort, contrary to the express orders of the flag-officer. The 'Cincinnati' and 'Carondelet' steamed up and flanked the batteries; the latter, being nearest to the fort, ran aground in that position, just as
the order was given for their engines to be stopped, and the 'Cincinnati' began to drift down the river. At first sight the 'Carondelet'
appeared to be steaming ahead of the flag-officer, and Foote immediately hailed her commander, with a few sharp technicalities
to keep in his station; but the 'Carondelet' was immovable: sticking fast to the flats, she stubbornly remained in her position ahead
of the other boats, notwithstanding all that her commander could
say or the engines do to back her off. Here was a scene! The flag-
officer in the midst of the excitement came forward in haste, trumpet
in hand, and called out again and again to stop the 'Carondelet'
(unaware of the fact that his own vessel was all the time drifting
down the river) until at last he gave up the undertaking in favor
of a junior officer, whose lungs (poor fellow) proved quite inade-

quate to the task of moving the 'Carondelet;' which with the cheers, orders, groans and general confusion; all the captain's efforts to explain his queer situation were confounded. At length the pantomime transformed itself into a comedy; but a satisfactory explanation was finally afforded by the action of the gunboat, sliding off the bank into deep water.

.　　.　　.　　.　　.　　.　　.　　.　　.　　.

"General Tilghman, with two or three of his staff, came off in a small boat to the 'Cincinnati' and formally surrendered Fort Henry to Admiral Foote, who sent for Captain Walke, introduced him to General Tilghman, and gave him orders to take command of the fort, until the arrival of General Grant, who soon after relieved him of his charge. Some of the cabins in the rear of the fort were still on fire, and the flames were put out by our men. Several of the 'Essex' 9-inch shell were found in the rear of the cabins unexploded. The first glance over the fort silenced all jubilant expressions of the victorious. On every side lay the lifeless bodies of the victims, in reckless confusion, intermingled with shattered implements of war. Our eyes then met each other's gaze with a sadness, full of meaning, that forbade any attempt to speak, and, in the quietness like to that of a graveyard, we walked slowly over the desolate scene.

"The largest gun of the fort was disabled, being filled with earth by one of our shells striking the parapet near its muzzle; the muzzle of another was broken by our shell; a third, with broken carriage and two dead men, was almost buried under the heaps of earth; a fourth burst, scattering the mangled gunners into the water and in all directions, scarcely one of them escaping. The surgeon of the fort labored with the few he could get to help him, to save the bleeding and dying. The scene was one which robbed us of all feelings of exultation. Some of our shell had pierced entirely through the breastwork; throwing tons of earth over the prostrated gunners, and then plunging ten feet into the earth beyond, or through the cabins in the rear: afterwards setting fire to them by their explosions. After the wounded were cared for, and the excitement had subsided, our men proceeded instinctively and quietly to draw the dead bodies of the victims from the water and the earth, and then buried them as well as they could."

The piercing of the *Essex'* boiler was a type of casualty which was not infrequent in Civil War gunboat actions; and it almost invariably resulted in horrible injuries. There is much confusion about the number of men in the *Essex* who were incapacitated this day, and Laning's figures are not correct. Some of the trouble arises from the fact that the gunboats' complements were partly filled out with soldiers at this time. In any case we have an official report, the figures of which were at least correct and complete as of the day following the battle. Altogether the *Essex* listed 10 killed, 5 missing, 8 scalded badly, 14 scalded, and 1 scalded slightly; total 38. Of the officers and pilots alone there were 3 dead, 1 scalded badly (died later), and 1 scalded slightly. One of the officer deaths was the only one caused by gunfire. Beyond this point we can assume reasonably that all the "missing" lost their lives, and that most of those "scalded badly" died later. Of the 19 soldiers on board, 13 were casualties. There never was a war that was fun for everybody. In order to close on a happier note, however, it may be mentioned that the casualties were negligible in all the remainder of the flotilla.

CHAPTER V

BLUE NAVY *VS.* GRAY ARMY

Now it happens that while Grant and Foote were making their preparations for taking Fort Henry, the Confederates decided that they did not have the strength to hold it anyway. So they began to pull out for Fort Donelson, leaving little more than the garrison of the fort to fight what was virtually a rear-guard action. Even Fort Heiman, a strong point across the river, was evacuated although it was a position dominating Fort Henry. However, due to the rains and the frightful condition of the roads and minor watercourses, Grant was so delayed, it will be remembered, that almost all the retreating forces got away. The Union army that was landed on the west bank of the river found Heiman completely devoid of men.

So, after the capitulation of Henry, the next move was against Fort Donelson, only ten miles away on the Cumberland. It was situated just below the village of Dover, Tennessee. Here there was no complication of a second fort across the river. Donelson was integral in itself and was well guarded against attack from both land and water. Grant organized the venture as rapidly as possible; he wanted to move before enemy reinforcements could be brought up. He felt positive that these would be pushed forward to the utmost, in view of the vital importance of the place. A few days elapsed, but he moved on February 12 and invested the fortifications with a numerically inferior body of men! He did this, and succeeded with impunity, because he was sure of certain idiosyncracies of the Confederate general, Gideon Pillow, who was then virtually in charge. Meanwhile additional regiments in transports were coming around and up the Cumberland River along with the gunboats to take part in the offensive. There seems to be little evidence, however, of any plan for a well co-ordinated joint attack by army and navy. There had been one worked out for Fort Henry, even though the timing on that occasion did break down.

A very stirring attack was made on Donelson by the gunboats, and fortunately we have good firsthand accounts from both sides. Before reading them it is desirable to consider the guns in the Confederate batteries that were to oppose the boats, as the characteristics of these weapons were all-important. There were exactly two guns of long range, a 10-inch Columbiad and a 32-pounder rifled gun. Next there were eight 32-pounder smoothbores whose range was quite moderate. Lastly there were two 32-pounder carronades which were of no value except against wooden vessels at short range. While on the subject of guns this is a good place to point out what must be some sort of a typographical error in the words which are to be presented below from the pen of Captain Walke of the *Carondelet.* He speaks at one point of his expenditure of "10-inch and 15-inch shells." His bow guns, among the biggest aboard, consisted of one 8-inch smoothbore and two old 42-pounders which had been converted from smoothbores to rifles. These facts check with Walke's own and the official records.

There are many misconceptions about this important fight, especially on the part of the contestants on each side, about what occurred on the other side. Accordingly, pieces of the accounts will be sandwiched in with each other since this can be done, it is felt, to the advantage rather than to the detriment of the story. In general, each day's accounts will be completed before starting those of the following day; and each Confederate account will follow each Union account. Captain Walke contributes his description of the action in Volume I of the Century Company's *Battles and Leaders of the Civil War* as part of his "The Western Flotilla at Fort Donelson, Island Number Ten, Fort Pillow and Memphis." One of the important artillery officers at the fort was Lieutenant H. L. (H. S.?) Bedford. After supervising the mounting of many of the river guns, he commanded the 10-inch Columbiad. His story of the engagement was read before the Confederate Relief and Historical Association at Memphis; it was published later in Volume XIII of the *Southern Historical Society Papers* under the title "Fight Between the Batteries and Gunboats at Fort Donelson." Also there was a bluejacket in the *Carondelet* whose letter to his family has come down to us (quoted in Walke's *Naval Scenes and Reminiscences*). In order that the reader may not have to suffer the horrors of footnotes in addition to those of war, the source of the following extracts will be designated at the beginning of each one as follows: Commander Walke's passages will be preceded in each case by a "W," Lieutenant Bedford's by a "B," and those of the bluejacket by a "BJ."

As has been noted previously, the gunboats and transports were moving down the Tennessee and up the Cumberland on their way to Fort Donelson. They were badly strung out and the *Carondelet* was far ahead of the rest. She was in tow of the transport *Alps* in order to save fuel and time. As Walke wrote in an official dispatch (the parentheses being his): "I am (or the *Carondelet* is) very slow." On the morning of February 12, the first of her three days of fighting, the *Carondelet* was approaching her destination. And at this point we shall commence the firsthand reports with an extract from Captain Walke's story:

(W.) "When the *Carondelet,* her tow being cast off, came in sight of the fort and proceeded up to within long range of the batteries, not a living creature could be seen. The hills and woods on the west side of the river hid part of the enemy's formidable defenses, which were lightly covered with snow; but the black rows of heavy guns, pointing down on us, reminded me of the dismal-looking sepulchers cut in the rocky cliffs near Jerusalem, but far more repulsive. At 12:50 P. M., to unmask the silent enemy, and to announce my arrival to General Grant, I ordered the bow-guns to be fired at the fort. Only one shell fell short. There was no response except the echo from the hills. The fort appeared to have been evacuated. After firing ten shells into it, the *Carondelet* dropped down the river about three miles and anchored."

(B.) "On the morning of the 12th of February the finishing touches were put to the Columbiad, and the batteries were pronounced ready for gunboats. . . .

"As the artillerists, who were to serve the rifle and Columbiad, had no experience with heavy guns, most of them probably never having seen a heavy battery until that morning, it was important that they should be instructed in the manual of their pieces. Drilling, therefore, began immediately, but had continued for a short time only when it was most effectually interrupted by the appearance of a gunboat down the river, which subsequently was ascertained to be the Carondelet. She fired about a dozen shots with remarkable precision, and retired without any response from the batteries."

(W.) "But the sound of her guns aroused our soldiers on the southern side of the fort into action; one report says that when they heard the guns of the *avant-courier* of the fleet, they gave cheer upon cheer, and rather than permit the sailors to get ahead of them again, they engaged in skirmishes with the enemy, and began the battle of the three days following. On the *Carondelet* we were isolated and beset with dangers from the enemy's lurking sharp-shooters.

"On the 13th a dispatch was received from General Grant, informing me that he had arrived the day before, and had succeeded in getting his army in position, almost entirely investing the enemy's works. 'Most of our batteries,' he said, 'are established, and the remainder soon will be. If you will advance with your gunboats at 10 o'clock a. m., we will be ready to take advantage of every diversion in our favor.'

"I immediately complied with these instructions, and at 9:05, with the *Carondelet* alone and under cover of a heavily wooded point, fired 139 70-pound and 64-pound shells at the fort. We received in turn the fire of all the enemy's guns that could be brought to bear on the *Carondelet,* which sustained but little damage, except from two shots. One, a 128-pound solid, at 11:30 struck the corner of our port broadside casemate, passed through it, and in its progress toward the center of our boilers glanced over the temporary barricade in front of the boilers. It then passed over the steam-drum, struck the beams of the upper deck, carried away the railing around the engine-room and burst the steam-heater, and, glancing back into the engine-room, 'seemed to bound after the men,' as one of the engineers said, 'like a wild beast pursuing its prey.' I have preserved this ball as a souvenir of the fight at Fort Donelson. When it burst through the side of the *Carondelet,* it knocked down and wounded a dozen men, seven of them severely. An immense quantity of splinters was blown through the vessel. Some of them, as fine as needles, shot through the clothes of the men like arrows. Several of the wounded were so much excited by the suddenness of the event and the sufferings of their comrades, that they were not aware that they themselves had been struck until they felt the blood running into their shoes. Upon receiving this shot we ceased firing for a while.

"After dinner we sent the wounded on board the *Alps*, repaired damages, and, not expecting any assistance, at 12:15 we resumed, in accordance with General Grant's request, and bombarded the fort until dusk, when nearly all our 10-inch and 15-inch shells were expended. The firing from the shore having ceased, we retired."

(B.) "On the morning of the 13th drilling was again interrupted by the firing of this boat, and the same thing happened in the afternoon. It really appeared as if the boat was diabolically inspired, and knew the most opportune times to annoy us. Sometime during the day, probably about noon, she delivered her fire with such accuracy that forbearance was no longer endurable, and Lieutenant Dixon ordered the Columbiad and rifle to respond. The first shot from the Columbiad passed immediately over the boat, the second fell short, but the third was distinctly heard to strike. A cheer of course followed, and Lieutenant Dixon, in the enthusiasm of the moment, ordered the 32-pounders to open fire, although the enemy was clearly beyond their range. The Carondelet, nothing daunted, continued the action, and soon one of her shells cut away the right cheek of one of Captain Bidwell's guns, and a flying nut passed through Lieutenant Dixon's head, killing him instantly. In this engagement the flange of one of the front traverse wheels of the Columbiad was crushed, and a segment of the front half of the traverse circle was cupped, both of which proved serious embarrassments in the action next day."

(W.) "At 11:30 on the night of the 13th Flag-Officer Foote arrived below Fort Donelson with the iron-clads *St. Louis, Louisville,* and *Pittsburgh,* and the wooden gun-boats *Tyler* and *Conestoga.* On the 14th all the hard materials in the vessels, such as chains, lumber, and bags of coal, were laid on the upper decks to protect them from the plunging shots of the enemy. At 3 o'clock in the afternoon our fleet advanced to attack the fort, the *Louisville* being on the west side of the river, the *St. Louis* (flag-steamer) next, then the *Pittsburgh* and *Carondelet* on the east side of the river. The wooden gun-boats were about a thousand yards in the rear. When we started in line abreast at a moderate speed, the *Louisville* and *Pittsburgh,* not keeping up to their positions, were hailed from the flag-steamer to 'steam up.' At 3:30, when about a mile and a half from the fort, two shots were fired at us, both falling short. When within a mile of the fort the *St. Louis* opened fire, and the other iron-clads followed, slowly and deliberately at first, but more rapidly as the fleet advanced. The flag-officer hailed the *Carondelet,* and ordered us not to fire so fast. Some of our shells went over the fort, and almost into our camp beyond. As we drew nearer, the enemy's fire greatly increased in force and effect. But, the officers and crew of the *Carondelet* having recently been long under fire, and having become practiced in fighting, her gunners were as cool and composed as old veterans. We heard the deafening crack of the bursting shells, the crash of the solid shot, and the whizzing of fragments of shell and wood as they sped through the vessel. Soon a 128-pounder struck our anchor, smashed it into flying bolts, and bounded over the vessel, taking away a part of our smoke-stack; then another cut away the iron boat-davits as if they were pipe-stems, whereupon the boat dropped into the water. Another ripped up the iron plating and glanced over; another went through the plating and lodged in the heavy casemate; another struck the pilot-house, knocked the plating to pieces, and sent fragments of iron and splinters into the pilots, one of whom fell mortally wounded, and was taken below; another shot took away the remaining boat-davits and the boat with them; and still they came, harder and faster, taking flag-staffs and smoke-stacks, and tearing off the side armor as lightning tears the bark from a tree. Our men fought desperately, but, under the excitement of the occasion, loaded too hastily, and the port rifled gun exploded. One of the crew, in his account of the explosion soon after it occurred, said:

(BJ.) "We fought desperately for about two hours and a half, within less than half a mile from the fort, when the rifled gun I was serving with shell exploded, knocking us all down, killing none, but wounding over a dozen men, and spreading dismay and confusion among us for a short time. For about two minutes I was stunned, and at least five minutes elapsed before I could tell what was the matter. When I found out that I was more scared than hurt (although suffering from the gunpowder which I had inhaled), I looked forward and found that our gun had burst, and was lying on the deck split in three pieces. Then the cry ran through the boat that we were on fire, and my duty of pump-man called me to the pumps. While there, two shot entered our bow-ports, and killed four men, and wounded about a dozen. They were borne past me, three with their heads off, and a fourth with . . . . The sight almost sickened me, and I turned my head away.

"Then came our master's mate, Brennan, revolver in hand, threatening to shoot us if we did not go to our quarters immediately. I told him that our gun had burst, and that we had caught fire from the enemy's shell on the upper deck. He then said, 'Never mind the fire; go to your quarters.' There were six of us at the pumps at the time, and we accordingly obeyed his order.

"Then I took a station at the starboard tackle of another rifled bow gun, and remained there until the close of the fight. While running the gun out, we trampled in the blood and brains of an esteemed shipmate; but such are the horrors of war."

(W.) "The carpenter and his men extinguished the flames.

"When within four hundred yards of the fort, . . . our pilot-house was struck again and another pilot wounded, our wheel was broken, and shells from the rear boats were bursting over us. All four of our boats were shot away and dragging in the water. On looking out to bring our broadside guns to bear, we saw that the other gun-boats were rapidly falling back out of line. The *Pittsburgh* in her haste to turn struck the stern of the *Carondelet,* and broke our starboard rudder, so that we were obliged to go ahead to clear the *Pittsburgh* and the point of rocks below. The pilot of the *St. Louis* was killed, and the pilot of the *Louisville* was wounded. Both vessels had their wheel-ropes shot away, and the men were prevented from steering the *Louisville* with the tiller-ropes at the stern by the shells from the rear boats bursting over them. The *St. Louis* and *Louisville,* becoming unmanageable, were compelled to drop out of battle, and the *Pittsburgh* followed; all had suffered severely from the enemy's fire. Flag-Officer Foote was wounded while standing by the pilot of the *St. Louis* when he was killed. We were then about 350 yards from the fort.

"There was no alternative for the *Carondelet* in that narrow stream but to keep her head to the enemy and fire into the fort with her two bow-guns, to prevent it, if possible, from returning her fire effectively. The enemy saw that she was in a manner left to his mercy, and concentrated the fire of all his batteries upon her. In return, the *Carondelet's* guns were well served to the last shot.

Our new acting gunner, John Hall, was just the man for the occasion. He came forward, offered his services, and with my sanction took charge of the starboard-bow rifled gun. He instructed the men to obey his warnings and follow his motions, and he told them that when he saw a shot coming he would call out 'Down' and stoop behind the breech of the gun as he did so; at the same instant the men were to stand away from the bow-ports. Nearly every shot from the fort struck the bows of the *Carondelet*. Most of them were fired on the ricochet level, and could be plainly seen skipping on the water before they struck. The enemy's object was to sink the gun-boat by striking her just below the water-line. They soon succeeded in planting two 32-pound shots in her bow, between wind and water, which made her leak badly, but her compartments kept her from sinking until we could plug up the shot-holes. Three shots struck the starboard casemating; four struck the port casemating forward of the rifle-gun; one struck on the starboard side, between the water-line and plank-sheer, cutting through the planking; six shots struck the pilot-house, shattering one section into pieces and cutting through the iron casing. The smoke-stacks were riddled.

"Our gunners kept up a constant firing while we were falling back; and the warning words, 'Look out!' 'Down!' were often heard, and heeded by nearly all the gun-crews. On one occasion, while the men were at the muzzle of the middle bow-gun, loading it, the warning came just in time for them to jump aside as a 32-pounder struck the lower sill, and glancing up struck the upper sill, then, falling on the inner edge of the lower sill, bounded on deck and spun around like a top, but hurt no one. It was very evident that if the men who were loading had not obeyed the order to drop, several of them would have been killed. So I repeated the instructions and warned the men at the guns and the crew generally to bow or stand off from the ports when a shot was seen coming. But some of the young men, from a spirit of bravado or from a belief in the doctrine of fatalism, disregarded the instructions, saying it was useless to attempt to dodge a cannon-ball, and they would trust to luck. The warning words, 'Look out!' 'Down!' were again soon heard; down went the gunner and his men, as the whizzing shot glanced on the gun, taking off the gunner's cap and the heads of two of the young men who trusted to luck, and in defiance of the order were standing up or passing behind him. This shot killed another man also, who was at the last gun of the starboard side, and disabled the gun. It came in with a hissing sound; three sharp spats and a heavy bang told the sad fate of three brave comrades. Before the decks were well sanded, there was so much blood on them that our men could not work the guns without slipping.

"We kept firing at the enemy so long as he was within range, to prevent him from seeing us through the smoke."

(B.) "On the morning of the 14th, dense volumes of smoke were seen rising from down the river; it was evident that transports were landing troops. Captain Ross became impatient to annoy them, but having no fuse shells to his guns, he came over to the Columbiad and advised the throwing of shells down the river. The commander declined to do so without orders, whereupon Captain Culbertson, who had succeeded Lieutenant Dixon in the command of the batteries, was looked up, but he refused to give the order, upon the ground that it would accomplish no good, and that he did not believe in the useless shedding of blood. Captain Ross, not to be outdone, set himself to the task of procuring the necessary order and returned to the Columbiad about 3 o'clock P. M. with a verbal order from General Floyd to harass the transports. In obedience to this order, we prepared to shell the smoke. A shell was inserted, the gun was given the proper elevation, the lanyard was pulled, and the missle went hissing over the bend of the river, plunged into a bank of smoke, and was lost to view. This was called by an army correspondent, claiming to have been on one of the gunboats, 'a shot of defiance.' Before the piece could be reloaded, the prow of a gunboat made its appearance around the bend, quickly followed by three others, and arranging themselves in line of battle, steamed up to the attack. When they had arrived within a mile and a half of the batteries, a solid shot having been substituted for a shell, the Columbiad began the engagement with a ricochet shot, the rifle gun a ready second. The gunboats returned the fire, the right center boat opening, the others following in quick succession. After the third discharge the rifle remained silent on account of becoming accidentally spiked. This had a bad effect on the men at the Columbiad, causing them considerable uneasiness for their comrades at the upper battery. The Columbiad continued the action unsupported until the boats came within the range of the 32-pounders, when the engagement became general, with the ten guns of the batteries opposed to the twelve bow guns of the ironclads, supplemented by those of the two wooden boats that remained in the rear throwing curvated shells. As the boats drew nearer, the firing on both sides became faster, until it appeared as if the battle had dwindled into a contest of speed in firing. When they arrived within three hundred yards of the lower battery they came to a stand, and then it was that the bombardment was truly terrific. The roar of cannons was continuous and deafening, and commands, if necessary, had to be given by signs. Pandemonium itself would hardly have been more appalling, but neither chaos nor cowardice obtruded themselves. . . . The Columbiad was rigidly impartial, and fired on the boats as chance or circumstances dictated, with the exception of the last few shots, which were directed at the Carondelet. This boat was hugging the eastern shore, and was a little in advance of the others. She offered her side to the Columbiad, which was on the left and the most advanced gun of the batteries. Several well-directed shots raked the side and tore away her armor, according to the report of Lieutenant Sparkman, who was on the lookout. Just as the other boats began to drift back, the Carondelet forged ahead for about a half length, as though she intended making the attempt to pass the battery, and it is presumable that she then received the combined fire of all the guns.

". . . After the battle three of the gunboats were seen drifting helplessly down the stream, and a shout of exultation leaped from the lips of every soldier in the fort. It was taken up by the men in the trenches, and for a while a shout of victory, the sweetest strain to the ears of those who win, reverberated over the hills and hollows around the little village of Dover.

"While the cannoniers were yet panting from their exertion, Lieutenant-Colonel Robb, of the Forty-ninth Tennessee, who fell mortally wounded the next day, ever mindful of those around him, sent a grateful stimulant along the line of guns."

(W.) "The 15th was employed in the burial of our slain comrades. I read the Episcopal service on board the Carondelet, under our flag at half-mast; and the sailors bore their late companions to a lonely field within the shadows of the hills."

(BJ.) "I had the last solemn duty to perform for them on earth, namely, marking their rough head-boards with the initials of their names. I was present at their burial. A Catholic priest was passing by at the time, and thought that he would say a few words over them. Our officer checked him, and told him to wait a little longer, as another body would soon arrive from the gunboat 'St. Louis.' After its arrival, he asked the attention of those gathered around him. He made a few remarks about the deceased seamen, in which he said that 'although they did not die like Christians, they died like heroes in the defense of their country and their flag.' He then read the prayers for the dead, and ordered us to cover them over. They were all buried in a row, with their faces to the West. Their names were Albert Richardson, of Baltimore, Albert Markham, of Mississippi, William Duff, Joseph G. Leacock, and Charles W. Baker, all of Philadelphia. The first four mentioned belonged to the 'Carondelet,' and Baker to the 'St. Louis.'"

(W.) "As the last service was ended, the sound of the battle being waged by General Grant, like the rumbling of distant thunder, was the only requiem for our departed shipmates."

This land battle of the fifteenth had been initiated by the besieged army, much to the surprise of General Grant. He had noted their passivity while in superior force. Now that the advantage in numbers was on his side he felt sure they would not attack—at least not right away. But he was mistaken; and the attack came when he was down the river conferring with the wounded Flag Officer. The beleaguered force tried to break out to the south. Commencing with the utmost promise the Confederate movement bogged down in spite of the demoralization suffered by the National units which bore the brunt. Grant got back to the scene of action, effected a reorganization, and instituted a strong counterattack all along the line. His victory was so complete that the whole Confederate army surrendered unconditionally the following day, except for a few thousand who had slipped away during the night by river and on horseback along the bank.

There are two important factors involved in the gunboat action. Ignorant of the ranges of the various pieces of enemy artillery, Foote did not take advantage of a situation which offered the possibility of a complete victory almost without any loss whatsoever to his fleet. The excellent preliminary shooting of the *Carondelet* demonstrated what could be done while lying out of range of all but two of the enemy guns. With deliberate shooting, it would not have required a very long time for the four boats together to put out of action practically every gun opposed to them, meanwhile undergoing the shelling of only two guns even at the start. And it will be remembered that the Confederates' rifle, by rarest chance, was accidentally spiked after firing only three rounds on the big day; thus there remained only one gun with a long range— the Columbiad. The boats alone would have been a serious threat to the main fort if they had succeeded in silencing all the river batteries, and had thus been enabled to pitch shells into the fort without opposition. But the Federal boats shortened the range to the point where even the Rebel carronades could reach. With little doubt, too many envisaged a repetition of the Fort Henry cleanup. The result was as we have just read—a fearful hammering of at least two of the four ironclads. The flagship *St. Louis* alone was hit fifty-nine times. The important specific factor of the defeat, however, lay in the damage suffered by the steering gear of two of the boats. This put half of the force out of action completely for a period long enough to cause the decisive loss of the day.

Note further the great importance of the time element in this operation. The Confederate guns were ready just a couple of hours before the first appearance of the *Carondelet*.

In spite of the battered condition of the flotilla, the *St. Louis* and *Louisville* moved up to the attack the next afternoon, the day of the land fighting. Although the damage they inflicted was insignificant, their moral effect under all the circumstances was great. They demonstrated to both sides that the fleet was still a going concern despite the disaster of the day before.

Only 12 Federals had been killed in the big attack, a splendid testimonial to the defensive strength of the ironclads; but this number included, unfortunately, 3 more pilots. And the 42 wounded included Flag Officer Foote who was already demonstrating his ability and his value to the Navy of the West. Walke was incorrect, however, in stating that the *Louisville*'s pilot was wounded; fortunately he was not a casualty.

The great importance of the capture of the two forts can be handled in one summary. Immediately after the surrender of Fort Henry, the wooden gunboats swept up the Tennessee and captured or destroyed a very valuable collection of steamers and stores. In two days they traversed the whole depth of Tennessee, skirted the corner of Mississippi, and steamed through Alabama to the stopping point formed by Muscle Shoals. The capture of Fort Donelson permitted the gunboats to ascend the Cumberland as far as they liked, and again much material of military value was taken. However, there was little on that river above Nashville, which city fell nine days after Donelson. The capture of the combined Henry-Donelson position forced the withdrawal of Confederate forces from virtually all of Kentucky and a good part of western Tennessee as well. The event was of tremendous strategic importance.

Chapter VI

THE *CARONDELET* AT ISLAND NO. 10

WHEN A VESSEL bears such a lyrical name as *Carondelet* it is unfortunate that her closest association cannot be with a place sounding less prosaic than Island No. 10. Now if this name were only, for instance, *La Dixieme Ile* or the like, how much better it would be! We could then surely compose at least a roundelay out of the connection. But, poetry or prose, we must not fail to trail along with this very active gunboat, and now it is to Island No. 10.

With the capture of Forts Henry and Donelson the whole Ohio-Tennessee-Cumberland water system fell completely into Northern hands, as has already been noted. This made the ironclads wholly available for the one really vital job of the Western Navy, i. e., the opening of the Mississippi River. Foote had established his base at Cairo, Illinois, it should be remembered, where the Ohio flows into the Mississippi. The latter, with all its tributaries, was of course free of enemies above this point. From here to the mouth, however, it had to be cleared. As the crow flies, this distance is less than 500 miles; but considering the involved windings, the course of the river is just about 1,100 miles in length. It was a prodigious undertaking, especially with fortified and easily fortifiable positions at many points along the way. It is almost exclusively on the east bank that these places are found.

Now, the chief object of "opening the Mississippi" was not primarily to restore to the northwestern States their outlet for foreign trade, or even to assist in domestic trade. But to have the river safe again for traffic would aid the Federal military and naval forces very appreciably; and the most valuable achievement of all would be the separation of the seceded States west of the river from those east of it. All of the industrial strength and most of the man power of the Confederacy lay east of the Mississippi. West of it lay Texas, Arkansas, and part of Louisiana—not to mention the Choctaw

Nation. And that was all. In this vast area there were considerably less than a million free whites and scarcely a railroad. However, it was a great source of food supply for the easterly region after war broke out. So, in effect, it became the mission of the North's navy to *blockade* the east bank of the great river in the same respect in which the seacoast was being blockaded from Cape Henry to the Mississippi Delta. Because of lack of ships, scarcely an attempt to blockade the coasts of Louisiana and Texas was made till August, 1862. But if the supplies which might enter the ports of those States from abroad could be stopped at the Mississippi, they could be of no assistance to the Confederate Government.

So, Foote started the long pull down the river soon after Donelson fell. The first position to be reckoned with was the high fortified bluff at Columbus, Kentucky. In the course of Grant's operation at Belmont, Missouri, mentioned earlier, it will be remembered that reinforcements came to his foes from across the river. They came from Columbus which is just below Belmont. This strong position, mounting 140 guns, had to be evacuated by the Confederates when Henry and Donelson fell, because it was then outflanked. Union forces occupied it on March 4.

The first withdrawal of the Confederates down the Mississippi River was not great in distance, and they took with them many of their guns for further use. They made their next stand at Island No. 10, so named because it is the tenth one down the river from the mouth of the Ohio. It lies just where the Kentucky-Tennessee border strikes the river from the east. This spot was eminently suited for blocking the river. Fortifications had been established on the high ground of the island and on the left bank of the stream; and their guns commanded a stretch of river above them several miles in length. Just above Island No. 10 there is a long straight stretch of the river flowing south. About at the island the river turns sharp right, through a horseshoe turn of 180 degrees to the north. Then after about seven miles it makes a second sharp, flat, horseshoe turn of 180 degrees, the course thus becoming south again. Two narrow peninsulas are therefore formed, about two or three miles across. Island No. 10, nearly two miles in length, lay a bit past the middle of the first U-turn and was on the outer arc of the bend at the period we are considering. Its guns could fire upstream effectively by shooting over the low narrow tip of the first peninsula, i. e., the one pointing south. Even the several sources of information of the Confederates themselves conflict as to the ordnance in their batteries. It seems reasonable to conclude, however, that there were mounted upwards of fifty guns altogether, about half of which were quite powerful pieces. Those located on the riverbank were all on the Tennessee shore just below the Kentucky border, and not in Kentucky as stated in narratives which follow.

In the middle of March, Flag Officer Foote dropped down the river with a strong and numerous fleet which included eight ironclad gunboats, and ten mortar boats each mounting one heavy mortar. He got to work on the enemy on the seventeenth of the month but he set a very long range and the effect was slight. He could not treat these opponents in the cavalier manner in which he had handled Fort Henry. Meanwhile a Union army was working down the right bank and had reached a point below the big flat S of the river. It was commanded by General John Pope, not to be confused with the unfortunate skipper of the U. S. S. *Richmond* whom we met at the Head of the Passes. He had established his headquarters at New Madrid, Missouri, which is on the outside of the second bend of the river. When he got down there he found the "control of the sea" in the hands of Commodore Hollins, C. S. N., whose makeshift collection of gunboats included our old friends the *Ivy* and the *McRae*. It was not a strong squadron in any respect, and few members of it were in the vicinity at any one time; but it was much stronger than the nothing which the Federals had there. For, all of Foote's boats were stopped by Island No. 10.

The river was high, as was the water in all the surrounding country; so the large body of troops holding the Confederate batteries were cut off from all directions but the south, and were in touch with the outside world solely via the left bank of the river and friendly watercraft. Pope held the other bank a mile away but his batteries were ineffective in preventing supplies, etc., from reaching the enemy, especially at night.

Foote pounded away at long range, the gunboats as well as the mortar boats tied up to either bank; no results. The opposition here was Fort Donelson many times over, and he dared not go closer. In an almost epic piece of work the army started to extend a bayou all the way across the first peninsula by cutting a "canal" through a flooded forest. The presence of the trees in the proposed channel meant that their trunks had to be cut off at a distance below the surface of the water equal to the depth of channel desired—a baffling job. The object of the canal was to enable men and supplies to be carried all the way to the army by water instead of marching and hauling part of the way through swamplands. This canal was not going to be able to take a gunboat, however; so even the future was not brightened in any important respect by its construction. Pope began to get impatient. If he could have even one ironclad he could accomplish everything; without it nothing. But even a close approach to those vast batteries would seem to ensure the destruction of anything afloat.

Foote's wound was not healing properly and this more than likely reduced the aggressiveness of his measures, for the bombardment was continued at an ineffectively long range. One very important point should be remembered, however. On the previous occasions the gunboats were fighting upstream, this time down. Moreover the river was high, the current swift; nor was the speed through the water of any of the boats anything to boast about. Should any one of them cast off from her moorings, go into action and then become disabled, she was lost. Instead of drifting back away from the enemy as at Fort Donelson, she would drift ahead under the enemy's guns and be destroyed or captured. For, it must not be forgotten that these boats carried little armor except forward; none at all aft. So Foote was loath to fight under way; and there were not any suitable moorings much less than two miles from his targets. Thus he was getting nowhere. Pope was becoming more vocal in his pleas. Foote sounded out his officers on March 20. But Fort Donelson was too fresh in the minds of all. Walke alone disagreed with the opinion that nothing could be done without prohibitive risks.

The high water was hindering the defenders as well as the attackers. Their northernmost battery, more than a mile above the next one, was isolated by the water and swamps to such a degree that it could no longer be manned. Only a few sentries were left there to keep up a bluff. In ignorance of this situation a boat expedition from the fleet went after this battery on the night of April 1–2. The circumstances being as just described, they had no difficulty in swarming over it and spiking the six guns which they found there. Though the opposition was nil, the conception of the attack was very gallant; and the situation was at least partly simplified by the elimination of this battery from the picture.

Two weeks of bombardment had now been carried on, and almost the sole result had been a heavy expenditure of ammunition. Something else had to be tried. That something could be little else than an attempt to run the batteries and thus give General Pope his gunboat—if successful. Even so, who could say that the surviving vessel would be able to cope alone with whatever Rebel gunboats might be brought against her, even including possibly the famed *Manassas?* Foote held another council of war. The outcome was that Walke volunteered to make the attempt with the *Carondelet;* and Foote approved. This obviously brought everything very much to a head.

Fortunately for all of us the St. Louis *Democrat* had a man aboard the *Carondelet* when she made the try. Captain Walke approves his account as "the most correct and faithful" one that had yet been published (1877). Also there was a New York *Times* reporter with the fleet, who recorded the picture of the *Carondelet's* start. Just below are given five extracts from the pens of these writers; each of the former's excerpts will be preceded by "St. L. D.," and each of the latter's by "N. Y. T." For better understanding of this and subsequent chapters, it should be pointed out that "wheelhouse" refers to the *paddle*-wheel housing and not to the pilothouse where the steering wheel is located. With these minor preliminaries out of the way the rostrum will now be turned over to our eyewitnesses for their descriptions of the most important scene of the drama of Island No. 10.

(St. L.D.) "Yesterday morning [April 4] preparations began on the 'Carondelet.' Planks from the wreck of an old barge were brought on board, with which the deck of the boat was covered, to resist plunging shot; all surplus chains were coiled over the most vulnerable parts of the boat; an 11-inch hawser was wound round the pilot-house as high up as the windows; the hammock nettings were well packed with hammocks; gun carriages were taken apart, and cord wood was brought up from the hold for the purpose of constructing barriers about the boilers, and many other minor preparations made during the day to fit the vessel, so far as possible, for the ordeal through which she was to pass.

"Wm. R. Hoel, first master of the 'Cincinnati,' a gentleman of twenty-one years' experience on the Mississippi (and whom we may parenthetically state is now making his 194th trip to New Orleans), came on board the 'Carondelet' at 9, A. M., and relieved Richard N. Wade, the first master of the boat. A consultation was immediately held with the pilots, in which the course of the channel, and the location of the bars, were taken into consideration. It had been previously determined to run down on the Missouri side of the island, and to add to the practicability of this, last Thursday afternoon the fleet shelled the rebel floating battery, for the purpose of driving it from the command it held on that channel.

"At dusk, twenty-four sharpshooters, Company H, 42nd Illinois, commanded by Captain Hollenstelm, who dropped down in cutters and transports, and came at dusk on board of the 'Carondelet,' were mustered on deck, inspected, received their orders (which were to co-operate with the crew in repelling boarders), and then taken to the gun-deck, there to remain until called upon; observing the strictest silence in the mean time.

.   .   .   .

"At 8 o'clock the boat left her anchorage, and passed up the shore for a mile, where, partly concealed between two transports, was a barge containing coal and baled hay. This was immediately made fast to the port side, it being the part to be chiefly exposed to the enemy's batteries. The hay had been placed in layers on the wrong side of the barge (the outer one); the crew was soon employed in shifting it where it would afford greater protection, and at the same time enable the gunboat to control it much easier. One course of bales was laid over the casements astern, as they were to be presented to the enemy for a long time after passing the batteries, and liable to receive all the shots sent after us, without being iron-plated, or able to resist heavy cannon balls.

"The barge and the hay came up to the top of the broadside portholes, and would have been of much service had the batteries to be passed been on a parallel with the gunboat; but such was not the case here, for both on the mainland and head of the island they stand upon a bank twenty or thirty feet high, and in firing into a passing boat it becomes necessary, as subsequently demonstrated, for them to depress their guns. . . .

"The condition of the weather was anxiously looked forward to, and every perceptible change in the atmosphere or wind observed, and the consequences carefully calculated, as they were to bear on the success or defeat of the enterprise. Late in the day there was every prospect of a clear, moonlight night; something very undesirable, . . . which would have given the enemy timely notice of our approach, and enabled him to serve his guns with as much accuracy as in daylight. Under these circumstances, it was concluded to wait until the moon had gone down; and then, be the auspices what they might, attempt the execution of a project, the abandonment of which would have been a great disappointment, after the preliminaries had attained such a degree of maturity. At sundown the indications grew more favorable; the atmosphere became suddenly hazy, the wind veered to the north-west, and a set of black clouds, rapidly increasing in width, bordered the horizon from the north-west, strongly evidencing an approaching storm.

". . . Commodore Foote's injunctions concerning quietness and suppression of all lights aboard were . . . strictly observed, the guns were run back, and the ports closed; the sailors, *cap-a-pie,* with pistols, cutlasses, boarding-pikes, and muskets. Hand-grenades had been provided, and the hot-water hoses were connected with the boilers, and held in readiness to drench with scalding water those who might attempt to board the boat, and overcome the crew; the engineer had orders to cut the cold-water supply, and the injector pipe, if it became likely to fall into the enemy's hands. This, in case of necessity, would have been resorted to instead of burning the vessel; for it would not only have given to the crew better means of escape, but averted the terrible loss of life that inevitably would have resulted from the firing of the boat, and the explosion of the magazine.

"The hour approaches. At 10 o'clock the moon went down; the storm, which had been thickening and gathering for several hours, was now about to burst upon us, and, greatly encouraged by so opportune a period for starting, the captain passed the word 'All ready,' and the sailors were sent on shore to loosen the lines. In a few moments we were under way, and after a little difficulty in rounding with the cumbersome barges, fairly stood 'out for New Madrid.' The machinery was so adjusted as to permit the escape of the steam through the wheel-house, and thus avoid the puffing which results from its passing through the steam pipes. So silently did we proceed that it was scarcely known on board that the boat was under way, and we thought some of the officers were almost unbelievers when they asked the engineer, through the speaking pipes, if he was 'going ahead on her.' "

(N.Y.T.) "At 10 o'clock she cast loose, and started slowly down the stream. At the same time heavy clouds had overspread the sky, and a genuine tropical (in size) thunder-storm came howling upon the river. It did not rain in the ordinary meaning of the term, but whole gulfs of water came pouring down in masses. Nor did it thunder and lighten in the usual meaning given to those words, but it roared at us as if all the electric batteries of north, south, east and west, had concentrated their forces, and were bellowing at us in unison, while the lightning in each broad flash was so vast and so vivid, that it seemed as if the gates of some hell like that of Milton were opened and shut every instant, suffering the whole fierce reflection of the infernal lake to flash across the sky.

"At such a time the *Carondelet* lifted her anchor, and slowly swung into the stream, watched, through the almost blinding flashes, by thousands of eager eyes, whose owners, regardless of the driving storm, crowded the decks of the other gunboats and transports, to watch the heroic undertaking.

"Slowly she swung round till hauled down stream, and then she pushed straight ahead, keeping well over towards the island. We could see her almost every second—every brace, port, and outline could be seen with startling distinctness enshrouded by a bluish-white glare of light, and then her form for the next instant, would become merged in the intense blackness that lay upon the river like a pall.

"With beating hearts, we saw her arrive opposite to, and pass the first battery on the Kentucky shore, without a demonstration from the enemy! But just below was another battery, whose guns had often pitched their immense balls a distance of four miles; and with hearts, whose beatings could almost, it seemed, be heard beneath our jackets, we watched her slowly approaching, in checkers of darkness and flame, the dreaded works."

(St. L.D.) "For the first half mile everything went still and smooth beyond even the most sanguine anticipations, and the probability of passing the batteries unobserved was being remarked by some, when the soot in the chimneys caught fire, and a blaze five feet high leaped out from their tops, lighting brightly the upper deck of the vessel and everything around. The word was hastily passed to the engineer to open the flue-caps, after which the flames subsided; but not until the rebels had the fairest opportunity to discover our approach and prepare a reception. This was a serious mishap, because no signal, even by appointment, could so perfectly reveal our intentions; and what contributed to misfortune was the time of its happening, which was before any of their batteries had been passed, giving them ample time to communicate from one point to another before we came within range. Notwithstanding all this, strange as it may seem, no alarm among the rebels was discovered to follow, and we were consoling ourselves over the remissness of the rebel sentries, when, to our great astonishment, the chimneys were fired again, as if a treacherous deity was presiding over the fortunes of our boat.

"This repetition of what had seemed before an untoward event, was on deck thought to proceed from the mismanagement of the engineer, and it was with no little emphasis that the executive officer demanded 'why in h—l the flue-caps were not kept open.' A subsequent examination proved, however, that it was a matter over which the engineer had no control further than to suppress the fire when it occurred. The escape into the wheel-house of the steam, which, when passing through the smoke stacks moistened the soot, left it to be rapidly dried and ignited by the fire in the furnaces.

"The rebels took the alarm. The boat now presented a broadside to the upper fort, and the sentries there had not failed to discover the boat by the last accident, and alarmed the guards at the forts below by discharging their muskets. Immediately afterwards five rockets were sent up from the main land and the island, and were followed by a cannon shot from Fort No. 2. The stillness of the upper fort satisfied all those on board that the guns had been most effectually disabled by the spiking party. Had it not been so the rebels would have first opened upon us with cannon from that point, since it was first alarmed, and afforded an easy range. We concluded to rush by.

"But one course remained to be pursued by the officers of the 'Carondelet;' that was, to let on a full head of steam, and make the greatest possible haste by the rebel batteries, which were now momentarily expected to open fire from all their guns. To this end orders were hurriedly passed below to the engineers, and the speed of the boat was soon much accelerated. Mr. Wilson, one of the boatswain's mates, was stationed on the forecastle with lead and line, to give the soundings. Mr. Gilmore, one of the master's mates, was placed on the forward or upper deck to direct the pilots how to steer the boat.

"Just at this juncture, vivid flashes of lightning lit up the hurried preparations of the rebels as they charged and trained their guns, while peal after peal of thunder reverberated along the river, and the rain poured down in torrents."

(N.Y.T.) "A crashing peal of thunder—a blinding flash of light, which scarcely had disappeared when a broad blaze of flame burst from the fortifications, followed immediately by a second and third. A few instants later, and the reports came up to us dulled by the roar of the storm.

"No reply from the *Carondelet*. Slowly she steamed ahead, the sky all ablaze about her, the Kentucky shore vomiting fierce flames; the thunders of the storm and the roar of the rebel artillery commingling, as if heaven and earth had joined to crush the audacious intruder."

(St. L.D.) "Now was the time for coolness and heroism. Captain Walke deliberately giving orders; Captain Hoel stood firm on deck in a perfect shower of cannon balls and musket balls which were launched upon us, and as he discovered the outlines of the banks, or the course of the channel by the aid of the flashing lightning, his clear voice rang out his commands to the pilots, who steadily held the wheel. But once, we believe, during the perilous passage, did the watchful eyes of the captain suffer the boat to gain a precarious position; and then it was when a lengthened intermission between the flashes of lightning completely obscured our course, and the current, striking the cumbersome barge, sheered the vessel, and carried it towards a neighboring bar. The first glance of light, however, disclosed our situation, and the rapid command, 'Hard-a-port,' admonished us of our danger. The boat, nevertheless, soon regained the channel, and our fears were dispelled by remarks on deck, that 'all was going well,' and the anxiously-awaited reports, as they came up from the forecastle, 'No bottom.'

". . . When we got well out of the range of the enemy's land batteries, passed the first shock which greeted us from the *head* of the island, and were gliding down the north bank, the exultation began, and the most disparaging comments were made upon the enemy's wild firing. When the circumstances under which it was made are taken into consideration, however, we doubt whether our own gunners could have excelled it. The furious hurricane then raging, and the impenetrable darkness precluded a knowledge of our position, which every turn of the wheel changed. Our boat was not very fleet, and the barge in tow impeded a speed which might otherwise have been made, with the current in our favor. The consequence was, an exposure of *thirty minutes* to an uninterrupted fire from four batteries on the Kentucky shore, and one at the head of the island. The judgment which we were enabled to form from the shrieking of their shot, was that they flew from five yards to thirty yards over our heads; a few were heard to plunge in the water. One cause of the wild shooting was in over-estimating the distance of our boat. It was close along the bank, under their guns; and had this been fully understood, the rebels would have found it difficult to depress their guns to such a degree as to bear upon us, without having them dismounted by an angular recoil.

"After having passed the foot of the island without finding the battery there, which for several days had been reported as mounting a number of long-range guns, a feeling of security came over our officers, and they would have been glad to make it known to the crew, and afford them relief from a long and painful suspense, but it was not over yet. A reconnoissance on the preceding day disclosed the locality of a floating battery, three miles below the island, on the Tennessee shore, and this remained to be passed. A light was seen burning on it as we approached, and being in no wise prepared to engage it (although a feeling of this kind was exhibited after having thus far successfully accomplished our mission), the 'Carondelet' bore over to the Missouri shore, and ran by, being fired at only six or eight times from the floating battery. It was said that our shooting on Thursday, [April 3] when it was lying alongside of the island, cut its fastenings, when it floated down to the place we found it last night, and there it was overhauled and made fast by a rebel transport. It evidently evinced a disinclination to fight last night, by not firing at our boat while approaching, and reserving its fire until we had passed by out of range; and even the shooting was exceedingly stinted, as if through fear of provoking our return.

"Being out of danger from the enemy, the fact was made known to the sailors, who were relieved from the rigid silence, and permitted to join in the jubilant congratulations that passed around the boat. A little danger, however, was still to be encountered, that of our batteries at New Madrid, and the colors under which we sailed before starting being mistaken and fired upon as rebels.

"Signal guns, according to pre-arrangement, were to be fired in case of success, as the boat rounded New Madrid bend; but the incessant thunder rendered it highly probable that our guns might be mistaken for it, and a little delay was occasioned, to avoid this error. Our friends at the fleet, it was known, were anxiously waiting to hear the result of the hazardous enterprise; and it was feared that every moment's delay would dishearten, and lead them to expect disaster. Orders were given to get the guns in readiness and fire three times at intervals of one minute, and after a lapse of five minutes, to fire three guns. This was accordingly done, and the fact of the echo having borne the glad tidings back to the fleet, was made certain by a response from the flag-ship. At the fort, above New Madrid the signal was also understood, though a misapprehension had induced them to look for three perpendicular lights (red, white and blue, with blue in the center). The non-appearance of these, however, was not thought sufficient cause for shooting at the boat, and in a few minutes she was in the stream off New Madrid, when Captain Walke informed those on shore with a speaking trumpet, that she was the U. S. gunboat 'Carondelet.' A fire was soon kindled at the banks, and the best landing-place made known by the men at the fort. In rounding to, a misunderstanding occurred between the pilots and engineers, by which a stray 'turn ahead,' when it should have been 'turn back' was made, resulting in getting the boat hard aground, fifty yards out in the stream. The cannon forward were all shifted to the stern, the crew withdrew also, and with the bow thus lightened, the boat backed off and was made secure to the bank at 1, A. M., having been two hours in the passage and one hour aground. Purser Nixon, desiring to add to the joy of the gallant tars of the 'Carondelet,' asked and obtained permission of the captain to let them 'splice the main-brace.' This, though particularly forbidden by the regulations, was on this occasion accorded, because of the unrestricted enjoyment which should be allowed to follow all such happy issues, and when the boatswain's mate sounded 'grog, oh!' there never was a ship's crew merrier than the one on board the 'Carondelet.'

.   .   .   .

"At 8, A. M., Assistant Secretary of War Scott and General Pope came on board to congratulate Captain Walke. The boat's arrival, has been heralded all over the camps hereabouts, and Army officers have been flocking aboard all day, expressing their satisfaction at her presence and promise of future co-operation."

Allowing the smokestacks to "torch" was a serious lapse, but Captain Walke believed that it made little difference as it turned out—that the enemy could discover his vessel much more easily by the flashes of lightning, and that she was first detected during one of them.

The "floating battery" mentioned more than once was none other than the battling dry dock of other song and story. The dislodgment of this floating dock from her assigned position was one of the few worth-while accomplishments of the long bombardment.

The *Carondelet's* running of the gantlet was such a superlative success that the *Pittsburg* followed her down two nights later during another thunderstorm. With these two vessels available, Pope was in a position to ferry his troops across the river and block the only exit from the Confederates' defenses. The *Carondelet's* feat had changed the situation so suddenly as well as so completely that nearly everything fell into the bag. On April 7, the Confederates surrendered. Seven thousand men, the dry dock, and ten assorted boats were captured. Some of the vessels had first been sunk in an attempt to prevent capture, but they were soon raised. Very large quantities of ammunition and supplies were taken intact, and of course all the many guns.

Captain Walke had been ready and willing to take what was believed to be a long chance; and the midnight dash of the *Carondelet* made possible an absolutely complete victory.

CHAPTER VII

THE AFFAIR AT PLUM POINT BEND

FOOTE LOST no time after Island No. 10 surrendered, and pushed on down the river with his fleet, driving all Confederate watercraft before him. On April 13, he was brought up short by a fortification on the Chickasaw Bluffs, on the left bank of the stream. This had formerly borne the title of Fort Wright, but had been renamed Fort Pillow by its new occupants. Island No. 10 was approximately in the northwest corner of Tennessee, with Memphis in the southwest corner. Fort Pillow was about halfway between and constituted practically the only remaining land barrier between the Union fleet and Memphis. Foote brought his mortar schooners into action again and they began to pitch shells into the fort from behind a point on the other side of the winding river. Most of the time the ironclads were tied up at or opposite Plum Point, which is the next one upstream on the left bank.

Just at the time Island No. 10 was falling, General Grant won the Battle of Shiloh. He had been moving south from Fort Donelson simultaneously with Foote and on a parallel course. Corinth, Mississippi, and many other important cities and large areas lay at the mercy of Grant's army after its victory; but just at that point Henry W. Halleck took command in person and that was the end of the drive. As for the Mississippi, practically all of Pope's army was detached from the down-river movement and added to Halleck's force. After the success of the *Carondelet* at No. 10, Foote was ready to attempt the run past Pillow. Under the circumstances, however, no good prospect was in sight for taking the fort just then. A very small body of troops was on hand; there was no especially weak spot to attack; and, furthermore, the strength of the Confederate fleet below the fort was increasing to an unknown degree. The Union commander was not even certain that the *Manassas* and a still more powerful ironclad might not be present. So Foote marked time, continued a slow, long-range bombardment, awaited developments, and nursed his wounded ankle.

Shortly he was at least relieved of his worries about the maximum possible strength of the enemy fleet. For it was on the night of April 23–24 that Farragut and his big fleet of seagoing ships and gunboats pushed on up the river, which they had entered several weeks before. On this night they passed Forts Jackson and St. Philip, annihilated the Confederate fleet, and received the surrender of New Orleans and the forts too. All of the losers' ironclad vessels, built and building, were destroyed, including the *Manassas*. Of our old acquaintances the *McRae, Mosher, Music,* and *Jackson* also were lost. So there could not be much left up river.

A short while previously the Confederates had evacuated the Pensacola Navy Yard, not being able to maintain sufficient troops there to hold it. The total result was that, with the exception of Mobile Bay, the Union Navy now held everything on the Gulf all the way from Key West to the Mississippi River, inclusive. This was one half of the Gulf Coast and the half that counted.

Flag Officer Foote was becoming progressively incapacitated by his wound and finally he had to give up. On May 9, Captain Charles H. Davis reported as his relief, and on the same day Foote started home for rest and recuperation. Junius Henri Browne, who was a *New-York Tribune* war correspondent, describes the parting as follows, in a book which he wrote in 1865 called *Four Years in Secessia.*

". . . The Commodore had for several months been very feeble, and was often unable to go on deck for weeks at a time.

"When the day was appointed for the Commodore's departure there was quite a stir in the Fleet, and, as he was greatly beloved, his fellow-officers and the sailors generally deeply regretted the loss of their gallant commander.

"When the hour came for his going up the river, the deck of the Benton was crowded; and as the Flag-officer appeared, supported by Captain Phelps, he was greeted by tremendous huzzas. Old tars swung their hats, and not a few of their eyes moistened when they looked, as they supposed, upon the brave old Commodore for the last time, as indeed they did.

"The Flag-officer paused for a few moments, and, removing his cap, gave those near him to understand he would address them.

"The Commodore said he had asked to be relieved because he knew he could not fill his office in his existing condition of health. He was willing to sacrifice himself for his country, but he knew he would be injuring the cause by retaining his position any longer.

"He had been growing feebler and feebler every day, and his physician had often told him he could not improve while exposed to the excitements of the service and confined to the Flag-ship. He complimented the officers and crew of the Benton in the highest manner. He had always found them faithful, brave, and true, and had fondly hoped to remain with them until the War was over. That he could not was a cause of great regret; but wherever he went, he would bear with him the memory of the Benton and her gallant crew, and, if his life were spared, he would often revert to the scenes he had passed among them with mingled feelings of sorrow and of pride. The interview was impressive and affecting, and at the close the Commodore could hardly speak for emotion, and the tears, answered by many who were present, stole down his thin and pallid cheeks.

"An hour after this, the De Soto dropped down to the Flagship to convey the Flag-officer to Cairo, and he soon made his way, with the assistance of Captains Davis and Phelps, to the transport, where he was placed in a chair on the guards, looking toward the crew of the Benton, who stood, an anxious crowd, upon the deck.

"The Commodore was moved deeply, and was extremely nervous, laboring greatly to conceal his agitation; but he could not succeed; and he placed a palm-leaf, which he carried, before his face, to hide the gushing tears.

"As the De Soto moved away, the crew pulled off their caps and gave three loud and hearty cheers, at which the Flag-officer rose from his chair and said, in an excited manner and in broken accents: 'God bless you all, my brave companions! I know you will succeed in all you undertake, for such a cause, in such hands, can not fail. I had hoped to stay with you. I had rather died with you than go away; but I go for your good and the good of my country; and I can never forget you,—never, never. You are as gallant and noble men as ever fought in a glorious cause, and I shall remember your merits to my dying day.'

.   .   .   .

"So we parted from the gallant Flag-officer, and never saw him more."

Andrew Hull Foote never completely regained his health. A year later he received orders to an even more important job than the one he was just leaving. He was about to take over the command of the South Atlantic Blockading Squadron; and this had nothing to do with the South Atlantic Ocean; it was the squadron blockading the southern part of the Atlantic Coast of the Confederacy. He died without reaching his station.

Following the loss of their New Orleans fleet, the Confederates below Pillow had been busy forming a new squadron to challenge the Union superiority on the Father of Waters. The new "men-of-war," most of them river craft, were steamers with good speed which had had their bows greatly strengthened for use as rams. The ram bow was the principal offensive weapon on each boat. The vessels averaged but two guns apiece approximately, and little use was made even of these. For ordnance they depended almost entirely upon the rifles of sharpshooters. Practically their sole protection consisted of bales of cotton. They were among the first "cotton-clads." Eight of these craft swung into action in the fracas described below; seven Federal ironclads were in the vicinity. The author is again Eliot Callender who was still attached to the *Cincinnati*. It was he, it will be remembered, who described the dissection of the Confederate mine in the presence of Grant, Foote, and others. Still under the title of "What a Boy Saw on the Mississippi" he writes:

"Flag officer Charles H. Davis had assumed command. He found his fleet at Fort Pillow, and had not had time to inspect the eight boats under his command, when on the morning of the 10th of May, 1862, he awoke to find a lively amount of business on his hands. I have stated that the Federal fleet lay at anchor five miles above the fort, awaiting a movement of our army, with which they expected to co-operate; but in order that General Beauregard might not think we had forgotten him, a mortar-boat, throwing a shell thirty-nine inches in circumference, was made fast to the shore just above the point behind which the fort lay, and every half-hour during the day one of these little pills would climb a mile or two into air, look around a bit at the scenery, and finally descend and disintegrate around the fort, to the great interest and excitement of the occupants. One of the gun-boats would drop down every night and stand a twenty-four hour watch over this mortar-boat. On this memorable morning, the 'Cincinnati,' Commander Stembel, was lying just above the mortar, made fast to the trees; and with steam down, all hands were busy holy-stoning decks. It was a beautiful morning,—like one of those June days which so often bless our more northern latitudes. Nature had put on her loveliest garb. The woods were vocal with songsters, and the entire surroundings seemed so appropiate for a young man who had left his girl behind him to indite her a few words, that at least one young man on the 'Cincinnati' that morning was engaged in that very occupation. While deep in a logical argument proving that beyond question the stars paled whenever she stepped out of an evening, the hurried shuffle of steps on the deck overhead, the short and sharp command calling all hands to quarters, caused the writer to drop his pen and climb the companion-way. The sight that met his youthful eyes will never be effaced. Steaming rapidly around the point below us, pouring dense clouds from their funnels, came first one vessel, then two, then more, until six war-vessels under full head of steam came surging up the river barely a mile below us. Eight minutes would bring them alongside; while the 'Cincinnati,' with hardly enough steam to turn her wheel over, lay three miles away from the rest of the Union fleet, not one boat of which had enough steam up to hold itself against the current. The enemy's plan was undoubtedly to surprise (and I may say here that they did) the gun-boat that protected our mortar, sink or capture her, destroy the mortar, and get back under cover of the guns of the fort before the Union fleet above could come to the rescue. . . .

"The 'Cincinnati's' cables were slipped, and slowly she swung out into the stream. Her engineers were throwing oil and everything else inflammable into her fires, that the necessary head of steam might be obtained to handle the boat. On came the leader of the Confederate fleet, the 'General Bragg,' a powerful gulf steamer, built full in the bow and standing up twenty feet above the surface of the river. Her powerful engines were ploughing her along at a rate that raised a billow ten feet high at her bow. At a distance of not over fifty yards, she received our full starboard battery of four thirty-two-pound guns. Cotton bales were seen to tumble, and splinters fly; but on she came, her great walking-beam engine driving her at a fearful rate. When less than fifty feet away the 'Cincinnati's' bow was thrown around, and the two boats came together with a fearful crash. It was a glancing-blow that the 'General Bragg' gave us, and not the one she intended,—a right-angle contact would have sunk us then and there; but glancing-blow as it was, it took a piece out of our midships six feet deep and twelve feet long, throwing the magazine open to the inflow of water, and knocking everything down from one end of the boat to the other. The force of the blow fastened the 'Bragg's' ram temporarily into the 'Cincinnati's' hull. 'Give her another broadside, boys!' passed the word of command. The men sprang with a cheer to their guns, and the entire broadside was emptied into the 'Bragg' at such close range that the guns could not be run out of the ports. This broadside settled the 'Bragg,' for she lay careened up against us so that it tore an immense hole in her from side to side. She slowly swung off from the 'Cincinnati,' and as the command to 'Board the enemy!' was given, she lowered her flag. But it is doubtful how much 'boarding' we could have done,—for just at this moment the second Confederate ram, the 'Sumter,' reached the scene of action, and coming up under full head of steam, struck the 'Cincinnati' in the fantail, cutting into her three feet, destroying her rudders and steering apparatus, and letting the water pour into the hull of the boat. Before she struck us, however, our stern battery of two six-inch guns got two broadsides into her. And now came up the third Confederate ram, the 'General Lovell,' aiming for our port quarter. 'Haul down your flag, and we will save you!' yelled some one, when she was less than fifty feet away. 'Our flag will go down when we do!' was the response. We got but one gun to bear on her before the crash came. The 'Cincinnati' was raised by the force of the blow enough to throw her bows under. The water was pouring in from three directions; the engineers were standing waist-deep in the engine-room; the fires were being rapidly extinguished; and we had just one more round of ammunition in the guns, the magazine being flooded. The 'General Lovell' was filled with sharp-shooters, who picked off every exposed man, including Commander Stembel, who fell with a Minie-bullet through his mouth. First-master Hoel, who assumed command, came down on the gun-deck and called out, 'Boys, give 'em the best you've got! we ain't dead yet!' A cheer was his answer; and as every gun on the boat poured its iron hail into one or another of the enemy, the 'Cincinnati' rolled first to one side and then the other, gave a convulsive shudder, and went down bow-first and head on to the enemy. It was an exceedingly damp time for the crew of that boat. We all piled on the hurricane deck, and from that there was some tall and lofty scrambling for the wheel-house, which, thanks to the shallow place we were in, remained above water. And now, perched like so many turkeys on a corn-crib, we were enforced spectators of the exciting and magnificent scene around us. By this time our fleet above us had arrived at the scene of action, led by the flag-ship 'Benton.' Running into the very midst of the enemy's fleet, she gave them first her bow battery of nine-inch Dahlgren guns, and then, wheeling, her starboard, stern, and port broadsides. By the time her bow swung around, her guns were again loaded; and repeating her circling again and again, she delivered upon the enemy a withering sheet of death and destruction. Several of the Confederate rams tried to reach her, but were either intercepted by our other boats, who one after another joined the *melee*, or were literally beaten back by the storm of shot and shell that poured from her sides. Soon the air was so full of smoke that little could be seen. Every now and then a Confederate ram would rush past us within a stone's throw, and then a shell would burst over our heads or a solid shot plough up the water. But ten minutes more settled it. Two of the enemy's boats were floating broadside down the river,—the 'General Bragg,' whose inside we blew out, and one other. The other four were making their best possible time for the fort. We could not save our prizes, for we neither dared go after them, nor could we have towed them upstream if we had. The 'Cincinnati's' wheel-house was soon relieved of its dead and living freight, and an hour afterward, the air and the mighty flood had swept away every vestige of the conflict."

The Yankees had been caught napping again; not perhaps as seriously as at the Head of the Passes, but inexcusably just the same. Apparently not a picket boat or a scout of any sort was down the river to warn against attack in this or any other form. Not even the guard boat *Cincinnati* had sufficient steam up to enable her to protect herself let alone the mortar boat under her care. Few of the ironclads succeeded in getting into close action and, before they threatened seriously, the rams had done an immense amount of damage. The latter then withdrew as planned, as soon as they were menaced by superior force.

In such a jumbled free-for-all as this battle turned out to be, no one can ever be sure of the relative positions and performances of many of the participants during any part of it. Callender's tale of the *Benton's* feats, however, sounds like a touch of "flagship-itis."

Our chronicler cannot brush aside the decisiveness of the defeat as he—and many another—seems to attempt. There is no evidence to support his statement that the *Bragg* hauled down her flag. It is true that several of the attackers were disabled in some respects; however, in each case the damage was of a nature easy to repair. But the *Cincinnati* was definitely sunk, and it was only because she had succeeded in getting into shallow water that it was possible to salvage her readily. Also the *Mound City* was badly holed forward and just succeeded in running her bow onto a bank; otherwise she too might have gone actually to the bottom as did the *Cincinnati*. The latter was raised five days later, the *Mound City* the day after the fight. Although both these boats were back in commission the following month, the victory on May 10 very definitely rested with the Confederates. The casualties to personnel were negligible on both sides; Captain Stembel recovered from his wound. Under all the circumstances, the blame for the surprise lay on more than one pair of shoulders. In fairness to Davis, it should be pointed out that the attack was made less than twenty-four hours after he had arrived and taken over.

This was one of the very few affairs of the entire war that can properly be called a "fleet action." And it is about the only one in which the Confederates felt that they were sufficiently forewarned or forearmed to take the offensive. Always the Federals are found in superior force. Off Elizabeth City, North Carolina, it will be remembered, the Union ships attacked. At the Head of the Passes the Confederates attacked but their opponents ran. Below New Orleans, and on other occasions, the Federal ships met opposition on the water, but the vessels which opposed them were little more than auxiliaries to the forts. At Plum Point Bend, however, the Confederates made a "tip-and-run" attack upon a superior force and were wholly successful. In summation it should be noted that the only fleet fight in which the Confederates attacked was the only fleet fight the Confederates won.

CHAPTER VIII

ARMY RAMS AT MEMPHIS

IT WILL BE recalled that the advance of the Union armies stalled after their victory at Shiloh, Halleck displaying no initiative in driving his opponents farther southward. Finally Beauregard, the Confederate general holding Corinth, Mississippi, decided that his position was becoming too dangerous to maintain, however dilatory his enemies might seem; their numbers were becoming too superior. Maintaining to the last his bluff of confidence and security, Beauregard pulled out of Corinth on May 30, twenty days after the affair at Plum Point Bend. When Corinth fell, Pillow had to be evacuated as well as Fort Randolph some distance below it. Accordingly, the gunboat fleet pushed on downstream in early June. With the make-up of his immediate command continually changing, Davis now had only five ironclads available for his advance on Memphis. The Confederate gunboats fell back on the city, of which they now constituted the sole remaining defense. By river Memphis is the better part of a hundred miles below Fort Pillow.

Meanwhile, a new development was taking place, another anomalous one. An elderly civilian engineer named Charles Ellet, Jr., had for years been urging the construction of rams for use in war. The feats of the *Merrimac* sold his idea to the Federal Government where his own persuasive powers had failed. Soon after the events in Hampton Roads he was summoned to the War Department, given a commission as colonel, and told to go ahead and get together a fleet of rams on the Mississippi as quickly as he possibly could. This Army angle was a peculiar one which existed for a long time in the early part of the war. Even the commander of the gunboat fleet reported to an Army superior at this time. Probably the idea was that the co-operation was to be so close, intimate, and continuous that the fleet and army would act as one. The idea was not a good one.

The name of Ellet is almost inseparable from that of the Ram

Fleet. There were about *six* Ellets closely connected with it, either brothers, nephews, or son of Charles, Jr., the first commander. The latter flew his flag in the *Queen of the West*. His brother, Alfred W., commended the *Monarch*. That officer fortunately left us a tale of the Ram Fleet and its first action, called "Ellet and His Steam Rams at Memphis"; it appeared in *Battles and Leaders of the Civil War*, Volume I. Extensive extracts from this article are given below. A page by the ubiquitous Captain Walke will be included at the proper point. It is from his *Naval Scenes and Reminiscences*. For identification it will be preceded by the name "Walke"; the resumption of the main story will be marked "Ellet."

"The boats constituting the ram-fleet of the Mississippi River were not built for the purpose they were to serve; they were simply such river steamers as could be purchased under the urgency then pressing. Some were side-wheelers, others stern-wheel tugs, with strong machinery and great power, and were hurriedly strengthened and braced to sustain a severe headlong blow. In a letter to the Secretary of War respecting the rams, while they were being fitted out, Colonel Ellet wrote: 'The boats I have purchased are illy adapted for the work I shall require of them; it is not their strength upon which I rely, but upon the audacity of our attack, for success.'

"His idea of an effective 'steam-ram' was not a hermaphrodite thing, half ram, half gun-boat, nor did he favor those sharp knife-like prows which, if they cut a hole in an enemy, would plug it at the same time. He wanted a vessel of medium size, easy to handle, and of great speed; she should be built very strongly, fitted with machinery of great power, and have weight sufficient when projected against an enemy to crush the side of any vessel that could float. Colonel Ellet did not rely on heavy ordnance, and did not recommend arming his rams. At the Battle of Memphis there were no firearms on board the ram-fleet except a few short carbines and some pocket-revolvers; his reliance was upon the prow of his vessel. He desired, as far as possible, to protect the vulnerable parts of his ship, the boilers and engines, and with simply enough men as crew to handle the boat with certainty and dispatch, to run the gauntlet of any fire that could be precipitated upon him, and drive his ram deep into his unwieldy adversary.

.   .   .   .

"Colonel Ellet purchased a number of steamboats at different points on the Ohio River, the best he could find at the short time at his disposal. He took some old and nearly worn-out boats, strengthened their hulls and bows with heavy timbers, raised bulkheads of timber around the boilers, and started them down the river to Cairo as fast as they could be got off the ways. They were the *Dick Fulton, Lancaster, Lioness, Mingo, Monarch, Queen of the West, Samson, Switzerland,* and *T. D. Horner.*

"While the work was progressing, and before any one of the rams was nearly completed, information was received that the Confederate fleet had come out from under the batteries of Fort Pillow, had attacked our fleet of gun-boats lying near Craighead's Point, and had disabled two of them. Colonel Ellet received most urgent telegrams from the Secretary of War to hurry the rams forward at the earliest possible moment. In consequence of these demands, five of them were immediately dispatched down the river under my command, work upon them being continued as they proceeded and for several days after their arrival at Fort Pillow. The other rams followed, and about the 25th of May Colonel Ellet joined the fleet on board the *Switzerland,* and the ram-fleet was now ready for action.

"Colonel Ellet at once conferred with Flag-Officer Charles H. Davis on the propriety of passing Fort Pillow, and engaging the enemy's fleet wherever found. Flag-Officer Davis did not approve the plan suggested, but offered no objection to Colonel Ellet's trying the experiment. Accordingly, immediate preparations were begun for running the batteries with the entire ram-fleet. During this period of preparation, constant watch was kept upon the fort and the enemy's fleet. On the night of the 4th of June I crossed the timber point in front of the fort, and reported to the colonel commanding my conviction that the fort was being evacuated. About 2 o'clock in the morning I obtained permission, with many words of caution from Colonel Ellet, to run down opposite the fort in a yawl and, after lying off in order to become assured that the place was abandoned, to land, with the assurance that the rams would follow in case my yawl did not return before daylight. I landed with my little band, only to find the fort entirely deserted; and after planting the National colors upon the ruins of one of the magazines, we sat down to wait for the coming of daylight and the rams. They came, followed by the entire fleet, and after a short stop all proceeded down the river, the rams taking the lead, to Fort Randolph, where they delayed long enough to plant the National flag and to examine the abandoned fortifications, the gun-boats at this point taking the advance.

"After leaving Fort Randolph the ram-fleet proceeded without incident to within about twenty-five miles of Memphis, where they all rounded to and tied up for the night, with orders of sailing issued to each commander; instructions to be ready to round out at the signal from the flag-ship, and that 'each boat should go into the anticipated fight in the same order they maintained in sailing.' [Nelson before Trafalgar: "The order of battle will be the order of sailing."] At the first dawn of day (June 6th) the fleet moved down the river, and at sunrise the flag-ship rounded the bend at 'Paddy's Hen and Chickens,' and immediately after came in sight of the Federal gun-boats anchored in line across the river, about a mile above Memphis. Colonel Ellet promptly signalled his vessels to tie up on the Arkansas shore, in the order of their sailing, as he desired to confer with Flag-Officer Davis before passing further.

"The *Queen of the West* came to first, followed by the *Monarch* and other rams in regular succession. The *Queen of the West* had made the land, and passed out line to make fast; the *Monarch* was closing in just above, but had not yet touched the shore. At this moment, and as the full orb of the sun rose above the horizon, the report of a gun was heard from around the point and down the river. It was the first gun from the Confederate River Defense Fleet moving to attack us. Colonel Ellet was standing on the hurricane-deck of the *Queen of the West*. He immediately sprang forward, and, waving his hat to attract my attention, called out: 'It is a gun from the enemy! Round out and follow me! Now is our chance!' Without a moment's delay, the *Queen* moved out gracefully, and the *Monarch* followed. By this time our gun-boats had opened their batteries, and the reports of guns on both sides were heavy and rapid.

"The morning was beautifully clear and perfectly still; a heavy wall of smoke was formed across the river, so that the position of our gun-boats could only be seen by the flashes of their guns. The *Queen* plunged forward, under a full head of steam, right into this wall of smoke and was lost sight of, her position being known only by her tall pipes which reached above the smoke. The *Monarch*, following, was greeted, while passing the gun-boats, with wild huzzas from our gallant tars. When freed from the smoke, those of us who were on the *Monarch* could see Colonel Ellet's tall and commanding form still standing on the hurricane-deck, waving his hat to show me which one of the enemy's vessels he desired the *Monarch* to attack, —namely, the *General Price*, which was on the right wing of their advancing line. For himself he selected the *General Lovell* and directed the *Queen* straight for her, she being about the middle of the enemy's advancing line. The two vessels came toward each other in most gallant style, head to head, prow to prow; and had they met in that way, it is most likely that both vessels would have gone down. But at the critical moment the *General Lovell* began to turn; and that moment sealed her fate. The *Queen* came on and plunged straight into the *Lovell's* exposed broadside; the vessel was cut almost in two and disappeared under the dark waters in less time than it takes to tell the story. The *Monarch* next struck the *General Price* a glancing blow which cut her starboard wheel clean off, and completely disabled her from further participation in the fight.

"As soon as the *Queen* was freed from the wreck of the sinking *Lovell*, and before she could recover headway, she was attacked on both sides by the enemy's vessels, the *Beauregard* on one side and the *Sumter* on the other. In the *mêlée* one of the wheels of the *Queen* was disabled so that she could not use it, and Colonel Ellet, while still standing on the hurricane-deck to view the effects of the encounter with the *General Lovell*, received a pistol-ball in his knee, and, lying prone on the deck, gave orders for the *Queen* to be run on her one remaining wheel to the Arkansas shore, whither she was soon followed by the *General Price* in a sinking condition. Colonel Ellet sent an officer and squad of men to meet the *General Price* upon her making the shore, and received her entire crew as prisoners of war. By this time consternation had seized upon the enemy's fleet, and all had turned to escape. The fight had drifted down the river, below the city.

"The *Monarch*, as soon as she could recover headway after her conflict with the *General Price*, drove down upon the *Beauregard*, which vessel, after her encounter with the *Queen of the West*, was endeavoring to escape. She was thwarted by the *Monarch* coming down upon her with a well-directed blow which crushed in her side and completely disabled her from further hope of escape. Men on the deck waved a white flag in token of surrender, and the *Monarch* passed on down to intercept the *Little Rebel,* the enemy's flag-ship. She had received some injury from our gun-boats' fire, and was making for the Arkansas shore, which she reached at the moment when the *Monarch,* with very slight headway, pushed her hard and fast aground; her crew sprang upon shore and ran into the thick woods, making their escape. Leaving the *Little Rebel* fast aground, the *Monarch* turned her attention to the sinking *Beauregard,* taking the vessel in tow, and making prisoners of her crew. The *Beauregard* was towed by the *Monarch* to the bar, where she sank to her boiler-deck and finally became a total loss."

(Walke) "The people in tens of thousands crowded the high bluffs overlooking the river, some of them apparently as gay and cheerful as a bright May morning, and others watching with silent awe the impending struggle. The roar of cannon and shell soon shook the earth on either shore for many miles; first, wild yells, shrieks, and clamors, then loud, despairing murmurs, filled the affrighted city. The screaming, plunging shell crashed into the boats, blowing them and their crews into fragments; and the rams rushed upon each other like wild beasts in deadly conflict. Amidst all this confusion and horror, the air was filled with the coal and sulphurous blinding smoke; and, as the battle progressed, all the cheering voices on shore were silenced, every voice became tremulous and disheartened, as it became evident that their fleet was faltering, and one after another of their vessels sank or became disabled. The deep sympathizing wail which followed each disaster, went up like a funeral dirge from the assembled multitude, and had an overwhelming pathos; but still many gazed through their flowing tears, upon the struggle, until the last hope gave way, and then the lamentations of the bereaved burst upon the ear, in deep heart-rending cries of anguish.

"The die was cast, and the crowd of mourning spectators melted away, in unutterable sadness for loved ones lost, and their sanguine hopes of victory forever gone. The spectacle was one which subdued all feelings of resentment on the part of the victors, and awakened a natural sympathy towards the vanquished—their fellow-countrymen—on shore. The general grief and the weight of woe inflicted, on some of the spectators, was such as could arise only from a civil war, like that in which we were then engaged.

"The crowning scene, though less distressing, was more terrific and sublime than anything which had preceded it. In the hour of triumph and naval supremacy, when our gunboats were returning to Memphis, occurred the explosion of the 'Jeff. Thompson' magazine. In an instant, before any sound had reached our ears, the heavens were lighted up as by a magnificent coronal, its snow white crest reaching beyond the clouds. Then came the terrific roar, and the scene—one that can never be forgotten—was of surpassing beauty and grandeur."

(Ellet) "The others of the enemy's fleet were run ashore and fired by the crews before they escaped into the adjoining Arkansas swamps. . . . the *General Bragg* was secured by our gun-boats before the fire gained headway, and was saved. The *Van Dorn* alone made her escape, and was afterward burned by the enemy at Liverpool Landing, . . . in Yazoo River, in order to prevent her from falling into our hands. . . .

"After the *Monarch* had towed the *Beauregard* into shoal water, from which, it was hoped, she might be raised, I received the first intelligence, from a dispatch-boat bearing orders, that Colonel Ellet was wounded. The orders I received from him were: 'Continue the pursuit as long as there is any hope of overtaking the flying enemy.'

"One other episode of this day should not be omitted. Toward the close of the engagement, Colonel Ellet was informed that a white flag had been raised in Memphis, and he immediately sent his young son, Medical Cadet Charles Rivers Ellet, ashore with a party of three men and a flag of truce, to demand the surrender of the city. They landed in a row-boat and delivered Colonel Ellet's dispatch to the mayor, and received his reply; then, surrounded by an excited and threatening crowd, they proceeded to the post-office, ascended to the top of the building, and, while stoned and fired upon by the mob below, young Ellet lowered the Confederate colors and raised the National flag over the city of Memphis. This incident occurred a considerable length of time before the formal surrender of the city into the possession of the United States troops under command of Colonel G. N. Fitch.

"At first, Colonel Ellet's wound was not considered necessarily dangerous, but a few days showed us all how futile was the hope that our brave commander would ever again tread the decks of his victorious fleet. He continued to send dispatches and issue necessary orders from his bed as long as he could receive the reports of his subordinates. Finally, his rapidly failing strength gave way; the *Switzerland,* to which he had been removed, and on board which he had been joined by his heart-broken wife and his young daughter, left Memphis on the 18th of June, and as the vessel neared Cairo on the 21st, his gallant spirit passed away. He was accorded a state funeral in Independence Hall.

. . . .

"His devoted wife, striken by grief, survived him but a few days. Both are buried at Laurel Hill Cemetary, Philadelphia."

The author of the foregoing became the second commander of the Ram Fleet; later the Colonel's son, young Charles Rivers Ellet, was its commander for a brief time.

This battle was a wild and disordered melee, contested under a pall of heavy smoke. Accordingly it is particularly hopeless to make any positive determination of the movements and performances of each of the fifteen vessels engaged, let alone their relative positions at any instant.

The ironclads were slow in engaging the enemy. The reasons seem to include their lack of speed and handiness, especially in the current; also Davis' desire to delay matters till the rams should come up with him.

As to the battle itself one important item seems to be generally agreed upon contrary to Ellet's statement, and that is the manner in which the *General Price* was disabled. The *Beauregard* and *Price* pretty definitely collided with each other when their intended victim, the *Monarch,* slipped from between them at the critical moment. It is possible that the *Monarch* rammed some other enemy in addition to striking the *Beauregard* later.

Recapitulation of the fate of the Confederate vessels shows the *Lovell* and *Beauregard* sunk and the *Bragg, Sumter,* and *Little Rebel* captured. The *Price* sank but was raised; the *Thompson* was captured but blew up. The *Van Dorn* escaped. Apart from the fatal wounding of Colonel Ellet, the Federal losses were practically zero.

The Battle of Memphis had one very interesting connection with the engagement off Plum Point; the connection was the same as that between Farragut's passage of the New Orleans forts and "Pope's run." The fracas at the Head of the Passes gave the Confederates great encouragement and caused them, naturally, to discount their opponents. Accordingly, when Farragut started up the river, his chances of getting past Fort Jackson, Fort St. Philip, and the Confederate fleet, were gravely underestimated by his foes. Similarly, the unwieldy ironclads proved such easy victims of the Confederate rams above Fort Pillow that Commodore Montgomery felt his chances sufficiently good to risk his fleet in an effort to save Memphis. The chief error in the Confederates' calculations in each comparison was that they had complete surprise on their side in the first episode and not in the second. In fact, at Memphis, although Davis was weaker than at Fort Pillow, the surprise was all *against* the Rebels, as a result of the dash of Ellet's two rams. The effort of the River Defense Fleet was glorious but the failure was fatal and complete.

CHAPTER IX

THE *ARKANSAS* SAGA

THE BATTLE just fought, following the one below New Orleans, eliminated the last collection of Confederate vessels in the West that could by any definition be called a "fleet." So, Davis tied up at Memphis for three weeks and "took a blow." There was a small Union army working its way down through Missouri and Arkansas, and it was desirable that this should receive some assistance from the fleet. Now, the White River is the first of three great watercourses below Cairo which flow into the Mississippi from the west, the others being the Arkansas and Red rivers. It was determined that a force consisting both of gunboats and troop transports should be sent up the White. This river flows into the Mississippi practically together with the Arkansas, about half way between Memphis and Vicksburg. The White River, however, drains an area considerably to the north of the Arkansas's basin. Together with its tributaries it has hundreds of miles of navigable water, as is the case with the other rivers in this region.

The ironclads detailed for the expedition were the *Mound City* and *St. Louis,* also the wooden gunboats *Lexington* and *Conestoga* —two of the original three. There was only one regular fortification erected on the river; it was at St. Charles, Arkansas, eighty-eight miles from the mouth. This was attacked by water and assaulted by land on June 17, 1862. Among those captured was the Confederate leader Joseph Fry, the same "Captain Fry" who commanded the *Ivy* at the Head of the Passes. The troops did not lose a single man when they captured the fort, but the Navy suffered frightfully when a shot hit one of the boilers of the *Mound City.* She carried 175 men and of these only 25 went scatheless. One hundred and twenty-five lost their lives, most of them by scalding or drowning. The above figures are exact, though by coincidence they appear to be round numbers. This disaster came only a little over a month after the *Mound City* was rammed and nearly sunk above Fort Pillow. It was tough service.

The victory at St. Charles put the entire water system completely in the hands of the Union forces. Some of the boats pushed on upstream until stopped by low water 151 miles from the Mississippi. In fact, the falling of the river brought the expedition to an end. The St. Charles forts were destroyed and then abandoned. At least for the time, practically all enemy military resistance throughout the entire region disappeared, and the occupation of Helena, Arkansas, was an easy task.

It will be remembered that the Union fleet and an accompanying army had captured New Orleans in the latter part of April. From that point Farragut steamed northward unaccompanied by any land forces. As his progress could not be effective and conclusive, it was slow and halting. His ships moved up the river spasmodically, receiving the surrender of Baton Rouge and Natchez among other places. These cities were defenseless and, therefore, did not require the presence of an army to cause them to yield. But after advancing four hundred miles above New Orleans Farragut reached Vicksburg and that was an entirely different proposition. This city is located on high bluffs at a hairpin bend of the river. Being perfectly designed for defense, it had been turned into a regular fortress town by the Confederates. Accordingly, when Farragut demanded its surrender the answer, naturally, was "No." The garrison then was not large, but the troops with Farragut were none at all. Had even a moderately strong land force been pushed up the river as soon as possible after the fall of New Orleans, Vicksburg might have proved an easy victim. But this was not done and the protracted consequences will be seen.

The fleet arrived below Vicksburg almost the same day St. Charles was captured. But what to do? Importuned more than once by the Navy Department, Farragut agreed against his better judgment to force his fleet past the Vicksburg batteries. Though the risks were believed correctly to be many and grave, the feat was accomplished on the night of June 27–28; the only ships that did not get up failed because of misunderstood orders primarily. After he had passed Vicksburg, one of Farragut's next dispatches to the Department said, in effect, "So what?" Here he was with his heavy seagoing ships five hundred miles from deep water, and his line of supplies and fuel insecure; and, above all, no useful employment for his force. Davis' fleet joined him on July 1 after covering the four hundred miles from Memphis in two days. This made Farragut's presence above Vicksburg as unnecessary as it was unwise. The combined fleets lay in the Mississippi between the city and the mouth of the Yazoo River.

There was nothing left of the enemy now, afloat or ashore, on the entire Mississippi River except at Vicksburg. But there was very soon going to be. It was the C. S. S. *Arkansas.* This boat will be described in a good deal of detail because much ignorance and misapprehension exists to date concerning her construction and characteristics. The errors have been perpetuated by artists to a particularly unfortunate degree. In order to piece together her career as correctly and as grippingly as possible, several extracts will be quoted from each of four eyewitness accounts. First author in all respects is her commander, Lieutenant Isaac N. Brown, one of the best naval officers the Confederacy had; next, two of her lieutenants, George W. Gift and Charles W. Read; finally, Acting Master S. B. Coleman, U. S. N., of the wooden gunboat *Tyler,* Walke's old command. Captain Brown's story, "The Confederate Gun-Boat 'Arkansas,' " is in Volume III of *Battles and Leaders of the Civil War.* Gift's and Read's stories appeared in the *Southern Historical Society Papers,* Volumes XII and I respectively. Gift's is entitled "The Story of the Arkansas" and Read's is called "Reminiscences of the Confederate States Navy." Coleman read his *Tyler* experiences before the Military Order of the Loyal Legion, Commandery of the State of Michigan, and it was printed in Volume I of their *War Papers* under the title "A July Morning with the Rebel Ram 'Arkansas.' " The source of each selected extract will be denoted by the author's name at its start. We commence with one from the pen of the *Arkansas*'s commanding officer.

(Brown) "On the 28th of May, 1862, I received at Vicksburg a telegraphic order from the Navy Department at Richmond to 'proceed to Greenwood, Miss., and assume command of the Confederate gun-boat *Arkansas,* and finish and equip that vessel without regard to expenditure of men or money.' I knew that such a vessel had been under construction at Memphis, but I had not heard till then of her escape from the general wreck of our Missis-

sippi River defenses. Greenwood is at the head of the Yazoo River,
160 miles by river from Yazoo City. It being the season of overflow,
I found my new command four miles from dry land. Her condition
was not encouraging. The vessel was a mere hull, without armor;
the engines were apart; guns without carriages were lying about
the deck; a portion of the railroad iron intended as armor was at
the bottom of the river, and the other and far greater part was to be
sought for in the interior of the country. Taking a day to fish up
the sunken iron, I had the *Arkansas* towed to Yazoo City, where
the hills reached the river. Here, though we were within fifty miles
of the Union fleets, there was the possibility of equipment. Within
a very short time after reaching Yazoo City we had two hundred
men, chiefly from the nearest detachment of the army, at work on
the deck's shield and hull, while fourteen blacksmith forges were
drawn from the neighboring plantations and placed on the bank
to hasten the iron-work. Extemporized drilling-machines on the
steamer *Capitol* worked day and night fitting the railway iron for
the bolts which were to fasten it as armor. This iron was brought
from many points to the nearest railroad station and thence twenty-
five miles by wagons. The trees were yet growing from which the
gun-carriages had to be made—the most difficult work of all, as
such vehicles had never been built in Mississippi. I made a contract
with two gentlemen of Jackson to pay each his own price for the
full number of ten. The executive officer, Mr. Stevens, gave the
matter his particular attention, and in time, along with the general
equipment, we obtained five good carriages from each contractor."

(Gift) "There was neither foundry or machine shop in the place.
The ship was in a very incomplete condition. The iron of her armor
extended only a foot, or a little more, above the water line, and
there was not a sufficiency of iron on hand to finish the entire ship.
Of guns, we had enough, but were short four carriages. In the matter of ammunition and outfit for the battery we were also very de-
ficient. It was fearfully discouraging, but Brown was undismayed.
He summoned the planters from the neighborhood and asked for
laborers, and all the blacksmiths' tools they could furnish. In a few
days we had several hundred laborers and their overseers. Numbers
of forges were sent in, and the work commenced. The hoisting
engine of the steamboat Capital was made to drive a number of
steam drills, whilst some dozens of hands were doing similar work

by hand. A temporary blacksmith shop was erected on the river bank, and the ringing of the hammer was incessant. Stevens went to Canton and got the four gun carriages. I have often been greatly amused when thinking of this latter achievement. He made no drawing before his departure, not knowing that he could find a party who would undertake the job. Being agreeably disappointed in this latter respect he wrote back for the dimensions of the guns. With two squares I made the measurement of the guns (all different patterns) and sent on the data. In a week or a little more Stevens appeared with four ox teams and the carriages. However it would take more space than is necessary to recite all that was done, and how it was done. It is sufficient to say that within five weeks from the day we arrived at Yazoo City we had a man-of-war (such as she was) from almost nothing—the credit for all of which belongs to Isaac Newton Brown, the commander of the vessel."

(Brown) "The finishing, armoring, arming, and equipment of the *Arkansas* within five weeks' working-time under the hot summer sun, from which we were unsheltered, and under the depressing thought that there was a deep channel, of but six hours' steaming between us and the Federal fleet, whose guns were within hearing, was perhaps not inferior under all the circumstances to the renowned effort of Oliver Hazard Perry in cutting a fine ship from the forest in ninety days. We were not a day too soon, for the now rapid fall of the river rendered it necessary for us to assume the offensive without waiting for the apparatus to bend the railway iron to the curve of our quarter and stern, and to the angles of the pilot-house. Though there was little thought of showing the former, the weakest part, to the enemy, we tacked boiler-plate iron over it for appearance' sake, and very imperfectly covered the pilot-house shield with a double thickness of one-inch bar iron. Our engines' twin screws, one under each quarter, worked up to eight miles an hour in still water, which promised about half that speed when turned against the current of the main river. We had at first some trust in these, not having discovered the way they soon showed of stopping on the center at wrong times and places; and as they never both stopped of themselves at the same time, the effect was, when one did so, to turn the vessel round, despite the rudder. Once, in the presence of the enemy, we made a circle, while trying to make the automatic stopper keep time with its sister-screw."

(Gift) "Our good ship had been gotten up under the peculiar circumstances of haste and incompetency, which so frequently characterized our Confederate navy. What she was designed for no man probably knows. I imagine that she was intended for a powerful iron-clad gun boat, with an iron beak for poking, and several heavy guns for shooting. But, before she had arrived at anything like a state of completion, the plan was altered, and she was made into an hermaphrodite-iron-clad. That is to say (I am speaking for the benefit of those learned in naval matters), instead of finishing the ship with an ordinary rail and bulwark all round, her sides were 'built on' amidships for fifty or sixty feet in length, so as to give an apology for protection to three guns in each broadside. The sides, it must be understood, were perpendicular. The ends of this 'castle,' or 'gun-box,' as Captain Brown dubbed it, were sloping or inclined, from which were thrust four more guns, two at each end. This gave us a battery of ten guns, which, by the way, were of all sizes and descriptions—to-wit: two eight-inch Columbiads; one eight-inch shell gun; two nine-inch shell guns; one smooth bore, 32-pounder, (63 cwt.,) and four rifle-guns, formerly 32-pounders, but now altered, three banded and one unbanded. Four of the carriages were mounted on railroad iron *chassis;* the six broadside guns were on carriages constructed at Canton, Miss., by parties who never saw or heard of such things before. The timber had not left the stump ten days when we received the carriages on board."

(Brown) "The *Arkansas* now appeared as if a small seagoing vessel had been cut down to the water's edge at both ends, leaving a box for guns amidships. The straight sides of the box, a foot in thickness, had over them one layer of railway iron; the ends closed by timber one foot square, planked across by six-inch strips of oak, were then covered by one course of railway iron laid up and down at an angle of thirty-five degrees. These ends deflected overhead all missiles striking at short range, but would have been of little security under a plunging fire. This shield, flat on top, covered with plank and half-inch iron, was pierced for 10 guns—3 in each broadside and 2 forward and aft. The large smoke-stack came through the top of the shield, and the pilot-house was raised about one foot above the shield level. Through the latter led a small tin tube by which to convey orders to the pilot. The battery was respectable for that period of the war: 2 8-inch 64-pounders at the bows; 2 rifled 32s (old smooth-bores banded and rifled) astern; and 2 100-pounder Columbiads and a 6-inch naval gun in each broadside,—10 guns in all, which, under officers formerly of the United States service, could be relied on for good work, if we could find the men to load and fire. We obtained over 100 good men from the naval vessels lately on the Mississippi, and about 60 Missourians from the command of General Jeff Thompson. These had never served at great guns, but on trial they exhibited in their new service the cool courage natural to them on land. They were worthily commanded, under the orders of our first lieutenant, by Captain Harris. Our officers were Lieutenants Stevens, Grimball, Gift, Barbot, Wharton, and Read, all of the old service, and Chief Engineer City, Acting Masters Milliken and Phillips, of the Volunteer Navy, and Midshipmen Scales, R. H. Bacot, Tyler, and H. Cenas. The only trouble they ever gave me was to keep them from running the *Arkansas* into the Union fleet before we were ready for battle. On the 12th of July we sent our mechanics ashore, took our Missourians on board, and dropped below Sartartia Bar, within five hours of the Mississippi. I now gave the executive officer a day to organize and exercise his men."[!!]

(Read) "Commodore Lynch now arrived from Yazoo City and proposed to go down with us. When he informed Captain Brown of his intentions, Brown remarked, 'Well, Commodore, I will be glad if you go down with us, but as this vessel is too small for two captains, if you go I will take charge of a gun and attend to that.' Commodore Lynch replied, 'Very well, Captain, you may go; I will stay. May God bless you!' The good old Commodore then called all the officers around him, and said he knew they would do their duty; and he hoped they would all go through the fight safely, and live to see our country free from her invaders. He then bade us all good-bye and returned to the city."

(Brown) "On Monday A. M., July 14th, 1862, we started from Sartartia. Fifteen miles below, at the mouth of Sunflower River, we found that the steam from our imperfect engines and boiler had penetrated our forward magazine and wet our powder so as to render it unfit for use. We were just opposite the site of an old sawmill, where the opening in the forest, dense everywhere else, admitted the sun's rays. The day was clear and very hot; we made fast to the bank, head down-stream, landed our wet powder (ex-

pecting the enemy to heave in sight every moment), spread tar-
paulins over the old saw-dust and our powder over these. By constant shaking and turning we got it back to the point of ignition
before the sun sank below the trees, when, gathering it up, we
crowded all that we could of it into the after magazine and resumed
our way, guns cast loose and men at quarters, expecting every moment to meet the enemy."

(Read) "The men of the 'Arkansas' were now all at their stations,
the guns were loaded and cast loose, their tackles in the hands of
willing seamen ready to train; primers in the vents; locks thrown
back and the lanyards in the hands of the gun captains; the decks
sprinkled with sand and tourniquets and bandages at hand; tubs
filled with fresh water were between the guns, and down in the
berth deck were the surgeons with their bright instruments, stimu-
lants and lint, while along the passage-ways stood rows of men to
pass powder, shell and shot, and all was quiet save the dull thump,
thump, of the propellers. Steadily the little ship moved onward towards her enemies. . . ."

(Brown) "I had some idea of their strength, General Van Dorn,
commanding our forces at Vicksburg, having written to me two
days before that there were then, I think he said, thirty-seven men-
of-war in sight and more up the river. Near dark we narrowly escaped the destruction of our smoke-stack from an immense overhanging tree. From this disaster we were saved by young Grimball,
who sprang from the shield to another standing tree, with rope's-
end in hand, and made it fast. We anchored near Haynes's Bluff at
midnight and rested till 3 A. M., when we got up anchor for the
fleet, hoping to be with it at sunrise, but before it was light we ran
ashore and lost an hour in getting again afloat."

(Gift) "Just before daylight we stopped the ship and sent a boat
on shore to obtain information from a plantation. Lieutenant
Charles W. Read was dispatched in charge of the boat. The expedition was fruitless, as the people had taken alarm and fled on
hearing a steamer in the river and a boat approaching their landing. An old negro woman alone remained to guard the house. Read
made some inquiry concerning the whereabouts of the people. She
could not tell. 'They have but just left,' he insisted, 'for the beds are
yet warm.' 'Dunno 'bout dat,' said the aunty, 'an' if I did, I wouldn't
tell.' 'Do you take me for a Yankee? Don't you see I wear a gray coat,'

said the Lieutenant. 'Sartin you's a Yankee. Our folks ain't got none dem gun-boats.'

"Getting no satisfaction, we proceeded; and when the sun rose we were still in the Yazoo.

"As it is now daylight, let me describe the scene on a man-of-war's deck, cleared for action, or at least that man-of-war, on that occasion. Many of the men had stripped off their shirts and were bare to the waists, with handkerchiefs bound round their heads, and some of the officers had removed their coats and stood in their undershirts. The decks had been thoroughly sanded to prevent slipping after the blood should become plentiful. Tourniquets were served out to division officers by the surgeons, with directions for use. The division tubs were filled with water to drink; fire buckets were in place; cutlasses and pistols strapped on; rifles loaded and bayonets fixed; spare breechings for the guns, and other implements made ready. The magazines and shell-rooms forward and aft were open, and the men inspected in their places. Before getting underway, coffee (or an apology therefor) had been served to the crew, and daylight found us a grim, determined set of fellows, grouped about our guns, anxiously waiting to get sight of the enemy.

"Stevens busied himself passing about the ship, cool and smiling, giving advice here and encouragement there. Our commander, Lieutenant Isaac Newton Brown, passed around the ship, and after making one of his sharp, pithy speeches, returned to his post with glass in hand to get the first sight of the approaching enemy."

(Brown) "At sunrise we gained Old River—a lake caused by a 'cut-off' from the Mississippi; the Yazoo enters this at the north curve, and, mingling its deep waters with the wider expanse of the lake, after a union of ten miles, breaks through a narrow strip of land, to lose itself finally in the Mississippi twelve miles above Vicksburg. . . . As the sun rose clear and fiery out of the lake on our left, we saw a few miles ahead, under full steam, three Federal vessels in line approaching. These, as we afterward discovered, were the iron-clad *Carondelet*, Captain Henry Walke, the wooden gunboat *Tyler*, Lieutenant William Gwin, and a ram, the *Queen of the West*, Lieutenant James M. Hunter [Joseph Ford]. The commander of the *Carondelet* and I had been friends in the old navy and messmates on a voyage around the world. Directing our pilot to stand for the iron-clad, the center vessel of the three, I gave the order not to fire our bow guns, lest by doing so we should diminish our speed, relying for the moment upon our broadside guns to keep the ram and the *Tyler* from gaining our quarter, which they seemed eager to do. I had determined, despite our want of speed, to try the ram or iron prow upon the foe, who were gallantly approaching; but when less than half a mile separated us, the *Carondelet* fired a wildly aimed bow gun, backed round, and went from the *Arkansas* at a speed which at once perceptibly increased the space between us. The *Tyler* and ram followed this movement of the iron-clad, and the stern guns of the *Carondelet* and *Tyler* were briskly served on us."

(Gift) "Owing to the fact that our bow-ports were quite small, we could train our guns laterally very little; and as our head was looking to the right of the enemy's line, we were compelled to allow them to begin the action, which was quite agreeable, as we had levelled all our guns with a spirit-level the day before, marked the trunnions, and agreed that we would not fire until we were sure of hitting an enemy direct, without elevation. The gunnery of the enemy was excellent, and his rifle bolts soon began to ring on our iron front, digging into and warping up the bars, but not penetrating. Twice he struck near my port, and still we could not 'see' him. The first blood was drawn from my division. An Irishman, with more curiosity than prudence, stuck his head out the broadside port, and was killed by a heavy rifle bolt which had missed the ship. Stevens was with me at the time; and, fearing that the sight of the mangled corpse and blood might demoralize the guns' crew, sprang forward to throw the body out of the port, and called upon the man nearest him to assist. 'Oh! I can't do it, sir,' the poor fellow replied, 'it's my brother.' The body was thrown overboard."

(Brown) "Grimball and Gift, with their splendid sixty-fours, were now busy at their work, while Barbot and Wharton watched for a chance shot abeam. Read chafed in silence at his rifles. The whole crew was under the immediate direction of the first lieutenant, Henry Stevens, a religious soldier, of the Stonewall Jackson type, who felt equally safe at all times and places. I was on the shield directly over our bow guns, and could see their shot on the way to the *Carondelet*, and with my glasses I thought that I could see the white wood under her armor. This was satisfactory, for I knew that no vessel afloat could long stand rapid raking by 8-inch shot at such short range. We soon began to gain on the chase, yet from time to time I had to steer first to starboard, then to port, to keep the inquisitive consorts of the *Carondelet* from inspecting my boiler-plate armor. This gave the nearer antagonist an advantage, but before he could improve it he would be again brought ahead. While our shot seemed always to hit his stern and disappear, his missiles, striking our inclined shield, were deflected over my head and lost in air. I received a severe contusion on the head, but this gave me no concern after I had failed to find any brains mixed with the handful of clotted blood which I drew from the wound and examined. A moment later a shot from the *Tyler* struck at my feet, penetrated the pilot-house, and, cutting off a section of the wheel, mortally hurt Chief Pilot Hodges and disabled our Yazoo River pilot, Shacklett, who was at the moment much needed, our Mississippi pilots knowing nothing of Old River. James Brady, a Missourian of nerve and equal to the duty, took the wheel, and I ordered him to 'keep the iron-clad ahead.' All was going well, with a near prospect of carrying out my first intention of using the ram, this time at a great advantage, for the stern of the *Carondelet* was now the objective point, and she seemed to be going slow and unsteady. Unfortunately the *Tyler* also slowed, so as to keep near his friend, and this brought us within easy range of his small-arms. I saw with some concern, as I was the only visible target outside our shield, that they were firing by volleys. I ought to have told Stevens to hold off Grimball and Gift from the iron-clad till they could finish the *Tyler,* but neither in nor out of battle does one always do the right thing. I was near the hatchway at the moment when a minie-ball, striking over my left temple, tumbled me down among the guns. I awoke as if from sleep, to find kind hands helping me to a place among the killed and wounded. I soon regained my place on the shield. I found the *Carondelet* still ahead, but much nearer, and both vessels entering the willows, which grew out on the bar at the inner curve of the lake. To have run into the mud, we drawing 13 feet (the *Carondelet* only 6), would have ended the matter with the *Arkansas.* The *Carondelet's* position could only be accounted for by supposing her steering apparatus destroyed. The deep water was on our starboard bow, where at some distance I saw the *Tyler* and the ram, as if awaiting our further entanglement. I gave the order 'hard a-port and depress port guns.' So near were we to the chase that this action of the helm brought us alongside, and our port broadside caused her to heel to port and then roll back so deeply as to take the water over her deck forward of the shield. Our crew, thinking her sinking, gave three hearty cheers. In swinging off we exposed our stern to the *Carondelet's* broadside, and Read at the same time got a chance with his rifles. The *Carondelet* did not return this fire of our broadside and stern guns. Had she fired into our stern when we were so near, it would have destroyed or at least have disabled us.

"Though I stood within easy pistol-shot, in uniform, uncovered, and evidently the commander of the *Arkansas*, no more notice was taken of me by the *Carondelet* than had been taken of my ship when, to escape running into the mud, I had exposed the *Arkansas* to being raked. Their ports were closed, no flag was flying, not a man or officer was in view, not a sound or shot was heard. She was apparently 'disabled.'

"We neither saw nor felt the *Carondelet* again, but turned toward the spiteful *Tyler* and the wary ram."

Now that the *Arkansas* has completed the first phase of her action and disabled one opponent, let us allow Captain Brown and his men a breathing spell while we give consideration to a few matters. First of all, the meeting of the opposing forces took place by merest chance. The Union ships were seeking information about the *Arkansas* but never dreamt that she was, that very moment, on the warpath. For her part, she was on her way to destroy ships below Vicksburg, although of course aware of the presence of enemy forces afloat above the city.

The *Carondelet* definitely was handled very roughly. This was probably the result, in large part, of her fighting her vulnerable stern against the *Arkansas's* powerful bow. Her steering gear *was* carried away causing her to swing into shoal water. She did not take the bottom, however, until after the *Arkansas* had passed her, though that is not particularly important. There can be no doubt that the *Arkansas* could have captured her if she had stopped, but she did the wise thing in pushing on with as little delay as possible. The *Carondelet*, however, did not haul down her flag, and Captain Walke states that it was not shot away at any time either. She got afloat and rejoined the fleet later in the day.

It happens that the damaging of the *Carondelet's* steering gear nearly caused the loss of the *Arkansas*. When the latter's Yazoo River pilot was wounded, Captain Brown really did a smart thing when he ordered the helmsman to follow the *Carondelet,* naturally expecting her to keep in the channel. The latter, however, ran into shoal water accidentally and the *Arkansas* went along until almost aground.

With the first episode just ending, all the boats were out of the wide bayou and in the river proper. The *Tyler* had gotten well below the *Arkansas,* and the *Queen* was just below the *Tyler.* According to our chronicler both National vessels at this moment were headed upstream, though they were not necessarily moving through the water. And so we turn to the *Tyler* to hear her side of the next round.

(Coleman) "Our last view of the 'Carondelet' was through a cloud of enveloping smoke with steam escaping from her ports, and of her men jumping overboard.

"Until it was evident that the ram was intent upon continuing her journey down the river, we considered the capture of the 'Carondelet' as certain.

"She, however, turned her attention exclusively to the 'Tyler' from this on, and moved over to strike us.

"The 'Tyler' was a wooden vessel, originally a river steamboat, cut down and altered to suit her new character, and carried a broadside of six eight-inch sixty-four pounders [three on a side], and a thirty-two pounder Dahlgren in the stern, but her guns and machinery and boilers were unprotected against anything more formidable than musketry.

"Her opportune presence at Shiloh was, it will be remembered, of great service during that battle, when the Confederate advance on the left was checked by the fire of her guns and that of her consort, the 'Lexington.'

"She had covered the landing of Grant's troops and his retreat from Belmont, where he made his first fight; and did her share of the work at Ft. Henry and Ft. Donelson.

"A few weeks before the 'Mound City,' an armored vessel, had her steam-chest perforated while engaged with a battery up the

White River, and of her crew of one hundred and seventy-five men, one hundred and thirty were dead and twenty-five badly injured, within a few minutes after she was struck.

"There was nothing reassuring in the present situation, for we were even more vulnerable than the 'Mound City,' and it was evident that the 'Tyler' was no match for an armored vessel such as was her antagonist.

"Her main reliance, the 'Carondelet,' was already disabled and evidence was accumulating on the 'Tyler' that the 'Arkansas' ' guns were heavy and well served.

.   .   .   .

"The 'Queen of the West,' in the meanwhile, was a few hundred yards astern of the 'Tyler,' having kept about that distance since the engagement began, apparently waiting for orders.

"Capt. Gwin now called out to her commander, to move up and ram the 'Arkansas.' His only response to this was, to commence backing vigorously out of range, while Gwin was expressing his opinion of him through the trumpet in that vigorous English a commander in battle sometimes uses, when things do not go altogether right.

"The ram commander was badly scared and demoralized by the loss of the 'Carondelet,' and he let slip a golden opportunity, for he could have struck and sunk the enemy, had not his valor given way at the critical moment. He pointed his vessel for the fleet and the last we saw of him he was making off at the top of his speed, followed until he was entirely out of hearing by a storm of what the darkey called the 'wustest kind of language' from Gwin, who was boiling over with rage and mortification at the turn affairs had taken and the imminent danger he was in of losing his vessel. [Earlier, Walke had ordered the *Queen* to make for the fleet and report the approach of the *Arkansas*.] By the time the 'Tyler' got headed down stream and her engines moving, the 'Arkansas' was close up and throwing grape, while the 'Tyler' as she swung around, replied with each gun as it could be brought to bear, and with musketry from a detachment of sharpshooters we had taken on board the night before.

"Things looked squally. Blood was flowing freely on board, and the crash of timbers from time to time as the 'Arkansas' riddled us seemed to indicate that some vital part would be soon struck. In fact our steering apparatus was shot away, and we handled the vessel for some time solely with the engine[s] until repairs could be made.

"Here is where Gwin showed his high qualities as a commander. He was ablaze with the spirit of battle. All knew that the vessel might go down and all of us be killed, but there would be no surrender. In fact he made that reassuring remark to the first lieutenant in my presence, when that officer suggested such a possibility. We were fighting for existence and we all knew it.

"The 'Tyler' had been pounding the 'Arkansas' all this while, but with little apparent effect; but her smokestack, close to the armor, had been shot through and through, and the smoke pouring out had lessened the draft from her fires and slackened her speed and we began to gain a little on her. [Sixty-eight holes total in the stack this day.]

"There are few circumstances more trying than to be exposed to a heavy fire and not be able to hit back.

"The unpleasant features of battle are not so apparent while the fight is on; then, one is busy, his pride is aroused, and the strain upon his nerve enables him to look upon death and bloodshed with some little indifference; but exposed to danger, seeing your comrades shot down and idle meanwhile, is trying in the extreme. There is but one thing to do under such circumstances and that is to stand up manfully and take what comes. On board a man-of-war there is no other course. This trying ordeal we went through for the next hour, most of us with practically nothing to do but watch the gunners of the 'Arkansas' as they handled their battery, render such assistance as was practicable to the wounded encumbering our decks, occasionally sounding the pumps to see if we had been struck below the belt, and the crew of our one stern gun working it for all it was worth.

"The 'Tyler' at last turned out into the Mississippi with the ram close at her heels, and soon the smokestacks and masts of the fleet appeared in sight. The code signals were run up in warning of the character of the company we were keeping, though the firing constantly approaching nearer, had been so continuous that it was supposed they would be in readiness to give her a warm reception. This was not the case. In fact one of the naval officers, ashore at the time, remarked, when we first came in sight: 'There comes the "Tyler" with a prize.'

"The heavy firing had been heard of course, but it was supposed that the expedition was on its return and shelling the woods, and no preparations were made to meet the emergency.

"In the early days of the war we used to let off our surplus loyalty by shelling the woods, where we thought the enemy might be, when there was no enemy actually in sight to practice on.

"In fact there was hardly time to have gotten up steam, and the combined fleets were entirely taken by surprise. The first intimation of the situation came when the 'Tyler' and 'Arkansas' appeared in sight, exchanging fire and signals flying.

"As the 'Tyler' steamed along the line, the crews of the different men-of-war were crowding on deck in hurried efforts to cast loose their guns.

"The 'Tyler' passed under the stern of the 'Hartford' receiving a parting shot from the 'Arkansas,' freighted with death for one unfortunate who had rested his head against the bulwark, only to have it taken off. . . .

.   .   .   .

"The 'Tyler's' decks presented a shocking spectacle. During the fight she had been hulled eleven times, besides being cut up by grape, thrown at very close range, and by exploding shells. Her decks were literally running with blood, and the killed and wounded lay around in every direction.

"At the very commencement of the fight in the Yazoo, the 'Arkansas' had exploded a shell from one of her forward guns directly on our crowded deck. It had horribly mutilated and instantly killed a commissioned officer and five men, piling them up in one sickening heap. Four of them were headless, and for many feet on both sides of the deck, the wood-work was spattered with blood and shreds of flesh and hair, while few of us escaped without bloody evidences on our clothing and in our faces of the destruction of our comrades.

"The 'Tyler' had lost in the engagement four officers and twenty-one men, killed and wounded, while the injuries to the vessel were of such a character as to require extensive repairs before she was again able to enter into active service."

(Brown) "On gaining the Mississippi, we saw no vessels but the two we had driven before us. While following these in the direction of Vicksburg I had the opportunity of inspecting engine and fire rooms, where I found engineers and firemen had been suffering under a temperature of 120° to 130°. The executive officer, while attending to every other duty during the recent firing, had organized a relief party from the men at the guns, who went down into the fire-room every fifteen minutes, the others coming up or being, in many instances, hauled up, exhausted in that time; in this way, by great care, steam was kept to service gauge. . . .

"Aided by the current of the Mississippi, we soon approached the Federal fleet—a forest of masts and smokestacks—ships, rams, iron-clads, and other gun-boats on the left side, and ordinary river steamers and bomb-vessels along the right. It has been asked why the *Arkansas* was not used as a ram. The want of speed and of confidence in the engines answers the question. To any one having a real ram at command the genius of havoc could not have offered a finer view, the panoramic effect of which was intensified by the city of men spread out with innumerable tents opposite on the right bank. We were not yet in sight of Vicksburg, but in every direction, except astern, our eyes rested on enemies. I had long known the most of these as valued friends, and if I now had any doubts of the success of the *Arkansas* they were inspired by this general knowledge rather than from any awe of a particular name. It seemed at a glance as if a whole navy had come to keep me away from the heroic city,—six or seven rams, four or five iron-clads, without including one accounted for an hour ago, and the fleet of Farragut generally, behind or inside of this fleet. The rams seemed to have been held in *reserve,* to come out between the intervals. Seeing this, as we neared the head of the line I said to our pilot, 'Brady, shave that line of men-of-war as close as you can, so that the rams will not have room to gather head-way in coming out to strike us.' In this way we ran so near to the wooden ships that each may have expected the blow which, if I could avoid it, I did not intend to deliver to any, and probably the rams running out at slow speed across the line of our advance received in the smoke and fury of the fight more damage from the guns of their own men-of-war than those of the *Arkansas.*"

(Gift) "The first vessel which stood out to engage us was 'No. 6'

(Kineo), against which we had a particular grudge, inspired by Read, who desired us all to handle roughly any sea-going vessel we should see with 'No. 6' on her smoke stack, as that vessel was engaging the McRae, above Forts Jackson and St. Philip when Lieutenant Commander Huger was killed. Read, who was First Lieutenant under Captain Huger, and devotedly attached to him, saw the 'No. 6' by the flashes of the guns,—the fight occurred about dawn—and had ever since treasured the hope of getting alongside the fellow some day. This 'No. 6' came out like a game cock, steamed to the front to take the fire of a great monster from which 'mustangs' and river iron-clads were hiding and fleeing. I sent my powder boy to Read with a message to come forward, as his friend was in sight. He came leisurely and carelessly, swinging a primer lanyard, and I think I have never looked at a person displaying such remarkable coolness and self possession. On observing the numbers ahead his eye was as bright and his smile as genuine as if he had been about to join a company of friends instead of enemies. We were getting close aboard 'No. 6,' and he sheered with his port helm and unmuzzled his eleven-inch pivot gun charged with grape. It was hastily pointed, and the charge fell too low to enter our ports, for which it was intended. This broke the terrible quiet which hung over us like a spell. Every man's nerves were strung up again, and we were ready for the second battle. With a sharp touch of the starboard helm Brady showed me 'No. 6' straight ahead, and I gave him a shell through and through, and as we passed he got the port broadside. He did not follow us up. These two shots opened the engagement."

(Brown) "As we neared the head of the line our bow guns, trained on the *Hartford*, began this second fight of the morning . . . and within a few minutes, as the enemy was brought in range, every gun of the *Arkansas* was at its work. It was calm, and the smoke settling over the combatants, our men at times directed their guns at the flashes of those of their opponents. As we advanced, the line of fire seemed to grow into a circle constantly closing. The shock of missiles striking our sides was literally continuous, and as we were now surrounded, without room for anything but pushing ahead, and shrapnel shot were coming on our shield deck, twelve pounds at a time, I went below to see how our Missouri backwoods-men were handling their 100-pounder Columbiads. At this moment I had the most lively realization of having steamed into a real volcano, the *Arkansas* from its center firing rapidly to every point of the circumference, without the fear of hitting a friend or missing an enemy. I got below in time to see Read and Scales with their rifled guns blow off the feeble attack of a ram on our stern. Another ram was across our way ahead. As I gave the order, 'Go through him, Brady!' his steam went into the air, and his crew into the river. A shot from one of our bow guns had gone through his boiler and saved the collision. We passed by and through the brave fellows struggling in the water under a shower of missiles intended for us."

(Gift) "The shot struck upon our sides as fast as sledge-hammer blows. Captain Brown was twice knocked off the platform stunned, his marine glass was broken in his hand, and he received a wound on his temple; but recovering himself, he gallantly—no, heroically—resumed his place, and continued to direct the movements of his ship from a position entirely exposed to the fire of not only great guns, but thousands of sharp-shooters, who were pattering the balls all around and about him. The man of steel never flinched, but carried us straight and clear through. I know that this great battle, and the great commander, have been ignored by the *sect* which ruled the navy, but when the history of our *corps* is written, Brown will rank first. Some one called out that the colors had been shot away. It reached the ear of Midshipman Dabney M. Scales, and in an instant the glorious fellow scrambled up the ladder past Captain Brown, and fearlessly treading the terrible path of death, which was being swept by a hurricane of shot and shell, deliberately bent on the colors again, knotted the halyards and hoisted them up, and when they were again knocked away would have replaced them had not he been forbidden by the Captain. Midshipmen Clarence Tyler, aide to the Captain, was wounded at his post alongside the Captain. We were passing one of the large sloops-of-war when a heavy shot struck the side abreast of my bow-gun, the concussion knocking over a man who was engaged in taking a shot from the rack. He rubbed his hip, which had been hurt, and said they would 'hardly strike twice in a place.' He was mistaken, poor fellow, for immediately a shell entered the breach made by the shot, and bedding itself in the cotton-bale lining on the inside of the bulwark proper, exploded with terrible effect. I found myself standing in a dense, sufficating smoke, with my cap gone and hair and beard singed. The smoke soon cleared away, and I found but one man (Quartermaster Curtis) left. Sixteen were killed and wounded by that shell, and the ship set on fire. Stevens, ever cool and thoughtful, ran to the engine-room hatch, seized the hose and dragged it to the aperture. In a few moments the fire was extinguished, without an alarm having been created.

"The Columbiad was fired but once after its crew was disabled. By the aid of an army Captain (whose name, I am sorry to say, I have forgotten), belonging to a Missouri battery, Curtis and myself succeeded in getting a shot down the gun, with which we struck the Benton. The ill luck which befell the crew of the bow gun was soon to be followed by a similar misfortune to the crew of my broadside gun. An eleven-inch shot broke through immediately above the port, bringing with it a shower of iron and wooden splinters, which struck down every man at the gun. My Master's Mate, Mr. Wilson, was painfully wounded in the nose, and I had my left arm smashed. Curtis was the only sound man in the division when we mustered the crew at quarters, at Vicksburg. Nor did the mischief of the last shot end with my poor gun's crew. It passed across the deck, through the smoke-stack, and killed eight and wounded seven men at Scales's gun. Fortunately, he was untouched himself, and afterward did excellent service at Grimball's Columbiad. Stationed on the ladder leading to the berth-deck was a Quartermaster named Eaton. He was assigned the duty of passing shells from the forward shell-room, and also had a kind of superintendence over the boys who came for powder. Eaton was a character. He had thick, rough, red hair, an immense muscular frame, and a will and courage rarely encountered. Nothing daunted him, and the hotter the fight, the fiercer grew Eaton. From his one eye he glared furiously on all who seemed inclined to shirk, and his voice grew louder and more distinct as the shot rattled and crashed upon our mail.

"At one instant you would hear him pass the word down the hatch: 'Nine-inch shell, five-second fuse—here you are, my lad, with your rifle shell, take it and go back quick—what's the matter that you can't get that gun out?' and, like a cat, he would spring from his place and throw his weight on the side tackle, and the gun was sure to go out. 'What are you doing here, wounded? Where are you hurt? Go back to your gun, or I'll murder you on the spot

—here's your nine-inch shell—mind, shipmate (to a wounded man), the ladder is bloody, don't slip, let me help you.'

"I have thrown in this slight sketch to show that our men were beginning to straggle, so badly were we cut up. But still the ship was not disabled; seven guns were yet hammering away, and the engines were intact. But steam was down to a terribly low ebb. The party who had fitted up the boilers had neglected to line the fire front with non-conducting material; the consequence was that when a heavy fire of coal was put in the whole mass of iron about the boilers became red-hot and nearly roasted the firemen, who had also got a tub of ice-water, of which they drank freely. The result was that we had to hoist them all out of the fire-room during the action, and Grimball headed a party to supply their place."

(Brown) "It was a little hot this morning all around; the enemy's shot frequently found weak places in our armor, and their shrapnel and minie-balls also came through our port-holes. Still, under a temperature of 120°, our people kept to their work, and as each one, acting under the steady eye of Stevens, seemed to think the result depended on himself, I sought a cooler atmosphere on the shield, to find, close ahead and across our way, a large iron-clad displaying the square flag of an admiral. Though we had but little head-way, his beam was exposed, and I ordered the pilot to strike him amidships. He avoided this by steaming ahead, and, passing under his stern, nearly touching, we gave him our starboard broadside, which probably went through him from rudder to prow. This was our last shot, and we received none in return.

"We were now at the end of what had seemed the interminable line, and also past the outer rim of the volcano. I now called the officers up to take a look at what we had just come through and to get the fresh air; and as the little group of heroes closed around me with their friendly words of congratulation, a heavy rifle-shot passed close over our heads: it was the parting salutation, and if aimed two feet lower would have been to us the most injurious of the battle. We were not yet in sight of Vicksburg, but if any of the fleet followed us farther on our way I did not perceive it.

.   .   .   .

"The connection between the furnaces and smoke-stack (technically called the breechings) were in this second conflict shot away, destroying the draught and letting the flames come out into the shield, raising the temperature there to 120°, while it had already risen to 130° in the fire-room. . . . We went into action in Old River with 120 pounds of steam, and though every effort was made to keep it up, we came out with but 20 pounds, hardly enough to turn the engines.

.   .   .   .

"The *Arkansas* continued toward Vicksburg without further trouble. When within sight of the city, we saw another fleet preparing to receive us or recede from us, below: one vessel of the fleet was aground and in flames. [A mortar schooner, destroyed to eliminate the possibility of her capture by the *Arkansas*.] With our firemen exhausted, our smoke-stack cut to pieces, and a section of our plating torn from the side, we were not in condition just then to begin a third battle; moreover humanity required the landing of our wounded—terribly torn by cannon-shot—and of our dead."

(Gift) "We got through, hammered and battered though. Our smokestack resembled an immense nutmeg grater, so often had it been struck, and the sides of the ship were as spotted as if she had been peppered. A shot had broken our cast-iron ram. Another had demolished a hawse-pipe. Our boats were shot away and dragging. But all this was to be expected and could be repaired. Not so on the inside. A great heap of mangled and ghastly slain lay on the gun deck, with rivulets of blood running away from them. There was a poor fellow torn asunder, another mashed flat, whilst in the 'slaughter-house' brains, hair and blood were all about. Down below fifty or sixty wounded were groaning and complaining, or courageously bearing their ills without a murmur. All the army stood on the hills to see us round the point. The flag had been set up on a temporary pole, and we went out to return the cheers the soldiers gave us as we passed. The Generals came on board to embrace our Captain, bloody yet game. This ends our second battle."

(Brown) "We were received at Vicksburg with enthusiastic cheers. Immediate measures were taken to repair damages and to recruit our crew, diminished to one-half their original number by casualties, and by the expiration of service of those who had volunteered only for the trip to Vicksburg.

"We had left the Yazoo River with a short supply of fuel, and after our first landing opposite the city-hall we soon dropped down to the coal depot, where we began coaling and repairing, under the fire of the lower fleet, to which, under the circumstances, we could make no reply. Most of the enemy's shot fell short, but Renshaw, in the *Westfield,* made very fine practice with his 100-pounder rifle gun, occasionally throwing the spray from his shot over our working party, but with the benefit of sprinkling down the coal dust. Getting in our coal, we moved out of range of such sharp practice, where, under less excitement, we hastened such temporary repairs as would enable us to continue the offensive. We had intended trying the lower fleet that evening, but before our repairs could be completed and our crew reinforced by suitable selections from the army, the hours of night were approaching, under the shadows of which (however favorable for running batteries) no brave man cares from choice to fight."

CHAPTER X

THE *ARKANSAS* SAGA (CONTD.)

ARRAGUT decides immediately to run his fleet back past the batteries before dark and destroy the ram en route; if he fails in the latter he can at least protect the ships below from attack by the *Arkansas*. From the port main yardarm of the flagship *Hartford* he suspends his heaviest anchor; this he will drop on the *Arkansas* if she should come alongside. The start is delayed.

(Gift) "As soon as dark began to set in it was evident that the enemy meant mischief.

"Everything was under way, and soon the guns from the upper battery opened quick and sharp, to be replied to by the broadsides of the heavy ships coming down—the Richmond (Alden) leading. Our plucky men were again at their quarters, and steam was ready, should we be compelled to cast off and take our chances in the stream against both fleets. About that time things looked pretty blue. It is true that we were under the batteries of Vicksburg, but practically we had as well have been a hundred miles from there. The guns were perched on the high hills; they were not provided with sights, and if ever they hit anything it was an accident or the work of one of Brooke's rifles. [Not then in position at Vicksburg.] This we well knew, and stripped this time for what we supposed would be a death struggle. The sea-going fleet of Farragut was to pass down, drag out and literally mob us; whilst the iron-clad squadron of Davis was to keep the batteries engaged. Down they came, steaming slowly and steadily, and seemed to be on the look-out for us. But they had miscalculated their time. The darkness which partially shrouded them from the view of the army gunners completely shut us out from their sight, inasmuch as our sides were the color of rust and we lay under a red bank; consequently, the first notice they had of our whereabouts came from our guns as they crossed our line of fire, and then it was too late to attempt to check up and undertake to grapple with us. They came by singly, each to get punished, as our men were again feeling in excellent spirits. The Hartford stood close in to the bank, and as we spit out our broadside at her, she thundered back with an immense salvo. Our bad luck had not left us. An eleven-inch shot pierced our side a few inches above the water-line, and passed through the engine-room, killing two men outright (cutting them both in two) and wounding six or eight others. The medicines of the ship were dashed into the engine-room, and the *debris* from the bulkheads and splinters from the side enveloped the machinery. The shot bedded itself so far in the opposite side that its position could be told by the bulging protuberance outside. On account of my disabled arm I had turned over my division to Scales, and remained with Captain Brown on the platform. To be a spectator of such a scene was intensely interesting and exciting. The great ships with their towering spars came sweeping by, pouring out broadside after broadside, whilst the batteries from the hills, the mortars from above and below, and the iron-clads, kept the air alive with hurtling missiles and the darkness lighted up by burning fuses and bursting shells. On our gun-deck every man and officer worked as though the fate of the nation hung on his individual efforts. Scales was very near, and I could hear his clear voice continually. He coaxed and bullied alternately, and finally, when he saw his object in line, his voice rose as clear as a bell, and his 'ready! fire!' rang out like a bugle note. The last vessel which passed us was that commanded by Nichols ('Bricktop') [the *Winona*] and she got one of our shots in her out-board delivery. He pivoted his eleven inch gun to starboard, heeled his vessel to keep the leak above water, and drifted past the batteries without further damage.

"We had more dead and wounded, another hole through our armor and heaps of splinters and rubbish. Three separate battles had been fought and we retired to anything but easy repose. One of our messmates in the ward-room (a pilot) had asserted at supper that he would not again pass through the ordeal of the morning for the whole world. His mangled body, collected in pieces was now on the gun-deck; another had been sent away to the hospital with a mortal hurt. The steerage mess was short four or five members, whilst on the berth deck many poor fellows would never again range themselves about the mess-cloth."

(Read) "The next morning (July 16th) at nine o'clock the enemy opened on us from all their mortar-boats above and below town, throwing their huge 13-inch shells thick and fast around us. As the mortar-shells fell with terrible force almost perpendicularly, and as the 'Arkansas' was unprotected on upper-decks, boilers amidship, a magazine and shell-room at each end, it was very evident that if she was struck by one of those heavy shells, it would be the last of her. Her moorings were changed frequently to impair the enemy's range; but the enterprising Yankees shelled us continually, their shell often exploding a few feet above decks and sending their fragments into the decks.

"When the 'Arkansas' started down the Yazoo her crew were seamen with the exception of about fifty soldiers—volunteers from a Missouri regiment. The seamen had been on the Yazoo swamps some time, and in consequence were troubled with chills and fever. Many had been killed, a large number wounded, and a greater portion of the remainder sent to the hospital on our arrival at Vicksburg. The day after we reached the city the Missouri volunteers, who had agreed to serve only for the trip, went on shore and joined their commands; so we were not very short-handed. Captain Brown asked General Van Dorn to fill up our complement from the army, which he readily assented to do, provided the men would volunteer, and make application for transfer through proper channels. At first quite a number volunteered, but when they got on board and saw the shot-holes through the vessel's sides, and heard sailors' reports of the terrible effect of shell and splinters, and were made aware of the danger of the mortar-shell that fell continually around the ship, those volunteers found many pretexts to go back to their commands; many took 'shell fever' and went to the hospital. As a general thing, soldiers are not much use on board ship, particularly volunteers, who are not accustomed to the discipline and routine of a man-of-war. A scene that occurred on board the 'Arkansas' one day at Vicksburg is illustrative. We were engaged hauling the ship into a position near one of our batteries; but having but few sailors to haul on the wharf we were progressing slowly, when Lieutenant Stevens, the executive officer, came on deck, and perceiving a crowd of volunteers sitting on deck playing cards, he said, rather sharply, 'Come, volunteers, that won't do; get up from there and give us a pull.' One of the players looked up at Lieutenant Stevens and replied, 'Oh! hell! we aint no deck hands;' and eyeing the man sitting opposite to him, was heard to say, 'I go you two better!'

"Both of our surgeons being sick, Captain Brown telegraphed out into the interior of Mississippi for medical volunteers. In a day or two a long, slim doctor came in from Clinton; and as he was well recommended, Captain Brown gave him an acting appointment as surgeon, and directed him to report to Lieutenant Stevens for duty. It was early in the norning when he arrived; the enemy had not commenced their daily pastime of shelling us; the ship's decks had been cleanly washed down, the awnings spread, and everything was neat and orderly. The doctor took breakfast in the ward-room, and seemed delighted with the vessel generally. Before the regular call to morning inspection the officer of the powder division started around below to show the new medical officer his station during action, and the arrangement for disposing of the wounded, etc., etc. In going along the berth-deck the officer remarked to the doctor that in a battle there was plenty to do, as the wounded came down in a steady stream. The 'medico' looked a little incredulous; but a few minutes afterwards, when he perceived the road through which an 11-inch shell had come, his face lengthened perceptibly; and after awhile, when the big shell began to fall around the vessel, he became rather nervous. He would stand on the companion-ladder and watch the smoke rise from the mortar-vessels, and would wait until he heard the whizzing of the shell through the air, when he would make a dive for his state-room. As soon as the shell fell he would go up and watch out for another. Occasionally, when a shell would explode close to us, or fall with a heavy splash alongside, he would be heard to groan, 'Oh! Louisa and the babes!' "

(Brown) "In time we became accustomed to this shelling, but not to the idea that it was without danger; and I know of no more effective way of curing a man of the weakness of thinking that he is without the feeling of fear than for him, on a dark night, to watch two or three of these double-fused descending shells, all near each other, and seeming as though they would strike him between the eyes.

"In three days we were again in condition to move and to menace at our will either fleet, thus compelling the enemy's entire force, in the terrible July heat, to keep up steam day and night. An officer of the fleet writing at this time, said: 'Another council of war was held on board the admiral's [flag-ship] last night, in which it was resolved that the *Arkansas* must be destroyed at all hazards, a thing, I suspect, much easier said than done; but I wish that she was destroyed, for she gives us no rest by day nor sleep by night.' We constantly threatened the offensive, and our raising steam, which they could perceive by our smoke-stack, was the signal for either fleet to fire up. As the temperature at that season was from 90° to 100° in the shade, it was clear that unless the *Arkansas* could be 'destroyed' the siege, if for sanitary reasons alone, must soon be raised.

"The result of our first real attempt to resume the offensive was that before we could get within range of the mortar fleet, our engine completely broke down, and it was with difficulty that we regained our usual position in front of the city."

(Gift) "On the morning of the 22d of July, a week after our arrival, we were awakened early in the morning by the drum calling us to quarters. Great commotion was observed in the fleet above. Everything seemed under-way again, and it was evident that we were soon to have another brush. On our decks were not men enough to man two guns, and not firemen enough to keep steam up if we were forced into the stream! Rather a doleful outlook! We were moored to the bank, head up the river, as a matter of course. The fires under the boilers were hastened, and every possible preparation made for resistance. In a few minutes we observed the ironclad steamer Essex ('Dirty Bill Porter' commanding) steaming around the point and steering for us. The upper battery opened, but she did not reply. Grimball unloosed his Columbiad, but she did not stop. I followed, hitting her fair, but she still persevered in sullen silence. Her plan was to run into and shove us aground, when her consort, the Queen of the West, was to follow and butt a hole in us; and thus the dreaded ram was to be made way with. On she came like a mad bull, nothing daunted or overawed. As soon as Captain Brown got a fair view of her, followed at a distance by the Queen, he divined her intent, and seeing that she was as square across the bow as a flatboat or scow, and we were as sharp as a wedge, he determined at once to foil her tactics. Slacking off the hawser which held our head to the bank, he went ahead on the starboard screw, and thus our sharp prow was turned directly for her to hit against. This disconcerted the enemy and destroyed his plan. A collision would surely cut him down and leave us uninjured. All this time we had not been idle spectators. The two Columbiads had been ringing on his front and piercing him every shot; to which he did not reply until he found that the shoving game was out of the question. Then, and when not more than fifty yards distant, he triced up his three bow port-shutters and poured out his fire. A nine-inch shot struck our armor a few inches forward of the unlucky forward port, and crawling along the side entered. Seven men were killed outright and six wounded. Splinters flew in all directions. In an instant the enemy was alongside, and his momentum was so great that he ran aground a short distance astern of us. As he passed we poured out our port broadside, and as soon as the stern rifles could be cleared of the splinters and broken stanchions and woodwork, which had been driven the whole length of the gun-box, we went ahead on our port screw and turned our stern guns on him, and every man—we had but seventeen left—and officer went to them. As he passed he did not fire, nor did he whilst we were riddling him close aboard. His only effort was to get away from us. He backed hard on his engines and finally got off; but getting a shot in his machinery just as he got afloat, he was compelled to float down stream and join the lower fleet, which he accomplished without damage from the batteries on the hills. He fired only the three shots mentioned. But *our* troubles were not over. We had scarcely shook this fellow off before we were called to the other end of the ship—we ran from one gun to another to get ready for a second attack. The Queen was now close to us, evidently determined to ram us. The guns had been fired and were now empty and inboard. *Somehow* we got them loaded and run out, and by the time she had commenced to round to. I am not sure, but I think we struck her with the Columbiads as she came down, but at all events the broadside was ready. Captain Brown adopted the plan of turning his head to her also, and thus received her blow glancing. She came into us going at an enormous speed, probably fifteen miles an hour, and I felt pretty sure that our hour had struck. I had hoped to blow her up with the thirty-two-pounder as she passed, but the gun being an old one, with an enlarged vent, the primer drew out without igniting the charge. One of the men, we had no regular gun's crews then, every man was expected to do ten men's duty, replaced it

and struck it with a compressor lever; but too late; his boilers were
past, and the shot went through his cylinder timbers without disabling him. His blow, though glancing, was a heavy one. His prow,
or beak, made a hole through our side and caused the ship to careen,
and roll heavily; but we all knew in an instant that no serious damage had been done, and we redoubled our efforts to cripple him so
that he could not again attempt the experiment. As did the Essex,
so he ran into the bank astern of us, and got the contents of the
stern battery; but being more nimble than she, was sooner off into
deep water. Returning up stream he got our broadside guns again,
and we saw that he had no disposition to engage us further. As he
passed the line of fire of the bow guns he got it again, and I distinctly
recollect the handsomest shot I ever made was the last at her. He
was nearly a mile away, and I bowled at him with the gun lying
level. It *ricochetted* four or five times before it dropped into his
stern. But it dropped there. As I have before said, the Essex was
drifting down stream unmanageable, and now would have been
our time to have ended her in sight of both squadrons, but we had
but seventeen men and they well-nigh exhausted. Beating off these
two vessels, under the circumstances, was the best achievement of
the Arkansas. That we were under the batteries of Vicksburg did
not amount to anything. I do not believe that either vessel was injured by an army gun that day. We were left to our fate, and if we
had been lost it would have been no unusual or unexpected thing.
The Essex used, in one of her guns that day, projectiles that were
probably never used before, to-wit: Marbles that boys used for playing. We picked up a hundred unbroken ones on our forecastle.
There were 'white-allies,' 'chinas,' and some glass marbles."

(Brown) "The closeness of this contest with the *Essex* may be in-
ferred from the circumstance that several of our surviving men had
their faces blackened and were painfully hurt by the unburnt powder which came through our port-holes from the assailant's guns."

After this latest unsuccessful attempt to destroy the *Arkansas* the
Federal fleets decided to give up the close blockade of Vicksburg
altogether. Everybody was getting sick. The few troops present
could do nothing. The level of the water was going down, instilling
increased fears in Farragut's mind of his big ships being held far
up the river till the following season. The close proximity of the

Arkansas necessitated the consumption of great quantities of coal in keeping up steam; and the heat from the boilers made life especially unpleasant. For it should be borne in mind that the only machinery units to use steam were the main engines and their auxiliaries. So the fires were not lit off unless a movement was in prospect. There was now such a vast mileage of riverbanks to patrol, against marauders of various sorts, that every available man-of-war was needed to ensure the safe passage of transports and other un-armed vessels. But the primary cause of the move was the sickness that was mounting to such heights in the bad climate around Vicksburg at this time of year. At one time, for instance, the *Brooklyn* had 68 on the sick list out of her complement of 300. The gunboat fleet had 40 per cent sick on July 25; and the small army had *only 25 per cent fit for duty*. Something had to be done quickly, and it was decided that all forces should withdraw, even if this should allow a much wider scope to the activities of the *Arkansas*.

(Brown) "Vicksburg was now without the suspicion of an immediate enemy. I had taken, with my brave associates, for the last sixty days, my share of labor and watchfulness, and I now left them for four days, only, as I supposed, to sustain without me the lassitude of inaction. Important repairs were yet necessary to the engines, and much of the iron plating had to be refastened to her shattered sides. This being fairly under way, I called, Thursday P. M., upon General Van Dorn, commanding the forces, and told him that, having obtained telegraphic permission from the Navy Department to turn over the command of the vessel temporarily to the officer next in rank, First Lieutenant Stevens, I would go to Grenada, Miss., and that I would return on the following Tuesday A.M., by which time the *Arkansas*, I hoped, would be ready once more to resume the offensive. Almost immediately on reaching Grenada I was taken violently ill, and while in bed, unable, as I supposed, to rise, I received a dispatch from Lieutenant Stevens saying that Van Dorn required him to steam at once down to Baton Rouge to aid in a land attack of our forces upon the Union garrison holding that place. I replied to this with a positive order to remain at Vicksburg until I could join him; and without delay caused myself to be taken to the railroad station, where I threw myself on the mailbags of the first passing train, unable to sit up, and did not change my position until reaching Jackson, 130 miles distant. On applying there for a special train to take me to Vicksburg, I learned that the *Arkansas* had been gone from that place four hours. Van Dorn had been persistent beyond all reason in his demand, and Stevens, undecided, had referred the question to a senior officer of the Confederate navy, who was at Jackson, Miss., with horses and carriages, furnished by Government in place of a flag-ship, thus commanding in chief for the Confederacy on the Mississippi, sixty miles from its nearest waters. . . . Ignorant or regardless of the condition of the *Arkansas,* fresh from Richmond on his mission of bother, not communicating with or informing me on the subject, he ordered Stevens to obey Van Dorn without any regard to my orders to the contrary.

"Under the double orders of two commanders-in-chief to be at Baton Rouge at a certain date and hour. . . ."

(Gift) ". . . we left Vicksburg thirty hours before General Breckinridge had arranged to make his attacks. The short time allowed to arrive at the rendezvous made it imperative that the vessel should be driven up to her best speed. This resulted in the frequent disarrangements of the machinery and consequent stoppages to key up and make repairs. Every delay required more speed thereafter in order to meet our appointment. Another matter operated against us. We had been compelled to leave behind, in the hospital, our chief engineer, George W. City, who was worn out and broken down by excessive watching and anxiety. His care and nursing had kept the machinery in order up to the time of leaving. We soon began to feel his loss. The engineer in charge, a volunteer from the army, had recently joined us, and though a young man of pluck and gallantry, and possessed of great will and determination to make the engines work, yet he was unequal to the task. He had never had anything to do with a screw vessel or short-stroke engines, and, being zealous for the good repute of his department, drove the machinery beyond its powers of endurance.

". . . At or near the mouth of Red river, the engines had grown so contrary and required to be hammered so much that Stevens deemed it his duty to call a council of war to determine whether it was proper to proceed or return. The engineer was summoned and gave it as his opinion that the machinery would hold out, and upon that statement we determined to go ahead. A few miles below Port Hudson he demanded a stoppage to key up and make all things secure before going into action. We landed at the right bank of the river, and I was dispatched with Bacot to a house near by to get information. After a deal of trouble we gained admittance and learned that the naval force of the enemy at Baton Rouge consisted of our particular enemy, the Essex, and one or two small sea-going wooden gunboats. This was very satisfactory. We learned, also, that Breckinridge was to attack at daylight; that his movements had been known for several days on that side of the river; yet it will be borne in mind that this important secret could not be entrusted to high officers of the navy until a few hours before they were to co-operate in the movement. At daylight we heard our gallant troops commence the engagement. The long rattle of the volleys of musketry, mixed with the deep notes of artillery, informed us that we were behind, and soon came the unmistakable boom of heavy navy guns, which plainly told us that we were wanted—that our iron sides should be receiving those missiles which were now mowing down our ranks of infantry. In feverish haste our lines were cast off and hauled aboard, and once more the good ship was driving towards the enemy. Like a war-horse she seemed to scent the battle from afar, and in point of speed outdid anything we had ever before witnessed. . . . We were in sight of Baton Rouge. The battle had ceased; our troops had driven the enemy to the edge of the water, captured his camps and his positions, and had in turn retired before the heavy broadsides of the Essex, which lay moored abreast of the arsenal. Our officers and crew went to quarters in high spirits, for once there was a chance to make the army and country appreciate us. Baton Rouge is situated on a 'reach' or long, straight stretch of river, which extends three of four miles above the town. We were nearly to the turn and about to enter the 'reach;' the crew had been mustered at quarters, divisions reported, and all the minute preparations made for battle which have before been detailed, when Stevens came on deck with Brady, the pilot, to take a final look and determine upon what plan to adopt in his attack on the Essex. It was my watch and we three stood together. Brady proposed that we ram the Essex and sink her where she lay, then back out and put ourselves below the transports and wooden gunboats as soon as possible to cut off their retreat. Stevens assented to the proposal and had just remarked that we had better go to our stations, for we were in a hundred yards of the turn, when the starboard engine stopped suddenly, and, before the man at the wheel could meet her with the helm, the ship ran hard and fast aground, jamming herself on to some old cypress stumps that were submerged. We were in full view from the position General Breckinridge had taken up to await our attack. All day long he remained in line of battle prepared to move forward again, but in vain. On investigation it was found that the engine was so badly out of order that several hours must be consumed before we could again expect to move. There lay the enemy in plain view, and we as helpless as a shear-hulk. Hundreds of people had assembled to witness the fight. In fact, many ladies in carriages had come to see our triumph. They waved us on with smiles and prayers, but we couldn't go. But Stevens was not the man to give up. A quantity of railroad iron, which had been laid on deck loose, was thrown overboard, and in a few hours we were afloat. The engineers had pulled the engine to pieces and with files and chisels were as busy as bees, though they had been up constantly then for the greater parts of the two preceding nights. At dark it was reported to the commanding officer that the vessel could be moved. In the meantime some coal had been secured (our supply was getting short), and it was determined to run up stream a few hundred yards and take it in during the night, and be ready for hot work in the morning. Therefore we started to move, but had not gone a hundred yards before the same engine broke down again; the crank pin (called a 'wrist' by Western engineers) of the rock-shaft broke in two. Fortunately one of the engineers was a blacksmith, so the forge was set up and another pin forged. But this with our improvised facilities used up the whole night. Meantime the enemy became aware of our crippled condition, and at daylight moved up to the attack. The Essex led, and came up very slowly, at a rate not to exceed two miles an hour. She had opened on us before the last touch had been given to the pin, but it was finished and the parts thrown together. As the ship again started ahead Stevens remarked that we were brought to bay by a superior force, and that he should fight it out as long as we would swim. The battle for the supremacy of the river was upon us, and we must meet the grave responsibility as men and patriots. His plan was to go up the river a few hundred yards and then turn on and dispatch the Essex, then give his attention to the numerous force of wooden vessels which had been assembled since the morning before. The pleasant sensation of again being afloat and in possession of the power of locomotion, was hardly experienced before our last and final disaster came. The port engine this time gave way, broke down and would not move. The engineer was now in despair, he could do nothing, and so reported. The Essex was coming up astern and firing upon us. We had run ashore and were a hopeless, immovable mass. Read was returning the fire, but the two ships were scarcely near enough for the shots to tell. We were not struck by the Essex, nor do I think we struck her. An army force was reported by a mounted 'home guard' to be coming up the river to cut off our retreat. Stevens did not call a council of war, but himself assumed the responsibility of burning the ship. I recollect the look of anguish he gave me, and the scalding tears were running down his cheeks when he announced his determination. Read kept firing at the Essex until Stevens had set fire to the ward-room and cabin, then all jumped on shore, and in a few moments the flames burst up the hatches. Loaded shells had been placed at all the guns, which commenced exploding as soon as the fire reached the gun deck. This was the last of the Arkansas."

Her career lasted only twenty-three days, but what a career! It included so much action that there probably never was another vessel that averaged anything like as much fighting per day as did the *Arkansas*.

CHAPTER XI

A MISSISSIPPI SURPRISE PARTY

THE *Arkansas* was destroyed less than two weeks after the withdrawal of the Union fleets from Vicksburg. After her elimination there remained afloat no threat to the hold which the Federal vessels now had on the entire river, except in the immediate vicinity of the city itself. It must be recognized, however, that this hold was not a tight one. Especially at this stage of the war there simply were not nearly enough armed vessels to patrol adequately such a length of stream as stretches from Cairo to the Gulf. It was impossible to prevent completely the transport of enemy supplies across the river from the western to the eastern part of the Confederacy. It was impossible to ensure at all points the safety of unescorted transports and other unarmed vessels.

The threats were various. Once in a while the Rebels would bob up with a craft such as the *Arkansas*, which would flash across the scene in a career that was brief but very upsetting to her opponents. Occasionally a battery would be established on an eminence commanding the river, and this would form a barrier to most vessels desiring to pass, until it was captured or destroyed—of which more in later chapters. Then there was the continual sniping from the banks at almost any point along the way against both Navy and noncombatant vessels. This covered a range extending from proper attacks with field guns by regular units of the Confederate land forces, all the way to musketry fire by individual citizens or guerrillas, i. e., irregularly constituted bands of unauthorized civilians. It was the reprisals taken by both the Union Army and Navy against this and similar forms of unlawful warfare that has caused probably more resentment in the South than all other incidents of the Civil War combined—resentment not yet extinguished.

Also, there was one more method by which the control of the river was at times impaired by the Confederates. An example will be given in the following story. This was one of the "Prize War

Stories" that were published by the *New York Weekly Tribune.*
The author was S. H. Brown, then writing from River View, West
Virginia. The incident took place during the few weeks throughout
which the previously described close blockade of Vicksburg was
maintained. Brown will provide the preliminaries of his story as
well as the yarn itself.

"I was only an able seaman then, but I had been with that grand
old sea-lion, Farragut, from the time we reached Ship Island in
March, had passed through the storm of shot and shell on the
morning of April 26th, when we ran past Forts Jackson and St.
Philip, clearing away the chain obstructions, meeting and sinking
the fire ships made of barges filled with pine wood, rosin, and tar,
blazing high above our topmast crosstrees. Thus, having either
destroyed or captured the Confederate gunboats and rams, we sailed
proudly up the Father of Waters with the glorious banner of the
Nation floating in triumph from our mizzen-peak, and we all felt
a thrill of pride as we thought of the joy the news would bring to
the hearts of the loyal people of our country; and every man of our
ship's company determined to show to the world what the men of
the American Navy could do in quelling rebellion at home as well
as sustaining the honor of the old flag on the sea.

"The surrender of New Orleans and its subsequent occupation
by our troops are matters of history now, but there were many events
connected with the passage of the fleet to Vicksburg and the landing
of supplies to the vessels after they reached there that have never
been written—instances of individual daring, night attacks upon
the transports running the gauntlet of shore batteries—that would
fill volumes if they were ever published.

"I remember well . . . the supply ship Houghton. She was a
small sailing bark, purchased by the Government, of about three
hundred tons. She had been fitted up by the Government with a
battery of five guns, four long thirty-twos in broadside and one
eleven-inch Rodman pivot gun on the forecastle. Her crew consisted
of an acting master, three master's mates, a surgeon, and sixty men.
I had been detailed by Captain Renshaw from the gunboat Westfield to take the place of one of the master's mates who was on the
sick-list. We had on board a full cargo of provisions, clothing, and
ordnance stores for the fleet above, and, in addition, had the fleet

paymaster on board with over $100,000 in gold for the crews of the
different ships in the fleet then lying just below Vicksburg. It was
known in New Orleans when we left that we had a very valuable
cargo, besides the money on board, and the news of our departure
was no doubt sent by the Confederates in the city to all the points
above, urging our capture if possible.

"We left the city early in July, and being a sailing vessel we had
to take an old river steamer called the Empire Parish to tow us up.
She made fast on the port side, and we took the precaution to pile
bales of cotton both forward and aft of her boiler and engines, and
also took the men's hammocks and hung them around the pilot-
house as a protection against the bullets of the sharpshooters who
lined the banks on both sides of the river all the way up. We had
passed Baton Rouge without molestation, except an occasional
rifle-shot from someone on the shore as a reminder that we were in
an enemy's country, when our steamer was disabled by the breaking of some portion of her machinery, and we came to anchor about
one hundred and fifty yards from the east bank of the river. After
endeavoring for some hours to make the necessary repairs it was
found that they could not be made without sending the steamer
back to Baton Rouge, and so after some temporary repairs, enabling
her to make the short distance, she steamed away, expecting to return by noon of the next day. But it required a longer time than
we expected to put the machinery in proper condition to make the
trip. . . .

"Nothing unusual occurred during the afternoon and night
after we were left, but the next morning, soon after eight bells had
struck, we noticed an old negro on the east bank who seemed by his
actions to wish to communicate with us for some reason, and it was
finally decided to send the second cutter ashore and see what the
old fellow wanted. He stood near the river bank and the moment
the cutter reached the shore, seeming very much frightened, he
hurriedly told us that there had been a large gathering the night
before at the house of his master, who was a colonel in the Confederate service, then at home on furlough, and the old fellow had
overheard the whole plan for our capture discussed and agreed
upon by the men assembled. They had full information as to what
kind of a prize they would secure if they succeeded in making
the capture. Their plan was to get as many batteaux and other

boats together as possible at a point on the river above us and have them manned with as many people as could be mustered for the service, headed by the colonel and some ten or more Confederate soldiers who had seen service and were then in the vicinity, some on furlough and some on detached service. The company were to meet at a point about one mile above, and as the night would be dark, there being no moon till late, they could float with the current almost noiselessly down upon us, dividing their force, part taking the port and part the starboard side. The bark lying very low, her plank-shears not over three feet above the water, they could climb right on board and have us captured before we were aware of any danger. . . . The old darkey after giving us this information seemed badly frightened for fear he would be found out. We offered to take him on board the ship with us, but he did not dare go. He said: 'S'pose day does come and kill you all an' take de ship and find old niggah dar, dey burn him alive shuah an' sartin. No, no, de old niggah go back to work in de cotton patch. Bime-by Massa Linkum come hisself and de ole niggah be free niggah den.' We told him all right, his old master should never know about it in any event, and went back to our ship.

"We lay there all that hot July day, and from out topgallant crosstrees we could see over the point of land above, and during the day descried a number of batteaux and other boats cross the river above and go behind the point of land, all filled with men; and occasionally we could see the glint of a musket or carbine as someone in the boat would change his position. Everything passed off quietly until the second dog-watch was out. Then all hands were called to quarters and the ship stripped for action and the necessary preparations made to give the surprise-party a different reception from the one they anticipated. The charges of shell were drawn from all the guns and a double stand of grape and canister were rammed home. Our bulwarks were hung on hinges which let them drop outboard, and left a clear flush deck from the fife-rail around the mainmast to the heel of the bowsprit; so, unless we objected, all the boarding party had to do was to leap out of their batteaux square on deck. We trained the broadside guns as far forward as possible with muzzles depressed so the charge would strike the water inside of fifty yards from the ship. Each man was armed with a brace of eight-inch navy revolvers, cutlass and belt. The entire battery was at full cock, primes in place, and we were ordered to stations and to keep silence.

"We had what seemed a long wait. One, two, three, four, and five bells struck, and still the silence was unbroken, save by the wash of the rapid current as it passed our cable, or the sudden blow of some heavy piece of driftwood against our cut-water. The strain on the nerves while awaiting the attack in perfect silence was intense. But soon after six bells had struck, the click of oars was heard up the river and we knew then that the struggle was near. We had no means of knowing the force of the attacking party, but we knew that if any number of them reached our deck unharmed it would be a desperate hand-to-hand fight for life. On they came, floating now with the current as silent as the grave, until within fifty yards of our bows, when they separated, about one-half of them going to each side or starting for those points, when with the rebel yell that was afterward so familiar to our boys, they made their grand rush for us. But suddenly, as if by magic, our battle-lanterns were lighted fore and aft, making the whole scene as bright as noonday, and disclosing to us what seemed to be a legion of shouting fiends filled with the spirit of the evil one, each man armed with whatever weapon had been most convenient—muskets, rifles, shot-guns, pistols, old cavalry sabres, short cutlasses, some with pieces of scythes, with sticks of wood for handles, others with long, ugly bowie-knives; in short, it was an expedition organized for murder and booty. At almost the same instant that our deck lights gave us the bearings of the two squads of boats came the clear ringing voice of our commander—an old veteran in the service—'Fire port and starboard batteries!' The officer in command of the pivot gun forward got his range on two of the largest batteaux, filled with men, and with one simultaneous roar our whole battery fore and aft exploded, carrying death and destruction in its wake. I am an old man now, but the screams of agony from those poor mistaken volunteers is as clear in my memory tonight, after the lapse of three and twenty years, as though I had heard them only yesterday. I have been often in battles since then, have seen my fellow men mangled by exploding shells, out of all human semblance, have heard the cries of pain from wounded animals, but never yet have heard anything to equal the yell of agony that broke the stillness of that terrible night after the sound of our artillery had died away. Our aim had been so accurate that five of their batteaux were blown to fragments. Many of the men were completely riddled with the canister and grape, and sank at once in the turbid waters; others, wounded and struggling for life, and grasping at anything to sustain them for a moment, were hurried by the swift current, shrieking from our sight, only to find graves under the remorseless tide. On the remaining boats, about one hundred men who were still unhurt, with a bravery worthy of a better cause, paying no heed to their wounded and drowning comrades, made a dash for us, and five of the boats, three on the port and two on the starboard side, had succeeded in grappling to the lanyards of our standing rigging or to the forward chain-plates and bobstays, when again that clear voice rang out above the din of conflict: 'All hands repel boarders, port and starboard!' The next five minutes witnessed a perfect fusillade of musketry, mingled with the clash of cutlass and sabre, the thud of the boarding-pike, the rebel yell, and the cheers of our men as the last of the attacking party leaped from our deck in the endeavor to reach the last boat, then some yards away, with the survivors pulling for dear life down stream.

"The struggle was over; it had been so brief and desperate that few of us realized that we had met and beaten off more than four times our number of brave and determined men, but such was the fact. Out of the whole party only four gained a foothold on our decks and three of them now lay there dead. One of them had been cloven from the shoulder to the waist with one blow of a cutlass dealt by the powerful arm of our boatswain's mate; another lay with part of a broken boarding-pike, thrust clean through his breast, still remaining in the ghastly wound, and the other had a pistol-shot through the brain. Of our own men only two were dead—Jack Grills, second captain of the pivot gun, and poor little Tommy French, a jolly, rollicking youngster, who had shipped in the navy in New York only a few months before. How well I remember him—always ready for duty, overflowing with good-humor, and liked by all. As we launched him and poor Jack from the gangway the next morning in their canvas shrouds, with a thirty-two pound shot at the feet of each, there was many a stifled sob and many a tear stole down the bronzed and weather-beaten faces of the grim tars, who had faced death many a time without the quiver of a muscle. We only had five wounded, and they were soon made as comfortable as possible under the skilful care of our surgeon; and before eight bells in the morning watch the decks had been washed down, guns run in and secured, ports triced up, the running rigging coiled down, and the usual routine of man-of-war life and duty begun again. The ship and treasure were safe, and the surprise party was a thing of the past."

One-hundred-pounder rifle, showing wheels and tackle on carriage, elevating screw (drapery not identified), firing lock with lanyard, and crude rear and "front" sights on breech and trunnion.

From *The Photographic History of the Civil War* (New York, 1912), courtesy of Albert Shaw.

The U. S. S. *Conestoga,* one of the first three Union gunboats on the western rivers, the others being the *Tyler* and *Lexington.*
From Henry W. Elson's *The Civil War Through the Camera* (Springfield, Mass., 1912).

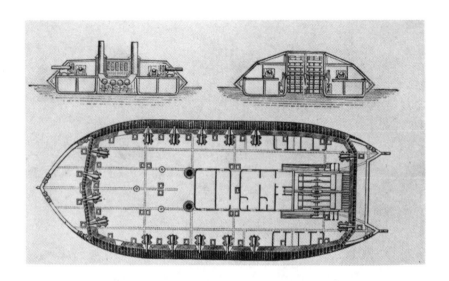

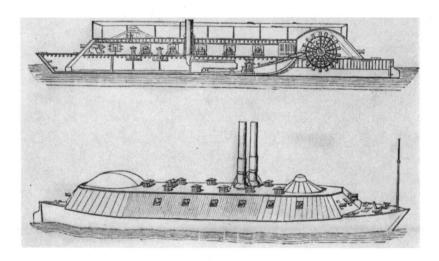

The U. S. ironclad gunboat *Benton*. The actual photograph of the *Benton* (following) shows that the water line was really higher on the hull than is indicated in these drawings.

From Alexander L. Holley's *A Treatise on Ordnance and Armor* (New York and London, 1865).

The U. S. S. *Benton,* one of the most powerful of the river gunboats, flew the flag of Davis and of Foote.

The steam sloop-of-war *Richmond,* Union flagship at the Head of the Passes.

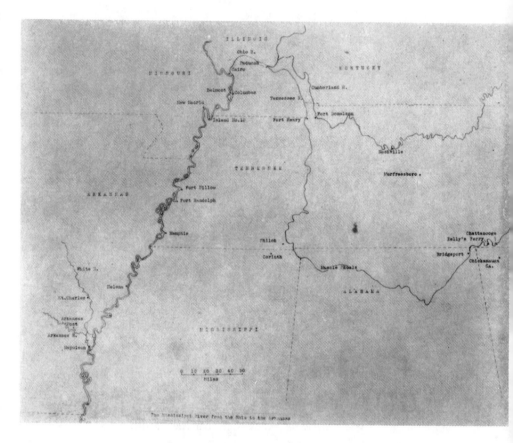

The Mississippi River from the Ohio to the Arkansas.

William D. "Dirty Bill" Porter commanded the *Essex* at Fort Henry.

Henry Walke, the aggressive commander of the U. S. Gunboats *Tyler, Carondelet,* and *Lafayette.*

The ironclad gunboat *Pittsburg* fought at Fort Donelson, Island No. 10, Yazoo River, Steele's Bayou, Grand Gulf, and Red River.

The U. S. S. *Carondelet* standing toward Island No. 10, a memorable venture, from a drawing by Captain Walke himself.

A. H. Foote, whose highly promising career was checked by a wound received at Fort Donelson.

The U. S. S. *Cincinnati* was handled very roughly above Fort Pillow.

Alfred W. Ellet commanded the Army Ram *Monarch* at the Battle of Memphis.
From *The Photographic History of the Civil War,* courtesy of Albert Shaw.

The C. S. gunboat *General Price* is typical of the vessels in Commodore Montgomery's "River Defense Fleet," which fought above Fort Pillow and at Memphis.

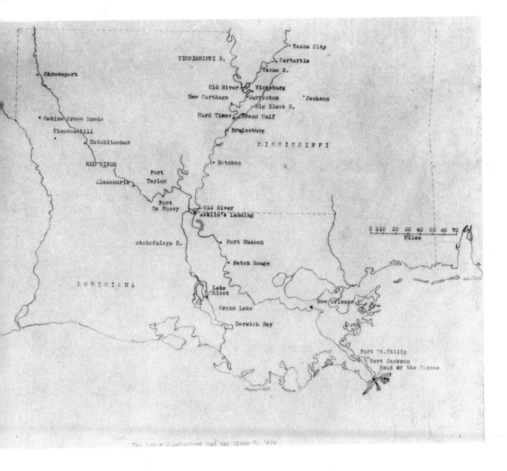

The Lower Mississippi and Red River valleys.

Bluejackets of the U. S. S. *Carondelet.*

From *The Photographic History of the Civil War,* courtesy of Albert Shaw.

The C. S. S. *Arkansas* passing the *Carondelet.* This sketch, by Captain Walke, is probably the most authentic representation of the *Arkansas* that has come down to us.

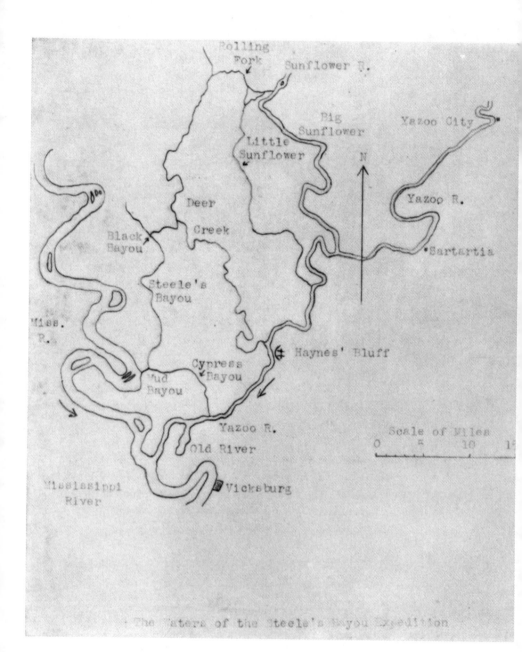

The waters of the Steele's Bayou expedition.

David Dixon Porter as a lieutenant. This photograph was taken a very short time before the future admiral made his distinguished war record.

Colonel Charles Rivers Ellet, at nineteen years of age, led the *Queen of the West*
up the Red River. He died eight months later.

From *The Photographic History of the Civil War,* courtesy of Albert Shaw.

A drawing of the U. S. river ironclad *Indianola*, by Dr. Oscar Parkes, distinguished English naval expert and ship artist.

George Dewey, the future "hero of Manila Bay," as he appeared during the Civil War.

From *The Photographic History of the Civil War,* courtesy of Albert Shaw.

The U. S. S. *Mississippi,* Perry's flagship at Tokyo. This photograph was taken at Baton Rouge only the day before the Port Hudson fight.

Vickburg, taken under fire.

"Training the howitzer upon them, I fired into the midst of the group."

The U. S. S. *Chattanooga,* flagship of the Cracker line.

The U. S. stern-wheel river monitor *Osage,* mounting two 11-inch guns, from a photograph taken on the Red River.

From *The Photographic History of the Civil War,* courtesy of Albert Shaw.

The U. S. tinclad *Cricket,* Porter's little flagship on the Red River expedition.
From *The Photographic History of the Civil War,* courtesy of Albert Shaw.

The U. S. river gunboat *Fort Hindman,* a typical "tinclad."

CHAPTER XII

GUNS ON THE BAYOUS

F OR SEVERAL months after the destruction of the *Arkansas,* affairs on the Mississippi remained in the status described in the last chapter: Vicksburg was practically unmolested; the National naval forces controlled all the rest of the river; but they did not yet have sufficient vessels to control it as completely as they desired. This imperfect control was supplemented, however, by the progressive extension of the blockade of the Gulf Coast beyond the mouths of the Mississippi, all the way to Mexico. In fact, for a time the blockade became very tight indeed. This was by virtue of the actual capture and possession of all the important ports such as Galveston, Texas, Corpus Christi, Texas, and Sabine Pass, the last forming the mouth of the Sabine River which separates Texas from Louisiana. Thus it became practically impossible to run supplies into the eastern Confederate States from abroad via Texas or Louisiana and thence across the Mississippi.

In the last quarter of 1862 there were stirrings indicating the resumption of major activities on the Mississippi River. The first of October marked the transfer of the gunboats to a status wholly under the direction of the Navy Department. The Ram Fleet was similarly shifted on November 7. David Dixon Porter, with the rank of acting rear admiral, took over the command from Charles H. Davis on October 15 and became an extremely prominent figure on western waters at this point. As has been mentioned before, D. D. Porter was the famous one of several sons of the famous Commodore David Porter of 1812 glory. He eventually became a full Admiral, a rank held, prior to World War II, only by Farragut, Dewey, and himself. Though not eminent in every respect—and who is?—he had many outstanding qualities. The ability he possessed along many lines was of great service to his country in the vital years of the war.

The main objective of the Union forces on the Mississippi was the capture of Vicksburg. Nothing that had been done previously in that direction had even scratched the surface of the problem. The first real move against the city began late in November, 1862. Porter moved down the river and anchored above the city. This time a real army followed and it was under Sherman. The land forces arrived in the latter part of December and went to work. The right flank of the Vicksburg defenses consisted of batteries crowning the heights along the Yazoo River, the outermost being Haines Bluff. Before the army arrived, Porter's fleet had worked its way up the Yazoo as far as practicable. That was not far enough. The Confederates had mined it heavily, with the result that the ironclad *Cairo* struck two mines and sank in such deep water that she could not be raised. Practically the sole cause of her loss, however, was the almost incredible bullheadedness of her commanding officer. At the very end of December a joint attack was made on the bluffs, with the army attempting a frontal assault. The effort was a complete failure thanks to the strength of the defenses and the flooded condition of the terrain over which the troops had to advance. The combined forces and leadership of Porter and Sherman were not equal to the task of cracking the Vicksburg line "the hard way." The attempt was made because no other way was at all feasible at that time.

Below the White River, the next big river system to enter the Mississippi on the west is the Arkansas. Its waters flow through territory far above Vicksburg; but these had not been cleared of the enemy when the White River was swept, although the two river valleys are practically adjacent. Fifty miles up the Arkansas was a strong point called Arkansas Post which the Confederates had renamed Fort Hindman. Around it centered activities of supplies and raids which were valuable to the South and had become most annoying to the North. The repulse at the Bluffs had depressed the morale of the Union forces above Vicksburg and a decision was made to kill two birds with one stone: send a joint expedition up the Arkansas River which would eliminate Fort Hindman and, in so doing, raise the spirits of the attacking forces. Strong enough units were selected to ensure success. The gunboats chosen included three ironclads.

The army was landed from its transports below Arkansas Post

on January 9, 1863, and the operation began. The ironclads gave the fort a fearful hammering on this day and the next; when the arrival of the army was delayed, the fort surrendered to the Navy before the troops arrived for their attack. Admiral Porter recounts the following occurrence which then took place, the source being his *Incidents and Anecdotes of the Civil War,* published by D. Appleton & Company.

"About an hour after the surrender, when the prisoners had all been secured, a large number of Union officers on horseback were seen approaching the fort. The marines had been posted as sentinels, and the sailors were taking the prisoners off to the gun-boats. An adjutant galloped up, and, jumping from his horse, sang out, 'Get out of this; everybody clear the fort. General Smith is coming to take possession. Clear out at once!' The naval officers were watching the approaching cavalcade from the summit of a mound. I was dressed in a blue blouse with nothing but a pair of small shoulder-straps to indicate my rank, and, stepping down, I said to the new-comer, 'Who are you, pray, that undertakes to give such orders here? We've whipped the rebels out of this place, and if you don't take care we will clear you out also!' At that moment General Smith rode in with the cavalcade. 'Here, General,' said the officer, 'is a man who says he isn't going out of this for you or anybody else, and that he'll whip us out if we don't take care!' 'Will he, be God?' said General Smith; 'will he, be God? Let me see him; bring the fellow here!' I stepped forward and said, 'Here I am, sir, the admiral commanding this squadron.' At this announcement Smith laid his right hand on the holster of his pistol. I thought, of course, that he was about to shoot me, but, instead of that, the general hauled out a bottle and said, 'Be God! Admiral, I'm glad to see you; let's take a drink!'

"This was the origin of my acquaintance with General A. J. Smith, resulting in a friendship which lasted through the war."

A. J. Smith was a fine fighter whose fame is less than he deserves, the reason no doubt being the multiplicity of "General Smiths" in the Civil War. For instance, it will be seen later that three of them figured in the Red River campaign alone.

The gunboats pushed ten miles beyond the fort and also took

the opportunity of sailing around and checking up on the White River, which had been swept the preceding June. The fort at St. Charles, the objective of that earlier expedition, was found empty. The gunboats ascended fifty miles beyond. Everything on both rivers of any war value was captured or destroyed. The affair was a complete success in all respects.

At the end of January, Grant took personal command of the army operating against Vicksburg. The combination of Grant, Porter, and Sherman is one almost impossible to surpass in U. S. military annals. But the rains had descended and now the floods came. While the water was high it was almost impossible to get at Vicksburg at all. The single immediately feasible way to do it was to withdraw all the way back to Memphis, reorganize the expedition, set out around to the east and south, and approach Vicksburg from the land side. This was ruled out, however, because of the effect which an apparent large-scale retreat would have on those engaged, on those at home, on the enemy, and on everyone else. Grant determined at least to keep his forces busy with one project after another, however pessimistic he might be about each one when it was undertaken.

On the west side of the river the land was so low that most of it was now under water. This made it necessary for the army to string out for *sixty miles* to find camping ground. At the same time it opened up possibilities of cutting water passages around Vicksburg; through these, men, supplies, and men-of-war might be moved to points below the city without coming under the fire of its batteries. One of the projects that was undertaken was a canal across the long, narrow peninsula opposite Vicksburg itself. The Yankees never succeeded in making it deep enough; nor was it quite out of range of the enemy's guns. (In 1876 the river cut its own way through the peninsula just outside of this canal.) Second, there was a vast network of bayous, lakes, etc., which might be tapped into the Mississippi above and below Vicksburg, and cleared and deepened sufficiently for use. Attempts along these lines were made but none succeeded.

On the east side of the river (above Vicksburg) there was not even enough high and dry land to camp an army, let alone operate it against any objective. The flooded terrain, however, did open up another alternative. There was a great deal of water in a great many places where little or no water had been seen for a long, long time. If some powerful men-of-war could be moved from the Mississippi into the Yazoo *above* Haines Bluff, a great advance would be made toward the capture of Vicksburg. And in any case literally hundreds of miles of navigable waterways would be at the mercy of the invaders—waterways ploughed by dozens of Confederate steamers many of which had escaped up the Yazoo after the disasters below New Orleans and at Memphis. Two Union expeditions of major proportions entered this network of bayous to the east of the Mississippi. One got in by cutting open the Old Yazoo Pass opposite Helena, Arkansas, which had already provided a channel in days gone by between the Mississippi and Coldwater rivers. Fortunately Admiral Porter himself accompanied the other expedition in person, the affair taking place in March, 1863. In his narrative, the expedition's route is called Cypress Bayou all the way to the Rolling Fork. Actually this watercourse from the Yazoo to the Rolling Fork bears the successive names of Cypress Bayou, Steele's Bayou, Black Bayou, and Deer Creek. Keeping this in mind we shall turn now to the Admiral's own description of the adventure as he gives it in his *Incidents and Anecdotes of the Civil War.*

"At one period of the siege the rains had swollen the Mississippi River so much that it had backed its waters up into its tributaries, which had risen seventeen feet, and, overflowing, had inundated the country for many miles.

"Great forests had become channels admitting the passage of large steamers between the trees, and now and then wide lanes were met with where a frigate might have passed.

"The ironclads drew only seven feet of water and had no masts or yards to encumber them, and but little about their decks that could be swept away by the bushes or lower branches of the trees. I had thoughts of trying the experiment of getting the vessels back of Vicksburg in that way, and sent Lieutenant Murphy in a tug to examine the woods as far as he could go, and to let me know the results of his cruise as soon as possible.

"Murphy soon returned with the most cheering news, and induced me to go with him and take a look for myself. General Grant accompanied me, and, prepared with lead-lines to measure the depth, we started off.

"A few miles up the Yazoo, before reaching Haines's Bluff, we came to an opening in the woods. Under the pilotage of Murphy, the tug Jessie Benton darted into the bushes, and the man at the lead took the soundings—nothing less than fifteen feet. Presently we reached an opening between the trees sufficiently wide to admit two ironclads abreast. I suppose it was an ancient road in the forest by which to haul cotton to the river.

"We followed this for five miles until we reached a forest of large trees without any undergrowth, but with width enough between them to admit the passage of our heaviest ironclad. This forest permitted us to steam along about five miles farther, when we came to a wide opening where there were but few trees. Here we found a bayou leading to the westward with from ten to twelve feet of water—more than enough for our purposes.

"We knew this bayou led into the Rolling Fork and the Sunflower River, though there was not generally enough water in it to float a canoe. We could not ascend it then for fear of alarming the inhabitants, or letting them know the news of our arrival in these woods and having it conveyed to Vicksburg.

"We saw all we wanted, and General Grant approved of the plan I proposed of going up with some ironclads, tugs, etc., and trying to get into the Sunflower; that would lead us into the Yazoo again, and we could come down and take Haines's Bluff in the rear.

"General Grant also determined to send General Sherman on the expedition with ten thousand troops, and said we could make a reconnoissance if we could do no more, for he saw from the first that there was no use in sitting down before Vicksburg and simply looking at it, or bombarding it to bring about a surrender; we would have lost time, and deposited our shell in the hills, increasing their weight in iron, without getting nearer to our object. . . .

"I determined to go myself, and, to make it a success, I omitted nothing that might possibly be wanted on such an expedition. I selected the ironclads Louisville, Lieutenant-Commanding Owen; Cincinnati, Lieutenant-Commanding Bache; Carondelet, Lieutenant-Commanding Murphy; Mound City, Lieutenant-Commanding Wilson; Pittsburgh, Lieutenant-Commanding Hoel, and four tugs; also two light mortar-boats built for the occasion, to carry each a thirteen-inch mortar and shells enough to bombard a city.

. . . .

"At the same time General Sherman prepared his contingent to accompany the expedition.

"General Grant was so much interested in this work that he went up to the end of the woods on one of the transports to see Sherman start on his march alongside of the gun-boats, and gave his personal attention toward pushing ahead those of Sherman's troops that had not reached us in the transports. These now and then got lost in the thick woods, and sometimes got their pipes knocked down.

"This was one of the most remarkable military and naval expeditions that ever set out in any country, and will be so ranked by those who read of it in future times.

"Here was a dense forest, deeply inundated, so that large steamers could ply about among the trees with perfect impunity. They were as much at home there as the wild denizens of the forest would be in dry times.

"The animals of all kinds had taken to the trees as the only arks of safety. Coons, rats, mice, and wild cats were in the branches, and if they were not a happy family, it was because when they lay down together the smaller animals reposed within the larger ones.

"It was a curious sight to see a line of ironclads and mortar-boats, tugs and transports, pushing their way through the long, wide lane in the woods without touching on either side, though sometimes a rude tree would throw Briarean arms around the smoke-stack of the tin-clad Forest Rose, or the transport Molly Miller, and knock their bonnets sideways.

"It all looked as though the world had suddenly got topsy-turvy, or that there was a great camp-meeting in the woods on board iron-clads and transports.

"The difficulty was to preserve quiet, so that our presence might not be detected by the enemy's scouts.

.   .   .   .

"I had little to fear of the rams at Yazoo City, as I knew their condition, through a truthful contraband, who informed me, 'Dey has no bottom in, no sides to 'em, an' no top on to 'em, sah, an' deir injines is in Richmon'.'

"We ran on, in line of battle, eight or ten miles through the open way in the trees, carrying fifteen feet of water by the lead-line. Let the nautical reader imagine an old quartermaster in the 'chains' of an ironclad steaming through the woods and singing out 'Quarter less three!' Truth is stranger than fiction.

"At last we came to a point where the forest was close and composed of very large trees—old monarchs of the woods which had spread their arms for centuries over those silent solitudes: Titans, like those in the old fables, that dominate over all around them.

"In the distance, between the trees, would spring into sight gray, sunless glens in which the dim, soft ripple of day seemed to glimmer for a second so fancifully, indeed, that it required but a slight stretch of imagination to see the wood-nymphs disporting in their baths.

"The sun seldom reached these woody glades, and, if it did, it was but to linger for a moment and disappear, like the bright star of eve, behind a silver cloud.

"It all looked like some infinite world in which we were adrift, where the sky, soft and serene (which we had been accustomed to see), had been furled in anticipation of a squall.

"Every turn of the wheels sent an echo through the woods that would frighten the birds of prey from their perches, whence they were looking down upon the waste of waters, wondering (no doubt) what it all might mean, and whom these mighty buzzards, skimming over the waters and carrying everything before them, could possibly be.

"Our line of battle was broken on approaching the large trees; then we had to go more cautiously. What, thought I, if the trees should become so dense that we could not pass between them; what would we do then? I solved the difficulty at once. 'Ram that large tree there,' I said to the captain of the Cincinnati; 'let us see what effect the old turtle will have on it.' It was an unnecessary act of vandalism to injure the old Titan, but it would shorten our road, and we would not be obliged to go meandering about to find a channel. We struck the tree while going at the rate of three knots an hour, and bounced off, but started it about twenty degrees from the perpendicular. The light soil about its roots had become softened by the water, and the tree had not much staying power. I backed again and gave it another ram, and the weight of eight hundred tons, with a three-knot velocity, sent it out of all propriety. I hailed the ironclad astern of me, and ordered her to bend a heavy chain to it and pull it down, which was accomplished in half an hour.

"I wanted to see what we could do at ramming and pulling at big trees, and our experience so gained came into play before we got through the expedition.

"It was all very pleasant at first, skimming along over summer seas, under the shade of stalwart oaks, but we had no conception of what we had before us.

"We had to knock down six or eight of these large trees before we could reach the point where Sherman was disembarking part of his troops. When I came up he was on a piece of high ground, on an old white horse some of his 'boys' had captured.

" 'Halloo, old fellow,' he sang out, 'what do you call this? This must be traverse sailing. You think it's all very fine just now, don't you; but, before you fellows get through, you won't have a smokestack or a boat among you.'

" 'So much the better,' I said; 'it will look like business, and we will get new ones. All I want is an engine, guns, and a hull to float them. As to boats, they are very much in the way.'

"At this point we ran up alongside higher land which looked like a levee.

" 'Is this the the last of it?' I asked Sherman.

" 'No,' he said; 'steam on about twenty yards to the west, and you will find a hole through a kind of levee wide enough, I think, for your widest vessel. That is Cypress Bayou; it leads into the Sunflower about seventy-five miles distant, and a devil of a time you'll have of it. Look out those fellows don't catch you. I'll be after you.'

"Sherman knew every bayou and stream in that part of the country better than the oldest inhabitants knew them.

"I pushed on, my fleet following, and soon found myself inside the bayou. It was exactly forty-six feet wide. My vessel was forty-two feet wide, and that was the average width of the others. This place seemed to have been a bayou with high levees bordering, reaching, indeed, above the vessel's guns.

"It had been made, I suppose, into a kind of canal to connect the waters of the Sunflower by a short cut with those of the Yazoo, near Haines's Bluff. All on the left of the levee was deep water in the woods. On the other side were cornfields. The levee had stopped the further encroachment of the flood. This bayou had not been used for many years for the purposes of navigation. It had almost closed up, and the middle of it was filled with little willows which promised to be great impediments to us, but, as there was nine feet of water in the ditch, I pushed on.

"Sherman told me he would follow me along the left bank of the ditch with his troops, and be up with me before I knew it, as he would make two miles to my one.

"It was intended from the first that we should travel along together for mutual support. We to transport him across rivers and marshes, he to keep off sharp-shooters, whom we could not reach with our guns on account of the high banks. We left Sherman at the point where we found him arranging his men, and I pushed into the bayou with my whole force, keeping one tug in the advance with one mortar-boat, the ironclads in the middle, and the other tugs and mortar-boat with the coal barge bringing up the rear.

.   .   .   .

"We had not entered the bayou more than half a mile before we saw the greatest excitement prevailing. Men on horseback were flying in all directions. Cattle, instead of being driven in, were driven off to parts unknown. Pigs were driven by droves to the far woods, and five hundred negroes were engaged in driving into the fields all the chickens, turkeys, ducks, and geese, and what were a few moments before smiling barn-yards, were now as bare of poultry as your hand. I had issued an order against capturing anything on shore, but the difficulty was to find out where the shore was, as apparently the Cypress Bayou ran right through the middle of a stable-yard.

"I informed the sailors that loot naturally belonged to the army, but that prize in the shape of cotton marked 'C. S. A.' belonged to them. A mile from the entrance to the bayou there were two piles of cotton containing six thousand bales, and placed opposite each other on the banks of the stream in which we were then just holding our way against its two-knot current.

"Suddenly I saw two men rush up from each side of the bayou and apply a lighted pine-knot to each pile. 'What fools these mortals be!' I said to an officer, 'but I suppose those men have a right to burn their own cotton, especially as we have no way of preventing them.'

" 'I can send a howitzer-shell at them, sir,' he said, 'and drive them away.'

" 'No,' I replied, 'that might kill them, and we don't want to do that except in battle.'

"So the two men went on with their work of destruction. They applied the torches to every part of the two piles, and in twenty minutes there was a column of smoke ascending to the skies, and the passage between the piles became very much obscured.

" 'How long will it take that cotton to burn up?' I inquired of a darkey who was asking permission to come on board.

" 'Two day, Massa,' the negro answered; 'sometime t'ree.'

"By this time all the outside of the cotton was blazing. 'Ring the bell to go ahead fast,' I ordered, 'and tell those astern to follow after me.' I was on board the Cincinnati. 'Go ahead fast the tug and mortar-boat,' and away we all went, darting through between the burning bales.

"All the ports were shut in and the crews called to fire quarters, standing ready with fire-buckets to meet the enemy's *fire.*

"It reminded me a little of the fire-raft at Fort Jackson, but we soon got used to them.

"The fellows on the tug wet themselves and boat all over very thoroughly, and as they darted through, being below the bank, they did not suffer much; but the paint was blistered on the boat, and the fire scorched the men.

"Myself, captain, and wheelman were the only ones on deck when the Cincinnati passed through, but the heat was so intense that I had to jump inside a small house on deck covered with iron, the captain following me. The helmsman covered himself up with an old flag that lay in the wheel-house. The hose was pointed up the hatch to the upper deck and everything drenched with water, but it did not render the heat less intolerable.

"The boats escaped with some blistering. The smoke was even worse than the heat, and I have often since imagined how a brave fireman feels when he is looking through a burning house in search of helpless people.

"Just after we passed through the fire there was a dreadful crash, which some thought was an earthquake. We had run into and quite through a span of bridge about fifty feet long, and demolished the whole fabric, having failed to see it in the smoke.

"There was a yell among the negroes on the bank, who looked on with amazement at the doings of 'Mas' Linkum's gun-boats.'

" 'What dey gwine ter do nex'?' said an old patriarch.

"The next we did was to stop and breathe after getting through that smoke, and look back and regret the loss of the cotton. The worst thing to be done with cotton is to burn it, especially when it is not your own.

"Here was the Confederate Government complaining of Northern oppression, and yet their own agents were riding around on horseback, setting fire to people's cotton to keep it from falling into our hands, while, if they had let it alone, it would not have been troubled by us, except by giving a receipt for it, and, when the war was over, the owners would have netted more than the full value of their property.

"This was one of the worst cases of vandalism I had yet seen.

"When all the vessels had passed through the flame and smoke we hauled up at a small collection of houses, where the negro women were running around screaming and driving in the pigs and poultry. A burly overseer, weighing over two hundred pounds, sat at the door of a log-hut with a pipe in his mouth. He was a white man, half bull-dog, half blood-hound, and his face expressed everything that was bad in human nature, but he smoked away as if nothing was the matter—as Nero fiddled while Rome was burning.

"He looked on us with perfect indifference; our presence didn't seem to disturb him at all. Doubtless he felt quite secure; that we didn't want anything so bad as he was.

"I called to him, and he came down in his shirt-sleeves, bare-headed, and looked stolidly at me as if to say, 'Well, what do you want?'

" 'Why did those fools set fire to that cotton?' I inquired.

" 'Because they didn't want you fools to have it,' he replied. 'It's ourn, and I guess things ain't come to such a pass that we can't do as we please with our own.'

" 'Tell them we won't trouble it,' I said; 'it is wicked to see such material going off like smoke.'

"In five minutes he had a dozen negroes at his side, and they were all sent up the bayou on a full run to stop the burning of cotton. He believed our word, and we did not disappoint him.

" 'And who are you?' I inquired of the man.

" 'I am in charge of this plantation,' he replied; 'this is the mother of my children'—pointing to a fat, thick-lipped negress who stood, with her bosom all bare and arms a-kimbo, about ten yards away— 'and these fine fellows are my children,' he continued, pointing to some light-colored boys who had followed him down.

" 'I suppose you are Union, of course? You are all so when it suits you,' I said.

" 'No, by G—, I'm not, and never will be; and as to the others, I know nothing about them. Find out for yourself. I'm for Jeff Davis first, last, and all the time. Do you want any more of me?' he inquired, 'for I am not a loquacious man at any time.'

" 'No, I want nothing more with you,' I replied; 'but I am going to steam into that bridge of yours across the stream and knock it down. Is it strongly built?'

" 'You may knock it down and be d—d,' he said. 'It don't belong to me; and, if you want to find out how strong it is, pitch into it. You'll find a hard nut to crack; it ain't made of candy.'

" 'You are a Yankee by birth, are you not?' I asked.

" 'Yes, d—n it, I am,' he replied; 'that's no reason I should like the institution. I cut it long ago,' and he turned on his heel and walked off.

" 'Ring "Go ahead fast," ' I said to the captain; 'we will let that fellow see what bridge-smashers we are.'

"In three minutes we were going four knots through the water, and in one more we went smashing through the bridge as if it was paper. I looked toward the overseer to see how he would take it, but he did not even turn his head as he sat at his door smoking.

"This man was but one remove from a brute, but there were hundreds more like him.

"We came to one more bridge; down it went like ninepins, and we steamed slowly on, forcing our way through small, lithe willows that seemed to hold us in a grip of iron. This lasted for an hour, during which we made but half a mile.

"But that was the last of the willows for a time. Had they continued, we would have been obliged to give it up. The small sprouts, no larger than my little finger, caught in the rough plates of the overhang and held us as the threads of the Lilliputians held Gulliver.

"Now we came to extensive woods again on either side, the large trees towering in the air, while underneath they looked as if their lower branches had been trimmed to give them a uniform appearance; but they had only been trimmed by the hand of Nature, whose fair impression fell on all about us. Man only marred the prospect there.

"The *banks* of the bayou were high with large, overhanging trees upon them, and the long branches of the latter stretched out into the stream, endangering our pipes and boats. The channel was here exactly the width of the ironclads—forty-two feet—and we had to cut our way with the overhang through the soft soil and the twining roots. It was hard and slow work. The brutal overseer felt quite sure that we would be bagged before night. He didn't know that Sherman was right behind us with an army, and an army, too, that was no respecter of ducks, chickens, pigs, or turkeys, for they used to say of one particular regiment in Sherman's corps that it could catch, scrape, and skin a hog without a soldier leaving the ranks. I was in hopes they would pay the apostate Yankee a visit, if only to teach him good manners.

"The gun-boats at this stage of the cruise, were following each other about a quarter of a mile apart. The only idea I can give of Cypress Bayou is to *fake* a string up and down a paper two hundred or more times. We did nothing but turn upon our course about every twenty minutes. At one time the vessels would all be steaming on different courses. One would be standing north, another south, another east, and yet another west through the woods. One minute an ironclad would apparently be leading ahead, and the next minute would as apparently be steering the other way. The tugs and mortar-boats seemed to be mixed up in the most marvelous manner.

"There was a fair road on the right of the bayou, along which Sherman's troops would have to march, and all that was required to make the situation look confusing and confounding was to have the soldiers marching beside the gun-boats.

"I was in the leading vessel, and necessarily had to clear the way for the others. The bayou was full of logs that had been there for years. They had grown soggy and heavy, and sometimes one end, being heavier than the other, would sink to the bottom, while the other end would remain pointing upward, presenting the appearance of *chevaux-de-frise,* over which we could no more pass than we could fly. We had to have working parties in the road with tackles and hook-ropes to haul these logs out on the banks before we could pass on.

"Again we would come to a 'Red River raft' that had been imbedded in the mud for ages. All these had to be torn asunder and hauled out with a labor that no one who had not tried it could conceive of.

"Then, again, we would get jammed between two large, overhanging trees. We could not ram them down as we did in the woods, with plenty of 'sea room' around us. We had to chop away the sides of the trees with axes.

"A great many of these large trees had decayed branches, and when the heavy ironclad would touch the trunk of one (though going only at the rate of half a mile an hour, which was the most we could make at any time in the ditch), the shock would be so great, the resultant vibration of the tree so violent, that the branches would come crashing on deck, smashing the boats and skylights and all the frame-work that they reached.

"An hour after entering the very narrow part of the ditch, where we really had not a foot to spare, we had parted with everything like a boat, and cut them away as useless appendages. Indeed, they were of no use to us, and only in the way. When we got rid of them we got along better.

"The vessels behind learned a good deal from our experience, and lowered their boats and towed them astern, though that did not relieve them entirely.

"Sometimes we would have to pass a dead tree, with its weird-looking branches threatening us with destruction in case we should handle it too roughly. We received quantities of dead branches, and we never knocked a dead *tree* without suffering terrible damages.

"No wonder the overseer took our going on so cooly. He expected that we would get jammed before we went a mile.

"That day, by sunset, we had made eight miles, which was a large day's work, considering all the impediments, but when night came—which it did early in the deep wood—we had to tie up to the bank, set watches, and wait until daylight, until which time we hoped to give our men to rest.

. . . .

"We stopped that evening about seven o'clock, and about an hour later we heard the chopping of wood in the forest. We had seen no one along the stream since we had left that burly overseer. The truthful and intelligent contrabands, in whom I was wont to repose confidence, were nowhere to be seen, whereat I marveled much, knowing their sociable disposition and the lofty aspirations they felt with regard to the liberty of their race.

"They were so faithful in adherence to their protectors that they would come in in crowds with wild inventions of moves on the part of the enemy if they could not find something real to tell.

"I missed these ingenious creatures, and wondered what had become of them. It was true we were hard to get at in this swamp, though there was a road on one side and a levee on the other; the southern side was an interminable waste of water and wood.

"I was always of an inquiring mind, and determined to find out what the wood-chopping meant. It seemed to me that there were a dozen axes at work.

"I put a twelve-pound boat-howitzer on the tug, and sent her ahead to see what was going on. In twenty minutes I heard the report of the howitzer, and then another, and another. Then a steam whistle was blown from the tug, and all was silent. No more axes heard cutting wood.

"In a very short time the tug was heard returning, snorting as if carrying a heavy pressure of steam, and every now and then giving some playful screams with the whistle. The forest fairly reverberated with the sound.

"The officer in charge reported that he had suddenly come upon a large body of negroes, under the charge of some white men carrying lanterns, cutting trees on the banks of the stream we were in; that they had felled a tree three feet in diameter, and this had fallen right across the bayou, closing the stream completely against our advance.

"There was the secret of our not meeting the truthful contraband. He was employed in hemming us in. He was too accustomed to implicit obedience to his master to refuse to do anything imposed upon him. He was too ignorant to have formed any opinions on the subject of doing something to deserve liberty. Oppression was second nature to him, obedience one of Heaven's first laws, and he helped to chop down those trees with as much glee as children would feel at setting fire to a hay-stack.

"There was but one thing to do: Move ahead and clear the channel of a tree across it, three feet in diameter, spreading its branches over an area of seventy by one hundred and fifty feet.

"We worked slowly with men in advance on the bank, with lanterns to show what dangers there were. We arrived at the fallen tree in less than an hour, and made arrangements while under way for removing it.

"It was not a matter of great labor. Two large snatch-blocks were strapped to standing trees as leaders. The largest hawser was passed through the snatch-blocks, one end made fast to the fallen tree, and the other end taken to a steamer. 'Back the ironclad hard,' and the obstruction began to move slowly over the water. In less than ten minutes it was landed clear across the road, so that Sherman's soldiers wouldn't have to march around it.

"A second application of this 'power gear,' and the route was again free.

"The Confederates didn't think of all that when they tried to bag us in that way. They forgot the ingenuity of American seamen.

" 'Now,' I said to the officer in charge of the tug, 'go ahead with all the speed you have, and see that no more trees are cut down to-night; and, though I shall be sorry to harm that faithful friend and brother, the contraband, if he continues to chop at any one's dictation you must give him shrapnel,' and off the tug started.

"We could already hear the faint strokes of the axes in advance of us, and no doubt the managers, having cut one tree down and supposing that they had blocked the game on us for the night, and not knowing our facilities for removing trees, had, as soon as they imagined themselves out of reach of the howitzer, set to work at cutting other trees, with the intention that we should never see the Sunflower, nor get in the rear of Vicksburg. The Confederates were energetic, and it was wonderful how soon they got their machinery to work.

"Some twenty minutes after the tug left us we heard the howitzer firing rapidly, and then all was quiet, excepting three steam whistles, which meant *all well*.

"At one o'clock that night the tug's small boat returned to us with the report that the choppers had commenced cutting about twenty of the largest trees, but that none had been completely felled; that they had captured two truthful contrabands, who informed them that the parties directing the cutting of trees were officers from Vicksburg; that they had pressed three hundred negroes into the work and made them use their axes with pistols to their heads, and gave them plenty of whisky.

" 'The officers are from Vicksburg!' I said; 'and we thought ourselves so smart! No doubt they started before we did, and got their instructions from Richmond. What next?'

" 'The officer' (Lieutenant Murphy) 'says, sir, he will continue on all night, and thinks no more trees will be cut down at present.'

"I didn't care about the trees. I was just then thinking how I would feel if they should block up the head of the pass with cotton bales and earth, and leave me and mine sticking in the mud at the bottom of the bayou.

"What a time, I thought, Sherman would have digging us out— but I was sure he wouldn't mind doing it.

"Nevertheless, we put out guards along the road, and slept as comfortably as if we had been at the Fifth Avenue Hotel. Somehow or other I didn't think the Confederacy could bag me as long as I had Sherman in company with his stalwart fellows—half sailor, half soldier, with a touch of the snapping turtle.

"At daylight next morning we moved ahead, and all that day toiled as men never toiled before. Our vessels looked like wrecks, and there was scarcely a whole boat left in the fleet. Evening found us fourteen miles ahead, but where was Sherman? There was only one road, so he couldn't have taken the wrong one.

"I had been rather precipitate in rushing ahead with the fleet, though I could not have been of any help to Sherman, but I would have had the services of the army to stop the tree-cutting, which I now had to do myself by sending out a detachment of two hundred men from the vessels. These men were ordered to march all night along the road while the tug covered them with her howitzer.

"It were vain to tell all the hardships of the third day. The plot seemed to thicken as we advanced, and old logs, small Red River rafts, and rotten trees overhanging the banks, seemed to accumulate.

"The dead trees were full of vermin of all sorts. Insects of every kind and shape, such as are seen only in Southern climes, infested these trees. Rats and mice, driven from the fields by the high water, had taken up their abode in the hollow trunks and rotten branches. Snakes of every kind and description had followed the rats and mice to these old arks of safety. These innocent creatures knew nothing of the insecurity of their adopted homes in presence of the butting ironclads. Small wonder. Who would have dreamed of such things in these regions?

"A canoe might have been seen, perhaps, of late years winding its way down these tortuous channels of a moonlight night, manned by a couple of dissipated darkies out on a coon-hunt, but navigation by anything larger in these waters was unknown.

"Sometimes, when we would strike against one of these trees, a multitude of vermin would be shaken out on the deck—among them rats, mice, cockroaches, snakes, and lizards, which would be swept overboard by the sailors standing ready with their brooms. Once an old coon landed on deck, with the life half knocked out of him, but he came to in a short time and fought his way on shore. Even the coons were prejudiced against us, and refused to be comforted on board, though I am sorry to say we found more Union feeling among the bugs of all kinds, which took kindly to the ironclads, and would have remained with us indefinitely had they been permitted to do so.

"Three days' hard work and no hope of seeing the Sunflower River! We had made one capture. Lieutenant Murphy had gone ahead and taken possession of an Indian mound as old as the deluge; no one remembered its age.

"Why had not the Confederates taken possession of the place and fortified it? It must have been because they thought it worthless. They showed themselves to be poor judges in such matters. But Lieutenant Murphy, who had been following engineering for some years before the war, saw some strong point in this mound (which I did not), and urged me to fortify it. At length he persuaded me to let him have four boat guns to place on the top of it. 'It would be,' he said, 'a *point d'appui* for Sherman's troops to assemble about in case they were attacked!'

" 'Where are the attacking forces to come from?' I inquired.

" 'Can't tell, sir,' said Murphy, 'but I think it a strong point.'

" 'Go ahead, then, and fortify it,' I replied; 'it will keep you employed.'

"We had arrived nearly at the head of the pass, or bayou, to what was called the Rolling Fork, and, after all our toil and trouble, did hope to see the road clear to Vicksburg in the rear.

"There was a small collection of houses at the point where we had stopped, and all the contrabands in the country were assembled there. The tree-cutters had disappeared and liberated from duty all those who had been pressed into service, but took all the axes away with them. The negroes were jubilant over being able to join 'Mass' Linkum's gun-boats.'

"We could readily have dispensed with their services. They were only an encumbrance to us. They could give us no information. They had never been taught to think or know anything but to hoe and pick cotton. That's all they were wanted for.

"We had steamed, or rather bumped, seventy-five miles, and had only six hundred yards to go before getting into the Rolling Fork, where all would be plain sailing; but I waited for all the vessels to come up to repair damages, and start together.

"I noticed right at the head of the pass a large green patch extending all the way across. It looked like the green scum on ponds.

" 'What is that?' I asked of one of the truthful contrabands.

" 'It's nuffin but willers, sah,' he replied. 'When de water's out ob de bayou—which it mos' allers is—den we cuts de willers to make baskits wid. You kin go troo dat like a eel.'

"I thought I would try it while the vessels were 'coming into port.' I sent the tug on ahead with the mortar-boat, and followed on after.

"The tug went into it about thirty yards, began to go slower and slower, and finally stuck so fast that she could move neither ahead nor astern. I hailed her and told them that I would come along and push them through. We started with a full head of steam, and did not even reach the tug. The little withes caught in the rough iron ends of the overhang and held us as if in a vise. I tried to back out, but t'was no use. We could not move an inch, no matter how much steam we put on. Ah, I thought, this is only a temporary delay.

"We got large hooks out and led the hook-ropes aft, and tried to break off the little twigs, but it was no use; we could not move. We got saws, knives, cutlasses, and chisels over the side, with the men handling them sitting on planks, and cut them off, steamed ahead, and only moved three feet. Other withes sprang up from under the water and took a fresher grip on us, so we were worse off than ever.

"Just as well, I thought, that Murphy seized upon that mound. It will be three or four days before we can get through here. He can hold it as a look-out, and if any sharpshooters should appear he can fire on them.

"Just then a rebel steamer was reported coming up the Rolling Fork and landing about four miles below. We will catch that fellow after dark, I thought. He has come up here after stores.

"This was the Vicksburg granary—full of everything in the way of grain, cattle, and poultry. 'Hog and hominy' was abundant.

"I went at it again, and worked hard for over four hours, but not one foot did I gain with that ironclad. I wished ironclads were in Jericho.

"While I was pondering what to do, and the negroes were looking on in admiration upon the ingenious devices we put into play to get rid of those willow fastenings, wondering to myself if the Confederacy had planted these willows on purpose to keep me out of the Sunflower River, I heard the faint reports of two guns, and directly after the shrill shriek of rifle-shot, which came from directions at right angles to each other. The shells burst over the Indian mound where Lieutenant Murphy was studying the strategy of war. They were Whitworth shells. I knew the sound too well to be mistaken. I had heard them before. There were two six-gun batteries with a cross-fire upon us.

" 'Now's your chance, Murphy,' said I to myself, 'to show some good practice. You did well in selecting that mound.'

"I forgot for a moment that we had only four twelve-pounder smooth-bores there, with a range of about twelve hundred yards.

"The two fields batteries were keeping up a rapid fire, and fifteen shells a minute were coming from the enemy's spitfires and bursting in all directions, throwing the pieces of iron and the bullets of the shrapnel down on the decks of the ironclads, where they rattled like hail.

"Here was a dilemma. We could not use our large guns; they were away below the banks, and lying so close to it that we could not get elevation enough to fire over.

"Suddenly I saw the sides of the mound crowded with officers and men. They were tumbling down as best they could; the guns were tumbled down ahead of them; there was a regular stampede. Murphy hadn't found the top of the mound a fine strategic point, and that was the reason why the Confederates had not adopted it.

"The fire from the enemy's Whitworths was incessant, and every one was running to cover.

"As the retreaters passed me I shouted to them to stop. The majority obeyed, but a number kept on. They had left their guns on the road.

"I made those who stopped bring the guns alongside my vessel. 'You shall have them no more,' I said; 'you don't know how to take care of them.'

"The shells from the enemy came so rapidly that it became annoying, so I ordered the mortars manned, measured the distance by the sound—2,800 yards on one range, and 2,600 on the other—and opened fire.

"The shells seemed to be well timed; they fell in the midst of the artillerists, and the two batteries ceased by mutual consent, while we not only kept up the fire there, but all through the woods where these parties were located.

"This little diversion being over, I set to work again to overcome the willows.

" 'What a dodge this was of the Confederacy,' I said to the captain, 'to plant these willows instead of a fort! We can take their forts, but we can't, I fear, take their willows.'

"I stepped out to the bank (where the negroes had assembled again as soon as the shooting was over) to see if I could learn anything about willows from these innocent people.

"All I could find out from them was that 'dey was mo' tougher'n ropes.'

" 'Why don't Sherman come on?' I said aloud to myself. 'I'd give ten dollars to get a telegram to him.'

" 'I'm a telegram-wire, Massa,' said a stubby-looking negro, coming up to me. 'I'll take him for half a dollar, sah; I'm de county telegraph, sah. I does all dat bizness.'

" 'Where's your office, Sambo?' I inquired.

" 'My name ain't Sambo, sah. My name's Tub, an' I run yer line fer yer fer half a dollar.'

" 'Do you know where to find General Sherman?' I said.

" 'No, sah, I don' know him. Ef he's in Vicksburg, I kin find him.'

" 'Can you carry a note for me without betraying it to the Confederates?'

" 'I don't understan' one of dem words, sah, but I'll take a note to Kingdom Kum if yer pay me half a dollar.'

"Then I told him who General Sherman was and where to find him. 'Go along the road,' I said, 'and you can't miss him.'

" 'I know nuff better 'an dat manner when I carry telegraph, sah. I don't go de road; I takes de ditches. It's nuff shorter and mo' safer. On de lef' han' comin' up dars all marsh an' wata, an' a kenoe kin allers git 'long dar. I'll go de way we nigs takes when we go chicken huntin'.'

" 'Where will you carry the dispatch?" I inquired.

" 'In my calabash-kiver, Massa,' he answered, pointing to his thick, wooly head.

"I wrote the dispatch and handed it to him. He stowed it away in a pocket in his hair, where it was as safe as a telegram traveling on a wire. I wrote:

" 'DEAR SHERMAN: Hurry up, for Heaven's sake. I never knew how helpless an ironclad could be steaming around through the woods without an army to back her.'

"I had no sooner got off the telegraph (as he called himself) than another steamer was reported as landing at the same place as the one which brought up the artillery.

"Upon examining her with the glass, it could be seen that she was full of troops. Those fellows would not have landed there if they had not known that we were blockaded.

"The stream, for some reason, began to run rapidly, and large logs began to come in from the Rolling Fork and pile up on the outside of the willows, making an effectual barricade. It was the water rushing down through the cut-off and creeks from the opening into the 'Old Yazoo Pass' of the Mississippi River. What was doing good to those fellows was bad for us. I wondered if they had found the Confederacy as smart as we had. I had no doubt of it. [They had.]

"Just then the two rifle batteries of the enemy opened again viciously from other positions, and it was reported to me that two thousand men had landed and were marching to get into our rear. Pleasant, that!

"I had sent the rear tug back to see if anything could be heard of General Sherman coming on. It returned with the information that ten miles in our rear the enemy were cutting down the largest trees across the pass, that eight had been felled within a short distance of each other, and the channel behind us was effectually blocked. I did not mind this so much, as I knew that Sherman was not far off.

"I found another telegraph man among the negroes, and sent him off to Sherman. He pursued the same method as his predecessor, but was captured by the enemy.

"We kept our mortars hard at work, but the artillery shifted position every three minutes, and were sending among us about twenty shells a minute. The men had to keep between decks.

"We were in the narrowest part of the pass; it was the same width as the ironclads. We fitted in nicely—too nicely!

"The Confederates had completely checkmated us. Every knight and pawn and castle was in check, and my vessel, the Cincinnati, was checkmated by the willows!

"There was nothing easier than for two thousand men to charge on us from the bank and carry us by boarding. Only the enemy didn't know the fix we were in. They didn't know how it was that we could fire those thirteen-inch shell, that would burst now and then at the root of a great tree and throw it into the air. They didn't know that we had only four smooth-bore howitzers free to work, that our heavy guns were useless, below the bank. So much for their not being properly posted. But I was quite satisfied that they would know all this before Sherman came up.

"We drove the artillery away about four o'clock in the afternoon. Then I sent a hawser to the tug, and another to the ironclad astern of me, while the latter made fast to another ironclad. Then we all backed together and, after an hour's hard pull, we slipped off the willows into soft water. *Laus Deo!*

"Then went forth the orders to unship the rudders and let the vessels drift down stern foremost, and away we all went together with a four-knot current taking us—bumping badly—down at the rate of two miles an hour—which was twice as fast as we came up. The enemy did not discover our retreat for some minutes, but when they did they made a rush for the Indian mound and took possession of it.

"After all, Murphy was right; it was a strategic point! But only with the Whitworth rifles, not with smooth-bores.

"I suppose we passed that fort twenty times in following the crooked pass, and the enemy were pouring it into us all the time, but they didn't do much harm.

"They were evidently greenhorns, and failed to understand that we were ironclad and didn't mind *bursting* shell. If they had fired solid shot, they might have hurt us.

"I cared very much more about that infantry than I did about the artillery. As our bow guns were bearing astern now and *up* the bayou, we could each of us give the enemy now and then, at the turns, a dose of nine-inch shrapnel, giving the same attention to their infantry, which we could see were marching in the direction we were pursuing. But our broadside guns were useless.

"The artillery kept up their fire for about two hours, and then I think they began to find out that our bow guns were bearing and doing them some injury.

"At dark we tied up at a point where we had about four feet of water between us and the bank, greased the ironsides, and, elevating the lower-deck guns after loading them with grape, we made the best of our position. I landed five hundred men with howitzers after dark, and placed them in position to enfilade any attacking party. Scouts were also thrown out to see if some of the enemy could be picked up, and the remainder of the crews slept on their arms at quarters. So passed the night; but Sherman's whereabouts were a continual source of conjecture to me. I was quite sure the Confederates had not captured him.

"About ten o'clock my scouts brought in four prisoners—two officers and two sergeants—and conducted them, at my direction, into the cabin.

"The commanding officer was quite a youngster, and when brought in was as stiff as a poker.

"He walked up to me and, presenting his sword, said, 'There, sir, you will likely recognize that; it is the sword of one of your officers who skedaddled off that Indian mound. We picked up two of them, and captured caps and shoes enough to fit out a regiment. Why, your fellows left a lot of ammunition behind then.'

" 'Yes,' I said, 'but you look tired; won't you sit down and take some supper with me? I have a cold supper and wine on the table.'

" 'I don't care if I do,' he answered, 'and I have the less compunction in taking it as it belongs to us anyhow. In two hours you will be surrounded and bagged. You can't escape. How in the devil's name you ever got here is a wonder to me.'

" 'I should like nothing better,' I said, 'than for your friends to try that kind of business; they would learn something. But sit down, gentlemen, and eat.'

"They did sit down, and ate with an appetite I never saw equalled.

" 'We have had nothing to eat or drink since noon,' said the youngster; 'we could eat our grandmothers and drink up Niagara Falls.'

" 'Drink some wine,' I said, and I shoved over the sherry to them. Their throats were dry as powder-horns. 'Help yourselves,' I said; 'don't stand on ceremony. You know it will all be yours when you surround us, and you had better get your share before the other fellows arrive.'

" 'Won't you drink with us?' asked the youngster.

" 'Yes,' I said, 'with pleasure. Tell me how Colonel Higgins is.'

" 'He's here,' replied the youngster, 'and came along on purpose to catch you. He says he'd give ten thousand dollars to do that.'

" 'Here's his health,' I said, and they all drank bumpers to Higgins.

" 'I can't drink with you any more now. I have to look out for these vessels; but, as you are prisoners, and have no responsibility, you may empty the bottle if you like, and there are the cigars.'

" 'You're a trump, and no mistake!' said the youngster; 'I would like to capture you myself.'

" 'Well, I promise you that if I surrender to any one it will be to you.'

"The quartette drank until they became very lively and loquacious, and boastful of what they were going to do.

" 'How far off are your troops?' I inquired.

" 'About four miles,' the leader answered. 'They will bag you at daylight.'

" 'That,' said I, 'is about a good distance. Sherman will be on them about three o'clock, and capture the whole of them.'

" 'Sherman!' he exclaimed; 'what has he to do with it?'

" 'Only,' said I, 'that he is at this moment surrounding your troops with ten thousand men.'

" 'Holy Moses!' he cried, 'we're sold. We didn't know anything about any troops. We thought it was something like that Yazoo River affair—a gun-boat excursion, and we like to have bagged *them*. They're wandering around in the ditches yet.'

"Having obtained all the information I desired, I went on deck, put a sentry over the cabin-door, had the stern-ports closed, and gave orders to call me at two o'clock.

"Then the shore parties were called on board, and we went on the *back track* for three miles. We either threw the enemy off the scent, or the captured officer deceived me about the contemplated attack. We heard nothing of them, and determined to go on down again.

"At the first start the leading vessel sunk the coal-barge, and there we were blocked and unable to move. It took hours to remove the coal and spread it out on the bottom.

"In the midst of the work we were attacked by the enemy's artillery in the rear.

"I was in the rear ironclad—bows upstream; we steamed up after the artillery, got within range, and with the bow guns scattered them like chaff. One of their guns was knocked over, and some of their men and cattle were hurt, but they were getting less timid and were gradually closing around the ironclads.

"The stream cleared of the coal, we bumped along, stern foremost, knocking down dead branches from the trees upon our decks, with the usual accompaniment of vermin, until we thought the limit of ill-luck had been reached by the vessels; but we looked worse before we got through.

"Sharp-shooters made their appearance in the morning. About sixty of them surrounded us. First it was like an occasional drop of rain. Then it was *pat, pat* against the iron hull all the time. The smoke-stacks seemed to be favorite marks to fire at. They no doubt took it for the captain, or the great motive power which kept us a-going.

"The sharp-shooters were not, as a rule, the brightest I have seen, but then they had bomb-shells falling among them, and now and then a tree, behind which they were, would suddenly be lifted out of the ground or canted sideways. The bomb-shells were demoralizing.

"I adopted a new plan. I turned *all* the guns into mortars by firing them at the greatest elevation (to clear the banks), and with very low charges. With short time-fuses and a range of about six hundred yards this had a good effect, and the sharp-shooters kept a long way off.

"The smoke-stacks still attracted considerable attention from them, though it was true they had wounded some of our people.

"Suddenly the Louisville, Captain Owen, brought up all standing. There were eight large trees cut down ahead of us—four from either bank, and they seemed to be so interlaced that it was apparently impossible to remove them.

"I sent out two hundred riflemen, and found that they were quite equal to the enemy. They drove them to a safe distance with the aid of the mortar fire. We had been firing heavily, great guns and mortars, for two days and nights, and thought Sherman must have heard us and been worried about us, but he had his troubles getting along as well as others. He was doing his best to come to our assistance. It may seem ridiculous for ironclads to be wanting assistance from an army, but without that army they would likely have been in an ugly scrape. Its proximity alone, without its immediate aid, made us perfectly at ease.

"Under fire from the sharp-shooters we removed the eight trees in three hours, and started to push on, when we found those devils had sunk two large trees across the bayou under water, and *pinned* them down.

"Another hour was spent in getting them up, and under renewed sharp-shooting. Every one was kept under cover except those it was absolutely necessary to expose. The captains and myself had to be on deck.

"We had no sooner got rid of these obstructions than we saw a large column of gray-uniformed soldiers swooping down on us from the woods.

"We opened mortar fire on them. They didn't mind it. On they came. They were no doubt determined to overwhelm us by numbers, and close us in. Their artillery was coming on with them. Now would come the tug of war. We were jammed up against the bank, and the stream was so narrow where we were we could not increase our distance from it. Their sharp-shooters had now taken up positions behind trees about one hundred yards from us, and our men were firing rapidly at them as they opened on us.

"We had picked up a few cotton-bales along the road to make defenses, and good ones they were.

"The sharp-shooters were becoming very troublesome about this time, when suddenly I saw the advancing column begin to fall into confusion; then they jumped behind trees, or fell into groups, and kept up a rapid fire of musketry. It looked as if they were fighting among themselves. But no! they were retreating before some one. They had run foul of Sherman's army, which was steadily driving them back.

"The enemy were much surprised at encountering such a force. They never dreamed of meeting an army of five or six thousand men. I believe there were more.

"I made signal to beat the retreat. We would have no more trouble now. But, just as I had given the order, half a dozen rifle bullets came on board, and one of them struck the first lieutenant, Mr. Wells, in the head while I was talking to him and giving him an order.

"He fell, apparently dead, at my feet. I called an officer to remove him, and *he* fell dead, as I supposed, on the other's body.

"Then an old quartermaster came, dragging a large quarter-inch iron plate along the deck, and stuck it up against a hog post. 'There, sir,' he said, 'stand behind that; they've fired at you long enough,' and I was wise enough to take the old fellow's advice. Poor old man! he was shot in the hand as he turned to get behind his cotton-bale.

"But that was about the last of it. In the course of half an hour Colonel Smith, of the 8th Missouri, rode up and told me his troops were in pursuit of the enemy, who were in full retreat, and that we should hear no more of them. Again *Laus Deo!*

"They were a perplexing set of fellows, these rebels, and showed a great amount of courage, considering the prestige of 'Mas' Linkum's gun-boats'; but then, it must be remembered, they had caught the ironclads in a ditch in the woods. They could hardly be said to be afloat.

"The Confederates never dreamed of finding us where they did, or they would have come provided with torpedoes, and left us all imbedded in the mud of Black Bayou, where in future ages mementos of us would be found, and as much be known of us as was known of the Indian mound which we *did not* find such a fine strategic point.

"But the rebs missed their opportunity, though they rather had the laugh on us. We had the satisfaction of knowing, however, that none of us had lost our heads, though at one time matters looked rather embarrassing.

"I didn't notice a single officer on that expedition who, though exposed almost at all times to an unpleasant fire from sharp-shooters, showed the least desire to avoid being shot, except when they hurried down so rapidly from the top of the Indian mound!

"I am happy to say that the two officers, who fell at my feet apparently dead, both recovered. Theirs were only scalp wounds, owing to the enemy's bad powder. They were both volunteers, and did good service all through the Rebellion.

" 'Old Tecumseh' came riding up, about half an hour after the last mishaps, on the old horse he had captured. He had received my county telegraph man, who explained to him pretty well how we were situated, and he had pushed on at night, by the aid of pine torches, through swamps and canebrakes, having undertaken a short cut recommended by the telegraph 'operator,' Mr. Tub, and found the travelling almost as bad as that experienced by the gunboats.

" 'Halloo, Porter,' said the general when he saw me, 'what did you get into such an ugly scrape for? So much for you navy fellows getting out of your element; better send for the soldiers always. My boys will put you through. Here's your little nigger; he came through all right, and I started at once. I had a hard time getting my troops over; some of them marched over from the Mississippi.

" 'This is the most infernal expedition I was ever on; who in thunder proposed such a mad scheme? But I'm all ready to go on with you again. Your gun-boats are enough to scare the crows; they look as if you had got a terrible hammering. However, I'll start at once, and go back with you; my boys will clean those fellows out.'

" 'Thank you, no,' I said, 'I have had enough of this adventure. It is too late now; the enemy are forewarned, and all the energies of the Confederacy will be put forth to stop us; they will fill all the rivers with torpedoes, and every hill will be turned into a heavy fort. They have the laugh on us this time, but we must put this down in the log-book as "One of the Episodes of the War." We will take Vicksburg yet, when it is more worth taking.'

" 'You are satisfied, then,' said Sherman, 'with what my boys have done for you and can do?'

" 'Yes, perfectly so,' I answered, 'and I never knew what helpless things ironclads could become when they got in a ditch and had no soldiers about. Won't you come aboard?'

" 'No,' said he, 'I must call in my men; they could not catch those fellows if they chased them a week. Good-morning,' and 'Old Tecumseh' rode off on his ancient horse, with a rope bridle, accompanied only by one or two aids.

"After Sherman had departed I went down into the cabin to see my prisoners. The cabin was dark, and they were sitting there very quiet.

" 'Well,' I said to the young officer, 'they have got us at last; we are surrounded.'

" 'I knew they would bag you in the end,' he replied; 'I felt that I was not going to be a prisoner yet. Well, sir, I will see that you are treated handsomely when you surrender.'

" 'Surrender to whom?' I said. 'What are you talking about?'

" 'Didn't you say you were surrounded?' asked the perplexed youth.

" 'Yes, I did,' I replied, 'but by Sherman's boys, and your fellows are skedaddling off as fast as they can go.'

" 'But not faster,' he retorted, 'than your fellows did down that Indian mound! But I'm sorry not to be able to take you to Vicksburg; they'd treat you kindly there.' With that he lay down and went to sleep.

"The game was up, and we bumped on homeward. The current was running very rapidly now, and the vessels were so helpless, dropping down stern foremost, that we could not protect them in any way. There was no knowing what part of them would strike the trees, or when huge dead branches would fall upon the decks. Every one remained between decks except those who were absolutely required above. There was still a chance of the enemy playing us a bad trick by blocking the head of the pass at Rolling Fork; there was plenty of cotton along the road to do it with, if they only should think of it. Twelve hundred bales of cotton would turn the water off from our bayou, and in an hour after we would be on the bottom. With these unpleasant possibilities before me, I continued on homeward, and protracted my run until eight o'clock that night, when I came up with the main body of Sherman's army, which was encamped along the road near the edge of the pass.

"Encamped! I say. They had no tents, but a plentiful supply of fence-rails and bonfires of pine-knots. The whole route for miles was all in a blaze.

"It was great fun for the soldiers to see our dilapidated condition. 'Halloo, Jack,' one fellow would sing out, 'how do you like playing mud-turtle? Better stick to the briny.'

"Another would say, 'You've been into dry dock, ain't you, and left your boats behind?'

" 'Don't go bushwhacking again, Jack,' said another, 'unless you have Sherman's boys close aboard of you; you look as if your mothers didn't know you were out.'

" 'Where's all your sails and masts, Jack?' said a tough-looking fellow who was sailor all over, though he had a soldier's uniform bent.

" 'By the Widow Perkins,' cried another, 'if Johnny Reb hasn't taken their rudders away and sent them adrift!'

" 'Dry up,' sang out an old forecastleman, 'we wa'n't half as much used up as you was at Chickasaw Bayou!' for which the old tar got three cheers. And so we ran the gauntlet until we reached the middle of the line.

" 'Where's General Sherman?' I inquired of some of the men.

" 'He's in his tent, sir, waiting supper for you,' answered one of them.

"Sherman's tent! As if he would have a tent when his soldiers were lying about on fence-rails.

"But I came to his tent at last; and, reader, I wish you could have seen it: it was three fence-rails set up in a triangle, but with only a small fly over the apex. It was raining hard at the time, and Sherman was standing leaning against one of the rails, while a large bonfire was blazing brightly before his 'tent'! 'You go on,' he said; 'I'll follow you tomorrow.' We passed the compliments, and I ran on down past the lines and tied up, having run the gauntlet of jokes that were showered on us by the soldiers.

"As we were getting made fast to the bank a canoe with two

soldiers in it tried to squeeze past us, but got stuck between us and the bank. They had a large pile of something in the bottom of the canoe covered over with a tarpaulin.

" 'What have you got in those bags?' I asked.

" 'General Sherman's baggage, sir,' said one; 'we've just brought it up from a transport.'

" 'General Sherman's baggage!' I said; 'how long has it been since he took to carrying baggage? Let me see what you've got there.'

" 'Only baggage, Admiral, I assure you,' said the speaker, 'except some turkeys we picked up for you on the road up here,' and he uncovered and displayed a pile of picked turkeys, geese, chickens, and sucking pigs.

" 'Where's the baggage?' I asked.

" 'Why, sir,' said the man, 'there was so much of it, it's coming up on a tug—a large carpet-bag of it, sir,' and he handed up one of each.

"The steward came, and took a turkey. 'Pass General Sherman's baggage,' I said to the captain, and the sailors, taking hold of the painter, pulled the canoe through.

"Sherman had a hard set of boys on foraging, and they enjoyed this trip up the bayou, where they were in the very midst of the enemy's granary, and the people of Vicksburg no doubt sighed when the Yankees found their way to the flesh-pots of the South. Most of them went without turkey, chicken, goose, or pig for many a day thereafter.

"There is not much more to be said about the Steele Bayou expedition; it didn't amount to much in effecting changes in the condition of Vicksburg, but we gained a lot of experience which would serve us in the future. We might, perhaps, have passed the willows if we had waited for the army, and got the soldiers to pull us through with ropes stretched along the bank; but to have delayed pushing astern would have assured the cutting down of five hundred trees by the enemy, and given them time to send to Vicksburg for torpedoes and have them planted all along that ditch.

· · · · · · · · · ·

"It was with the greatest delight that we got out of that ditch and into the open woods again, with plenty of 'sea-room' and no lee shores. We took our time, went squirrel-hunting in the few boats we had left, and got a fine mess of turkey-buzzards out of the old oaks which surrounded us.

"In ten days more we anchored again in the mouth of the Yazoo River and commenced to repair damages.

"I always carried a large steamer along with the squadron fitted as a carpenter's shop. She had a good supply of mechanics on board, with all that was necessary to repair a vessel after an action.

"In a week we were all built up again, were supplied with new boats from the store-ship, and, with our new coats of paint, no one would have supposed we had ever been away from a dock-yard.

"Some of the officers were talking of going again, and of the pleasure of the trip, as people who have gone in search of the North Pole, and have fared dreadfully, wish to try it once more."

CHAPTER XIII

QUEEN OF THE WEST

READERS of earlier chapters will recall that the charge at Memphis was led by the ram *Queen of the West*. She rammed and sank the *Lovell*, and this brought about the disruption of the Confederate fleet, which was soon annihilated. The *Queen* next appeared on the scene in a less glorious role when the C. S. S. *Arkansas* made her entrance. Accompanying the *Carondelet* and *Tyler*, the ram took no part in the action but steamed down the Yazoo to the main fleet to report the enemy's approach.

The *Queen of the West*, however, joined the *Essex* in that most dashing attempt to ram and destroy the *Arkansas* while she lay under the very guns of Vicksburg. The venture was unsuccessful on the part of both attackers, the *Essex* dropping below Vicksburg after her failure, whereas the *Queen* steamed back up river repassing the Confederate batteries. It should be remembered that she was wholly unarmored. A *New-York Tribune* reporter visited her after the ordeal, and this is his description of her condition (taken from J. Thomas Scharf's *History of the Confederate States Navy*, p. 330):

"The *Queen* presents a most dismantled and forlorn appearance, and is as nearly shot to pieces, for any vessel that will float, as can well be imagined. The many who have visited her since her terrible experience are with difficulty persuaded that not one of her crew was killed or dangerously wounded. She has the semblance of a complete wreck, and it will be necessary to send her North at once for repairs, though some think her injury too great for remedy—that she is not worth the mending.

"Shells exploded in her cabin, shivering her furniture, crockery, and state-rooms to pieces. The wardrobe of the crew was converted into rags, and hardly a whole garment or a pair of boots or shoes can be found on the boat. She is dented and damaged, and blackened and splintered, and singed and shattered, as if she had passed through a score of the fiercest battles, and presents as good an example of the amount of injury that may be done to a boat without absolutely destroying her as it would be convenient to present, or easy to discover in twelve months' service on the flotilla."

The *Queen*, however, was eventually repaired and placed back in active service. Meanwhile, Farragut had withdrawn his fleet down river, it will be recalled. The destruction of the *Arkansas* followed quickly, and no Confederate men-of-war remained to challenge the control of the Mississippi. The National vessels, however, held the waters in insufficient strength—often in no strength at all. Accordingly the Confederates took the opportunity of fortifying the high land at Port Hudson, Mississippi (east bank). Being little impeded they turned it into a barrier to river traffic which was second only to Vicksburg. For a time the combination of these two strong points allowed supplies to cross the stretch of river between them without much molestation from Union forces afloat. The big advantage of this circumstance from a Southern viewpoint was that the great Red River system empties into that same stretch of the Mississippi. The Red River and its multiplicity of branches formed the chief transportation network of that railless region, an area whose foodstuffs were of great importance to the Confederate armies struggling in the East.

In view of all the above factors, Admiral Porter decided that a gunboat should try to run down past the Vicksburg batteries. If she should succeed without having her military efficiency impaired she would be in a position to sweep all enemy watercraft from the surface of hundreds of miles of rivers; thus would the Confederates' West-East supply lines be crippled very severely. The *Queen of the West* was the boat selected. The favored commanding officer was Colonel Charles Rivers Ellet, now the third commander of the Ram Fleet; he was the young son of the original Ellet who had died of the wound received while leading his force to victory at Memphis. This new captain of the *Queen* was the same fellow who had gone ashore in a rowboat after the battle and received the initial surrender of the city. His new command was now more than merely a ram. She carried guns and had been provided with some protection. Accordingly, she was at this time essentially a gunboat.

In early February, 1863, the *Queen of the West* ran past the Vicksburg batteries and, as she went by, partly destroyed an important steamer that was moored at one of the city wharves. She then carried out a very brief but highly successful raid along the lines planned. She was now just below Vicksburg but just above some recently erected Confederate batteries at Warrenton, Mississippi. She was getting ready for her big trip; this time she was going to take along a coal barge, also a small captured steamer, the *De Soto,* now mounting a gun and provided with some iron and some cotton bales for protection. The *New-York Tribune* had a correspondent aboard the *Queen* and under the date of February 15 he gave the following account of the events that he witnessed.

"OUR DEPARTURE.

"We had intended to leave on Monday, the 9th inst., but certain repairs were at the last moment found necessary, and we were compelled to remain over the succeeding day.

"Col. Ellet decided to run the batteries by starlight, and just at dark the chimneys of the Queen of the West and the De Soto began to vomit forth huge columns of dense black smoke, and we knew that the time of our departure was approaching. Precisely at 9 o'clock we swung into the stream, the De Soto, around whose boilers and machinery bales of cotton had been placed, and on whose bow was mounted a huge 32-pound rifle, toward the batteries, the Queen of the West next, and the coal barge on the outside, all lashed together. In this position we floated down the river.

"Silently we floated by, every moment expecting to hear the scream and hiss of shot and shell, every moment looking for the explosion of the ugly missiles over our heads. We were abreast of the batteries, and began to wonder at their reticence. We were at point-blank range, the night was fine—why did they not fire? The suspense was terrible. Presently some one sang out, 'We are out of danger; we are below the batteries!' It is wonderful how this announcement affected us. Some who were crouching in abject terror became valiant in an instant. They mounted the hurricane deck and snapped their fingers for joy. What cared they for Rebel batteries?

"Speculations.

"We had passed the dreaded batteries without a shot, and began to bother our brains for an explanation. Some imagined that as the Queen had demonstrated her ability to pass them unharmed, the enemy had thought proper to remove the guns to the city, where they could do harm. Others, and among them Col. Ellet, thought they were removed to fortify the bridge across Big Black River, where the Vicksburg and Jackson Railroad spans it. Since the previous expedition down the Mississippi, and the consequent closing of the Red River country as a source of supply for the Confederate forces at Vicksburg, the integrity of this means of communication would naturally be religiously guarded. We finally settled down on this explanation, and the projected movement up the Big Black was abandoned, and we rapidly and carefully steamed down the Mississippi.

"Geographical and Historical.

"The mouth of the Big Black is 50 miles south of Vicksburg. On the bluffs to the south of this stream is the town of Grand Gulf, once a flourishing village of 1,000 inhabitants, and connected by rail with the village of Port Gibson, Mississippi. When Farragut's fleet passed up the river last Summer, the citizens had ugly habits, among them that of throwing shell at his transports. The old man became angry and burned the town. It is now desolate and nearly uninhabited, a bad commentary upon this fearful Rebellion, and a standing monument of the vengeance which Union officers are instructed to mete out to those who allow their patriotism in this direction to outrun their discretion.

"Ex-President Taylor's Plantation.

"Wednesday morning, Feb. 11, found us just below the mouth of the Big Black, and further on down the river, thirty miles north of Natchez, at what is called Taylor's Point, we landed to visit the plantation of ex-President Taylor. The family mansion is a quiet, homelike structure, embowered in a splendid grove of evergreens, and surrounded by cotton gins, negro quarters, and other appliances of Southern plantation life. The farm is an excellent one embracing an area of 2,000 acres of the finest cotton lands in the

State. It is now owned and cultivated by Dr. New, formerly of Kentucky, who purchased it of Jeff. Davis and the other heirs of Gen. Taylor. It is a beautiful home, just such a one as a gentleman of taste and refinement would select. Col. Ellet at first supposed the title to vest in the President of the Southern Confederacy, and hence intended to seize the cotton for breastworks and the negroes for deck hands. He did not care to trouble Dr. New.

"Natchez on the Hill.

"Thirty miles below Taylor's point, we rounded a sharp bend in the river, and 'Natchez on the hill' burst upon us in full loveliness like a disrobing goddess. The arrival of our little fleet naturally created considerable consternation, and, as we steamed up and down the river before the city, men in butternut, women in silks, old men and children, white and black, came out of their houses to gaze at us. Not a sound arose from that crowd of curious lookers-on —not a shout, cheer, or wave of handkerchief. All was silent as the grave.

" 'Natchez on the hill' and 'Natchez under the hill' present an inviting field to an enterprising commander, but I am told a sort of truce exists between the fleet and the citizens—according to the implied rather than the expressed terms of which, the former is expected not to shell the town so long as our boats are unmolested there. This tacit agreement has been regarded up to this time.

"We delayed but an hour or two at Natchez, and did not leave the boat to visit the city. It is doubtful if it were safe to do so. A little after noon we were on our way for Old River, sixty miles below.

"Topographical and Geographical.

"Old River is the channel followed by the Mississippi before the present cut-off was formed. It describes an arc of a circle whose diameter cannot be less than ten miles. Into this river, accessible from the Mississippi above and below the cut-off, the Red River empties, and from it, through the Atchafalaya, a large body of water passes, swift and deep, which finds an exit into Berwick Bay, and thence into the Gulf of Mexico. From this river there is an entrance into the Mississippi below Port Hudson, defended by a battery of four guns, near the point where the bayou, which connects the two, approaches the river. New Orleans can also be reached through the Atchafalaya, with no other obstruction than a battery at Butte la Rose.

"THE QUEEN IN THE ATCHAFALAYA.

"It was at the mouth of Old River that we tied up on Wednesday night, sending the De Soto to do picket duty a mile in advance. The night passed quietly, and at daylight on Thursday we started up Old River, moving cautiously, and calling at the plantations on the way. At 9 o'clock we entered the mouth of the Atchafalaya. Four miles down the river a long train of heavy army wagons, driven by negro teamsters and guarded by a squad of soldiers, was discovered moving along the river bank. We halted them, landed, and took possession. The soldiers escaped to the forests skirting the plantations. A detachment of Union soldiers commenced the work of destruction. Mules were unharnessed and turned adrift; harnesses were thrown into the river, and a few of the wagons cut down and rendered worthless. The rest were left until evening. The Queen then moved down the river to Simmesport, four miles below where Col. Ellet had heard of a Rebel transport. We arrived too late to capture her, but not too late to seize 70 barrels of beef belonging to the Valverde Battery, which the Minerva in her anxiety to escape had left behind.

"This was destroyed by cutting the hoops of the barrels and tumbling their contents into the river. Col. Ellet also captured a Rebel mail and important letters and dispatches at Simmesport, from one of which he learned of the occupation of Berwick Bay by Commodore Farragut. A few Confederate cavalry were quietly watching our movements from the bayou to the rear of the village, but a shell from our rifled Parrot bursting over their heads caused them to hunt their holes. From Simmesport we moved down the river a few miles and came in sight of another heavily-ladened train, which the negroes from the bank said also belonged to the Texas battery. Upon our approach the teamsters turned into the swamps just within reach of our shells. We had not men enough —scarcely twenty, all told—to send them after the fugitives, and were compelled to fire at them from the boat. This we did till the shades of evening began to gather, with what effect as regards wounding and killing we were unable to learn. One wagon laden with ammunition and officers' baggage fell into our hands. This was burned.

"GUERRILLAS FIRE INTO THE QUEEN.

"Night was approaching, and we turned the steamer's prow again toward Old River, where during the day the De Soto had waited for us. Just as we had reached the bend where the wagons were captured, and where we intended this evening to destroy them, while the most of us were at supper, all at once we heard the sharp report of musketry, and immediately First Master Thomas fell to the deck seriously wounded. A musket ball had passed upward, breaking his shin bones, and making its exit through the knee. From one of the brass guns on deck we replied, and also fired several rifle shots, but, protected by the levee, the rascals escaped injury. We abandoned our intention of landing, and kept on up the river, the Colonel muttering threats of vengeance.

"COL. ELLET'S VENGEANCE.

"Early Friday morning, a person came aboard the Queen and informed Col. Ellet that the firing the preceding night was done by the citizens living along the Atchafalaya, between its mouth and Simmesport. Col. Ellet accordingly determined to pay them a visit. He rounded to near Simmesport, and calling at the plantation of one Graves—who almost acknowledged that he had fired at us—he allowed him time to remove his family and furniture, and then burned the house, sheds, and quarters to the ground.

"The next plantation had, beside the dwelling-house and negro quarters, a magnificent sugar-mill upon it. These buildings were also burned.

"The third belonged to an old gentleman, who, with his son and two daughters, carried on the farm and worked the niggers. One of the young ladies admitted that the brother had fired upon the Queen, and only wished the one had been a dozen. She abused the Colonel and berated the Yankees. When she discovered that her abuse failed to move Col. Ellet, just as the flames began to curl around the housetop, like a brave and gallant girl, as she was, she sang, in a ringing, defiant tone, the 'Bonnie Blue Flag,' until forest and river echoed and reechoed with sweet melody.

"UP RED RIVER.

"Col. Ellet, on leaving the Atchafalaya, announced his intention to go down the Mississippi and attempt to open communication with Commodore Farragut below Port Hudson; but, on reaching the mouth, this intention was abandoned, and we turned our vessel into Red River. The air was as balmy as June in our Northern climate, the trees were decking themselves with green, men were walking about the hurricane deck in their shirt sleeves as we entered the Red. We could not help commiserating poor Northerners, shivering before coal fires—'on ice.' . . . Late Friday night we anchored at the mouth of Black River, as before, the De Soto thrown out as our advance picket.

"THE CAPTURE OF THE 'ERA NO. 5.'

"Saturday morning at daylight we raised anchor and proceeded up the river. We had heard that the enemy had lately constructed fortifications at Gordon's Landing, 85 miles from the mouth, called Fort Taylor. We had heard also that there were heavy guns at Harrisonburg, near the head of navigation on the Black River, and for a time Col. Ellet was undetermined which to attack. He finally settled upon the former, and we moved as rapidly as the tortuous nature of the stream and the ignorance of our pilots would admit, in the hope that we should reach the position and commence the attack before nightfall.

"The steamer Louisville, we also learned, had, just before we reached the mouth of the Black, passed up the Red with a 32-pounder rifled gun, intended for the gunboat W. H. Webb, then lying at Alexandria.

"We had, therefore, incentives for speed. At 10 o'clock the lookout reported a steamer descending the river, and shortly after the Era No. 5 hove in sight. She saw us as quickly as we discovered her, and was half turned around as if attempting to escape, when Col. Ellet ordered a shot to be sent after her. This took effect in her stern, passing through the cook-room, demolishing a stove, and slightly wounding the negro cook. The officers and passengers then came on deck and hoisted white sheets and waved white handkerchiefs in token of surrender. The Queen ran alongside and took possession. The Era No. 5 is a fine boat of 150 tons burden, belonging to the Red River Packet Company, and heretofore engaged in transporting supplies for the Confederate army. At that time she was laden with 4,500 bushels of corn intended for the Quartermaster's Department at Little Rock.

"This was to be taken to Camden, Ark., and to be transported thence by army wagons. Among the passengers were fifteen privates of the 14th Texas Cavalry, and three belonging to the 27th Louisiana, Lieut. Daly of the Texas State troops, and Lieut. Doyle of the 14th Texas. The citizens on board were set on shore without parole, the soldiers were set on shore with parole, and the officers were retained. Among the parties retained was a German Jew named Elsasser, who had upon his person $32,000 in Confederate money. Col. Ellet thought he was a Confederate Quartermaster, although he strongly insisted to the contrary, and brought him along. One man dressed in citizen's clothing, and claiming to be a non combatant, was on that account released without parole. We have since learned that he was one of Gen. Hindman's Brigadier-Generals. His name I did not learn. Our prisoners being thus disposed of, the fleet, now numbering three steamers, moved toward Gordon's Landing. Four miles from the landing in a direct line across the country but fifteen miles as the river runs, we left the Era, with three or four men to guard the boat and prisoners.

"The Situation.

"We reached the vicinity of Gordon's Landing just at sundown, and moved cautiously around the bend near the point, 400 yards beyond which the fort and batteries are situated.

"The Red River is here extremely tortuous, so much so that at a point four miles below the fort by river, we were only a mile from it by land. The batteries are entirely concealed from sight by dense forests until we approach within 400 yards of them, or until the nose of the steamer begins to show around the point upon which the negro cabins are built.

"The Attack upon the Queen of the West.

"We moved slowly up the channel, making the bend with considerable difficulty, until we reached the point below the negro quarters where the land is cleared, when we discovered a long line of dense black smoke moving up the river beyond the fort, indicating the hasty departure of a transport. Our gun upon the bow was immediately placed in position, and two percussion shells were sent in that direction. These exploding in the vicinity of the transport, which we afterward learned was the Doubloon coming down the river with corn, caused her to disappear toward Alexandria.

"The land makes out into the river on the point, leaving an extremely shallow place 20 feet or more from its extremity which pilots are careful to avoid. Our pilot, whether designedly or otherwise, I know not, ran the Queen aground, and at the same instant the batteries opened fire upon us. Recollect, we were not 400 yards from the fort, and immovable. The pilots tried in vain to back her off, but she would not budge an inch. Shot were flying, shell were bursting, and worse than all we could not reply. The enemy had our exact range, and every explosion told with fearful effect. Your correspondent sought the pilot-house, and thus became an unwilling witness of the terrible affair. Three huge 32-pounder shells exploded upon the deck and between the smoke stacks, not 20 feet from our heads.

"The Explosion.

"The air was filled with fragments of exploding shells, which flew before, behind, and all about us. Soon we heard a crash among the machinery below. Word was passed up that the lever which regulates the engines was shot away. Another crash, and we learned that the escape pipe was gone. Still another, and the steam-chest was fractured. The whole boat shook with the rush of the escaping steam, which penetrated every nook and cranny. The engine-room was crowded with engineers, firemen, negroes, and prisoners, who had sought that place under the impression that it was the safest. All this time, while we supposed we were blown up, and looked every moment to be launched into eternity, the batteries played upon the unfortunate vessel, and pierced her through and through. Men crowded to the afterpart of the vessel. Some tumbled cotton-bales into the river, and getting astride of them, sought to reach the De Soto, a mile below.

"The yawl was tied to the stern, and a man stood there with a loaded pistol threatened to shoot the first one who entered it. The cry was raised for Col. Ellet, and men were sent forward to look after him. The negroes, in their fright, jumped overboard, and many of the poor creatures were drowned. Some of our men were scalded. Word was sent to the De Soto to come along side to remove us. She came as near as she dare and sent her yawl, but before it returned she herself was compelled to move down the river out of range.

"Personal Experiences.

"As I have before stated, I was in the pilot house when the explosion occurred, and took the precaution to close the trap-door, thus keeping out a quantity of steam. There was still enough to make breathing almost impossible, that came through the windows in front of us. I had sufficient presence of mind to cram the tail of my coat into my mouth, and thus avoid scalding.

"Shortly we discovered that to remain would induce suffocation, and we opened the trap-door and blinded by steam sought the stern of the vessel. Groping about the cabin, tumbling over chairs and negroes, I sought my berth, seized an overcoat, leaving an entire suit of clothes, my haversack and some valuable papers behind, and emerged upon the hurricane deck. The shell were flying over my head, and here was obviously no place for me to remain. Looking over I saw the wooly pate of a negro projecting over the stern below me, and calling to him to catch my coat I swung myself over by a rope and landed directly upon the rudder. At this time it was suggested that a boat be sent to hurry up the De Soto, and among those who entered it was your correspondent. We reached it in about ten minutes, passing on the way several men on cotton bales, among them Col. Ellet and McCullogh of *The Commercial*. Almost exhausted, the occupants remained behind, while another crew was sent up to pick up survivors.

"Boarding the Queen.

"The yawl had reached the boat, and was busily engaged in picking up the crew, when three boatloads of Confederate soldiers cautiously approached the vessel and boarded her. Of course there was no resistance, and our boys became their prisoners.

"The De Soto, hearing several men shout from the shore 'Surrender,' was allowed to float down stream, picking up as she floated several who had escaped on cotton bales. When she reached a point ten miles below, the yawl overtook her with others who had been similarly preserved.

"DESTRUCTION OF THE DE SOTO.

"We reached the Era No. 5 and found her all right. Our coal barge was leaking badly and hard aground. Of course we had to leave it. The De Soto had unshipped both rudders, and became unmanageable, and it was concluded to destroy her, lest with her valuable gun she should fall into the enemy's hands. Her pipes were knocked out, a shovel-full of live coals placed in her cabins, and she was soon destroyed.

"ATTEMPTED ESCAPE.

"It was now 10 o'clock Saturday night, and if we would escape more intimate acquaintance with Southern society and Southern prison life, we must make every exertion now. With a sigh for the poor fellows left behind, and a hope that our enemies would be merciful, the prow of the Era was turned toward the Mississippi. The night was a terrible one—thunder, lightning, rain, and fog. I doubt if, under any other circumstances, Red River would be deemed navigable. All hands were set to work to throw overboard the corn to lighten her up, and we are slowly crawling down the river. We know to a certainty that we shall be pursued. The gunboat Webb is lying at Alexandria, and we know that she will start in pursuit of us whenever she learns of the destruction of the Queen and of the escape of a portion of her crew. Our only hope lies in reaching the Mississippi quickly, whence we shall make the best of our way to Vicksburg. The Webb is a model of speed, and can make fourteen miles an hour against the current. If we do not get aground, and if our machinery does not break, we hope to outrun her. If I am captured, a visit to Vicksburg will be my portion. We shall see.

"OUR LOSSES.

"The following is the loss by the capture of the Queen of the West, as far as I can ascertain:

"PRISONERS—Cyrus Eddison, 2d Master; Henry Duncan, 3d Master; David Taylor, Engineer (scalded); D. S. Booth, Surgeon; 1st

Master Thompson (wounded on the Atchafalaya); Adj. C. W. Bailey; one blacksmith, name unknown; George Andrews, James Foster, carpenters; L. C. Jarbon, Thomas Williams, David McCullom, Charles Launer, Carrol Smith, Ed. Hazleton, Charles Faulkner, John A. Bates, Norton F. Rice, Wm. Brown, Geo. W. Hill, soldiers; Mr. Anderson, of *The Herald,* and about 30 negroes.

"KILLED—George Davis jumped overboard from the De Soto and is supposed drowned.

"The above are the names of those who floated down the river and were not picked up by the De Soto. They will probably be captured by the next Confederate steamer in these waters, probably the Webb, as she pursues us.

"BOD.

"STEAMER ERA NO. 5, IN THE MISSISSIPPI,
"NEAR VICKSBURG, FEB. 21, 1863.

"We arrived in the Mississippi Sunday morning, about 10 o'clock, without serious accident. All day the rain and fog continued, and such was the thickness of the weather that we did not make 30 miles in 24 hours. The river was filled with drift and logs which impeded our progress and broke the buckets of our wheels. We were short of fuel, and were compelled to touch at Union Point and take on a few cords of wet, soggy wood, with which we found it impossible to make steam enough to carry us two miles an hour. When opposite Ellis Cliffs, our pilot, the same who ran the Queen aground at Gordon's Landing and thus caused her capture, ran the Era, although she was drawing but 18 inches of water, hard upon the opposite point. Here we laid for four mortal hours within ten feet of shore, liable to capture at any moment from guerrillas, until our carpenter could go into the woods, select a tree, and fashion a spar to shove us off. To crown our misfortunes, the starboard wheel was dropping to pieces. We had decided that to be captured was our destiny, and Col. Ellet was discussing the practicability of seizing skiffs and dugouts and attempting to run by the batteries at Port Hudson, 50 miles below.

"As soon as we were off the point, Col. Ellet placed the pilot who caused our troubles in arrest, and ordered Mr. McKay, the other pilot, to take the wheel. I had toward morning thrown myself upon a mattress in the cabin, in the hope of snatching a moment's rest, and had just dropped off into most refreshing slumber, when I heard some one shout, 'There's a gunboat ahead of us.' We at first supposed the Webb had passed us during the night and was lying to above to capture us. I rushed on deck, but as soon as I saw the smokestacks, just then visible through the lift of the fog, I knew we had escaped. It was the Union gunboat Indianola, sent down to coöperate with the Queen. You may be sure no men ever witnessed a more welcome sight than this same good steamer Indianola. It was a miraculous escape, as you will see. From the depths of despair we were raised to the heights of exaltation.

"We are, some of us, hatless, bootless and coatless. All of us were hungry. We had eaten nothing for the last 48 hours but a little stale and sour corn-meal, found in the bottom of a barrel on board the Era at the time of her capture. The good people of the Indianola acted the part of good Samaritans; they clothed and fed us, and made us comfortable. Capt. Brown invited Col. Ellet and the two Bohemians into his cabin, and regaled us with a delicious cup of coffee.

"We lay by the Indianola until noon, when it was decided to move below again, in the hope of meeting the Webb. We had scarcely moved three miles, when the lookout announced a steamer approaching. All hands were called to quarters, and prepared for action. The Era was sent ahead to reconnoiter, and her shrill and prolonged whistle showed that she too had seen the Webb. The engineers clapped on steam, hot-water hose was got ready, and a lively time was expected. At this time we were full three miles away. As we approached the Webb, she was lying in the eddy directly under Ellis's Cliffs, looking for all the world like a frightened race-horse. She moved a little, then halted, and then bounded away like the wind. At this moment the larboard bow gun was fired, and almost simultaneously the starboard gun. Both shots lacked elevation, and fell short. Long before the smoke cleared away, a long train of smoke was moving down the river at the rate of 20 miles an hour. This was the last of the Webb. Had we not met the gunboat, we should inevitably have been captured before we could have reached Natchez.

"The Webb, we have since learned, was accompanied by three large, first-class steamers, the Grand Duke, Grand Era, and Doubloon, each laden with soldiers, and each protected, as to her machinery, with cotton-bales. The Webb turned back these also, and, together, they steamed up Red River.

"Fog coming on, we were obliged to cast anchor, and were not able to move again until late on Tuesday afternoon. At 3 o'clock we were again under way, and anchored for the night at the plantation of Col. Ackley, near the mouth of Old River. This is one of the largest plantations on the Mississippi River, containing in its area over 20,000 acres of tillable land, and worked by over 1,000 negroes. The Colonel has 1,200 bales of cotton, which he would like to sell. Although claiming to be a Rebel, it is plain that his interests would be materially advanced by the opening of the Mississippi.

"At noon we started again to return to Vicksburg. We are now lying at the plantation of Dr. Jenkins, five miles above the mouth of Old River, taking on the Era 300 bales of cotton, which will be placed about our machinery and used as a protection from Rebel sharpshooters.

"The Indianola, just as we left her anchorage, entered the mouth of Old River, and shortly afterward we heard the report of four of her heavy guns. We suspect she has taken a prize.

"We left Dr. Jenkins's plantation on Wednesday evening. Friday morning the Era stopped abreast of St. Joseph's, Louisiana, and Col. Ellet seized a Rebel mail, from one of the letters of which, dated the 17th inst., we learned that since coming down the river the enemy had placed a battery at Grand Gulf, and proposed to dispute our passage. Sure enough, when opposite the bluffs a battery of two field-pieces opened upon us, and fired thirty shots, 6-pounders, all but one of which fell from five feet to a hundred short. That one struck a cotton bale, and glanced harmlessly off into the water.

"At New-Carthage, La., 20 miles north of Grand Gulf, the river is very wide, with a large island in its center. Both sides of the island can be navigated, but it is usual for boats to take the shute nearest New-Carthage. We were intending to do so in this instance, and were just turning the point of the island, when we saw a white puff of smoke, and at once a Minié bullet came whizzing through the cabin. This was followed by others in quick succession. Under almost any other circumstance, we should have thought the main attack was here, but it occurred to us that it was a ruse to drive us near New-Carthage. We suspected they had a battery there, and concluded to take the other shute. For three miles we were followed by 25 men, who neglected no opportunity to fire their deadly rifles at us. Fortunately, we were protected by cotton bales, and no one was injured. While abreast of the island the fires gave out, and we were forced to stop the engines and clean out. This took an hour. Steam was raised again, and we had just passed the upper point of the island, when a battery of three 12-pounders opened upon us most furiously.

"This time forty-six shots were fired. They passed before, behind, and over us, but not one struck us. There was a camp here—Camp Perkins—upon the plantation of Judge Perkins, member of the Confederate Congress, and several thousand men. It deserves to be cleaned out, and I judge will be attempted speedily.

"We were undisturbed until we reached the vicinity of Warrenton. We had hardly come within range before the shot and shell began to fall around us like hail. The night was somewhat dark and the Rebels did not shoot well. At all events, although we received twenty-four shots, not one of them injured us, and not a man was hurt.

"The Era No. 5 now lies at the old anchorage of the Queen of the West, having accomplished a feat the like of which has not been performed since the inception of the Rebellion. One hundred shots for an unarmed steamer within thirty-five miles is no trifle. She bears a charmed existence.

"BOD."

Readers will no doubt have concluded—and correctly—that a good many unwise acts were committed by the leader of this expedition in losing both his ships, not to mention the coal barge. However, one or two points that are not worth going into, are extenuating at least in some slight degree. And when all is said and done it must be remembered that Ellet at this time was only nineteen years old! His mistakes were undoubtedly due, in large part anyhow, to inexperience; accordingly the chief blame, if any, should rest upon Porter, who selected him for the job. Just to make a clean sweep: A few days after the return, the *Era* was scuttled, *by the Army,* to remove any danger of her falling into the hands of the enemy!

Charles Rivers Ellet died the following October.

And what of the *Indianola* after she parted with the *Era* on February 19? First, there appears to have been no significance to the shots which the *Era* had heard her fire just after the two boats separated. The *Indianola* blockaded the mouth of the Red for two days but dared not ascend without a Red River pilot. Word came down river telling of preparations being made against her by the enemy. The *Queen of the West* was ready for action again, this time under new masters. During the week that had passed since her capture, the single small piece of important damage had been repaired, namely the injury to her steam chest. The powerful side-wheeler *William H. Webb* had been strengthened for use as a ram. Her ordnance was inconsiderable but she was quite possibly, at the time, the fastest thing afloat. Besides these two "men-of-war," the *Indianola* heard about the Confederate "cotton-clads" with their loads of troops to be used as mass sharpshooters and as boarding parties. Lieutenant Commander George Brown, commanding the *Indianola*, had felt at first that he was able to handle whatever he might encounter. This rapid accretion of enemy strength, however, caused his discretion to take charge. He determined to start back up the Mississippi toward Vicksburg, hoping and expecting to meet en route a new consort moving down to help him.

The *Indianola* was a large, grotesque affair, one of the first of a new crop of ironclads that followed the original nine. Her deck was flat and little above water. Forward was an armored casemate in which were mounted two great 11-inch smoothbores. On the quarters were huge paddle-wheel houses with another casemate between them. In this one were two 9-inch guns. Amidships rose very tall twin stacks with a tower-like pilothouse between them and the forward casemate. Down the center line ran a high wall-like deck house which was so narrow that there was a great wide open space on the main deck on each side of it. The *Indianola* had twin screws in addition to her paddles. An engine for each wheel thus gave her four main engines.

The *Indianola* left the mouth of the Red River on the morning of February 21, 1863. The withdrawal was under way. Captain Brown's first concern was to build cotton-bale bulwarks around his low, wide, main deck which was so vulnerable to boarders. He obtained the cotton from two plantations, the latter one a bit up the

Mississippi from the mouth of Old River. He had two loaded coal barges alongside which delayed him terribly in any upstream pull. He determined to hold onto them, however. His own full bunkers would take him up to Vicksburg all right, but he knew the coal would be needed for any future operations of his own vessel and any approaching companion. He was not just running away from superior force. He strongly suspected that enemy vessels were coming after him and he knew that the drag of the barges would probably enable them to overtake him.

The *Indianola* finished building her cotton barriers on the twenty-second and really started up the river. At approximately the same hour the little Confederate flotilla of four vessels made a more or less accidental rendezvous twenty miles below the scene of the *Queen of the West's* capture. They were the *Webb*, the *Queen*, the *Grand Era,* and the *Dr. Beatty.* The two latter vessels were virtually "infantry boats," they might be called. (The *Grand Era* should not be confused with the *Era No. 5.*) The whole was under the command of Major Joseph L. Brent, C. S. A. They were eighty-five to ninety miles away from the *Indianola* at this point and they started after her. *The chase was on!*

Bear in mind several points in order to appreciate fully the circumstances under which this dramatic pursuit was carried on. First of all, "speed over the ground" is what counts, not speed through the water; obviously much better speed can be made downstream than up. The *Indianola* was slowed so seriously by her coal barges that she was not making good more than two or three knots over the ground. The swift *Webb* and the *Queen* were held back by the inferior speed of the "infantry boats." The *Indianola* suspected that the enemy was following her and gaining on her, but could not know how far behind they might be at any time. The Confederates knew the *Indianola* was retreating upstream, and from reports received along the way they could make some guess as to her lead. And so the hares went on after the tortoise.

The day of the twenty-second passed. The pursuers made good speed down to the mouth of the Red and fair speed on down to the mouth of Old River. Here was situated Acklin's plantation and "Acklin's Landing." Brent learned that his quarry was far ahead in hours but not hopelessly out of reach in miles. The night of February 22–23 wore on. The current was running three to four knots and the *Indianola* was making slow going of it. She had left the mouth of the Red River on the morning of the twenty-first and Captain Brown could not know but that the enemy might already be close behind. The *Indianola*'s people necessarily had to start worrying.

Next day, the twenty-third, the *Indianola* passed Natchez and was, of course, observed from the shore. When the Confederate flotilla arrived there Major Brent learned that his intended victim was only about half as far ahead as she had been at Acklin's Landing. He felt sure he would achieve his opportunity to attack unless another Union man-of-war got down to her first. The *Indianola* still looked for this happy circumstance to come to pass, but as time went on Captain Brown became less optimistic. However, he hung onto his barges, crawled on up the river, and the day of February 23 came to a close.

That night the Confederates knew there would be no immediate fight, but the Federals were aware of the increasing likelihood of such an event. The dawn of February 24 brought no reinforcement. The *Indianola* passed Grand Gulf around noon. This is at the mouth of the Big Black River; so Vicksburg was now within striking distance, even if no reinforcing gunboat did come down the Mississippi. But the overtaking flotilla reached Grand Gulf only four hours behind the Yankee. Brent had planned things so that he could attack at night in order that the heavy Federal ordnance might be neutralized as far as possible. During the day the heavy smoke of his four vessels was sighted from the *Indianola*. For the first time, Captain Brown was certain he was being pursued; and he knew he was being closed fast enough so that he would probably have to fight or let go the coal barges. He kept his bunkers full but he hung onto his barges. Considering the bends in the river and considering the fact that a stern chase is a long one, his enemies were still many river miles astern when he first spotted them. Nevertheless, he made all preparations for battle and kept half the crew on watch from this time on—"watch and watch." The Rebels passed Grand Gulf before sunset. Nothing but an engineering casualty could now prevent Brent from having a go at his prey that night.

The *Indianola* plodded ahead. Darkness fell. Still no consort. She was in for it now. The night was a dark one but not pitch black. The pilots could see their way. About 9:30 P.M. near New Carthage the

Indianola sighted several vessels about three miles astern of her. The long chase was near an end and only thirteen miles below the nearest Federal batteries. As it was to be guns against rams, Brown swung his vessel's head around toward the enemy. He kept his barges lashed alongside for protection, kept his more vulnerable stern away. The responsibility for defense was placed squarely upon the two heavy bow guns.

The distance between the opponents decreased rapidly as they headed toward each other. Two of the Confederate boats were ahead of the rest, and it was very clear that their intention was to pile in very close indeed. Captain Brown knew they must be the *Queen* and the *Webb*. It was too dark to determine their range with any accuracy; it was not even too easy to tell their exact bearings. Brown ordered his big guns to hold their fire until he was sure of hitting his attackers and hitting them hard. Reloading these monsters was a matter of minutes, so there would be time for no more than one round from each gun during any single onset.

On came the rams and at almost point-blank range the *Indianola* fired her two 11-inch guns. Two clean misses! Almost immediately afterwards the *Queen* struck. She had gotten far enough around so that her bow cut into one of the coal barges, cut all the way through it, and it sank a few minutes later. The *Indianola* was spared and the *Queen* tried frantically to disengage herself from the wreckage of the barge. While she was still trying to back clear, on came the *Webb* nearly alongside the *Queen* and smashed into the bow of the ironclad forward of the barge. The victim stood up to the blow quite well, as it was delivered against her strongest section. Both rams got clear, and the *Queen* ran almost out of sight as she steamed away into the murk. She was withdrawing some distance to get up speed for her next attack. Meanwhile, the *Grand Era* and the *Dr. Beatty* were lying off at varying distances firing fruitless volleys of musketry. Nor was the ordnance of the rams a factor at any time. An occasional long-range shot roared from the *Indianola* whenever her battery officers deemed there was enough time to fire and reload before the next attacker was upon them.

While the defenders of the *Indianola* were straining their eyes after the disappearing form of the *Queen,* her consort came around in a smaller circle. On she came, the *Indianola* slowly swinging her bow around to meet her. They met almost head on; the result was that the *Webb* cut in between the *Indianola* and her remaining barge, doing no damage to the gunboat as she rasped through, but cutting the barge completely adrift. No more buffers left to the *Indianola*. About this time the *Queen* was looming plainer and plainer; she had come around and was now rushing back for another blow. Again the bow of the *Indianola* was swung toward the charger. Another deafening blast from one of the 11-inch guns carried with it a hit but not a disabling one. The *Queen* came on and crashed in, but once more it was only on the bow; she glanced off again with no really serious damage to her opponent.

All was not well with the *Indianola,* however. With the darkness covering everything, no one could see much through the slits in the pilot tower. Captain Brown spent his time running to and fro on the topside, shouting alternately to the helmsman in the pilothouse, to the engineers down the engine-room hatch, and to the gunners in the forward casemate. And these gunners were not doing well. Some hits were scored but they were few in number and did not cause vital damage. On the other hand, the attackers were inflicting considerable damage upon themselves in the course of their enthusiastic collisions.

The two rams drew off once again, the *Indianola* reloaded, kept swinging toward her enemies—but now this became impossible. The two attackers were going off in different directions so as to make possible to least one smash into the side; or maybe into the stern, better still, with its vulnerable wheels and rudders and its weaker hull. Peering through the darkness, Captain Brown tried to keep his tormentors in sight, tried to keep his heading toward one of them anyway, ordered one of the after 9-inch guns manned. His crew was not large enough to serve all of his main battery at once; nor was there ever sufficient time available to train either of his forward guns so as to aim it through a side port. The *Queen* came down on him from astern; the *Indianola* could not swing around fast enough; she fired a stern gun; it scored a hit but the *Queen* came on. She crashed into the starboard quarter abaft the great side wheel, wrecked it and the starboard rudder, and started some serious leaks. First real blood!

The *Indianola* was sorely hurt, but both the rams by this time were groggy too. However, having escaped serious damage by gunfire, they were not so badly off as their lone opponent. The latter was terribly worried over her inability to blast the rams out of the water as they charged. It was not too easy even to see them well enough to fire with any accuracy, let alone with any frequency. Brown did not know that the collisions had caused serious damage to the rams themselves—almost as much as to his own vessel. He went to work to stop the leaks, succeeded fairly well, still had one rudder and three engines of sorts with which to maneuver. But his agility, slight at best, had been seriously impaired; he required valuable time to revamp his ship's organization to fit the altered and impaired conditions. The much-needed time simply was not available.

Meanwhile the *Webb* was maneuvering around with a view to striking still another blow. The turning of the *Indianola* caused by the *Queen's* drive made it necessary for the *Webb* to change her calculations; nor was it easy to determine from any distance either the exact heading or the speed of the *Indianola*. But she had been sore hurt by the *Queen*, and before she could get entirely ready again the *Webb* got a chance at the vulnerable after section. On she came at near full speed. The *Indianola* was pulling away, but the difference in the speeds was very great. The *Indianola* let go with a 9-inch—missed. C R A S H went the damaged but still formidable stem of the *Webb* clear into the weakened stern of the Yankee. Out of commission went all the remainder of the propelling machinery and steering gear, and the dark waters of the river flooded in through a great hole. Captain Brown saw that the game was up. With the crushed but game *Queen* bearing down for one more smash, and with the infantry vessels closing in to board, Brown sang out his surrender; he got the bow aground on the west side of the river as his ship was sinking.

With all the thousands of rounds of musketry and dozens of rounds of larger stuff that were fired on both sides this dark night, the casualties for the whole 90-minute battle totaled exactly 6 for the *Queen*, 1 for the *Webb*, and 2 for the *Indianola!*

It has been noted that Brown headed for the west bank of the river. This was done for the very good reason that the Union land forces held a certain control over that shore. The contrary was true of the east bank. The victorious Confederates were as well aware of the situation as the prisoners, and undertook immediately to tow the *Indianola* across. Slowed and hampered by the difficulties involved in such an undertaking, they almost lost her in deep water; they barely got her aground near the other bank some distance downstream in ten feet of water. She was considerably farther submerged than when they first took charge of her, and most of the stores aboard were ruined. But the move was extremely worth while; she could be completely raised and refitted without too much difficulty if the salvagers had a clear field. The work began with the coming of day.

After the battle the *Queen* came up to Warrenton after salvage equipment, and Porter learned that morning of her presence. He had heard the heavy, slow firing the night before. From these two facts he deduced correctly that the *Indianola* had been either captured or sunk. He had sent the *Queen* down to dominate the lower waters; she had been captured and her strength added to that of the *Webb.* Now the powerful *Indianola* had succumbed to the combination of the two, and possibly her strength also had been added to the other side. Here was a pretty kettle of fish. The only wise thing to do was to send down immediately a force so superior that there could be no question of its successfully destroying or driving to cover all the enemy. It would be unwise to send another single boat or two. Their fate might be the same as that of their predecessors; this procedure might continue indefinitely until the enemy had the whole river navy! But Porter did not have to ponder a decision between these two alternatives; he had available *nothing at all* to send. All his fleet was upstream patrolling the length of the river. He sent posthaste for every gunboat he could get; but that meant a very serious delay. Assuming the worst—that the *Indianola* had been captured, not sunk—it was imperative that Porter do something immediately; he realized the possibility (as was actually the case) of the *Indianola* being in the enemy's hands, damaged, but readily made fit again if the opportunity should be given.

The Admiral acted with great alacrity. He "turned to" every man available from his large collection of noncombatant vessels and from the new but unready gunboat *Lafayette.* He took an old flat-bottomed barge and built a dummy "ironclad" monitor! Log rafts increased its length to 300 feet. Bulwarks were raised; a large "casemate" of logs was constructed up forward, and from its ports glowered a number of "Quaker" guns. A "pilothouse" was erected, also two huge though light "paddle-wheel houses." Two smokestacks rose high above the deck; they consisted of barrels piled one upon the other. Each stack had at its base a big pot of burning tar and oakum. Even two old pulling boats were swung from unworkable but realistic-looking davits. Covered with a heavy coat of tar and with black smoke pouring from her funnels she was a fearsome-looking creature indeed—if not observed too closely! She even bore a slight resemblance to the *Lafayette*—designedly no doubt. With energy and enthusiasm the Navy's newest "ironclad" was completed just about twenty-four hours after the *Indianola* was captured. The total cost was reported to be eight dollars and sixty-three cents.

Almost immediately in the middle of the night of February 25–26, she started on her trip down the Mississippi. As was the case with all runners of Vicksburg batteries she was subjected to a long, spectacular, and deafening bombardment. She did not even deign to reply, but glided on unscathed, her heavy armor apparently fending off the big projectiles without a tremor. The telegraph wires out of Vicksburg soon became hot. A veritable monster is on her way! Defenseless vessels retreat down river! Get word through to the salvage party on the *Indianola* to blow her up before she is recaptured!

Blessed with perfect "piloting" the "Black Terror" headed into the west bank below Vicksburg, and grounded where a body of Yankee soldiers had gathered. Soon the *Queen of the West* by chance came some little way up the river from Warrenton on a scout. While still some miles away she too spied the new enemy. Neither the *Queen* nor the *Webb* was in any condition to fight a new battle, even with the strength of the two combined; least of all could the *Queen* tackle such a formidable opponent single-handed. She began a retreat which, later in the day, became general. The word of the new threat reached the *Webb*, the *Grand Era*, and the *Dr. Beatty* one by one, and also the *Indianola* herself by no means least. In the haste and the excitement the *Queen* smashed into the *Grand Era* making it necessary for the latter to get rid of seventy bales of cotton over the side. In the words of the *Era*'s sea-going Lieutenant Colonel: "my port end was cut into."

The army files pushed the "monitor" back into the current, and down the river she went in pursuit. She almost held her own with some of the enemy vessels whose steam was low. Then the new ruler of the waves went aground again. Orders from Vicksburg finally got through to the *Indianola*'s new crew to blow her up. They wanted to defend her to the last and already were possessed of two fieldpieces to assist the ironclad's own battery. But the orders to destroy were insistent; and there was the enemy hovering ominously just two and a half miles away (on a mudbank!). The *Indianola* was already deserted by all of her new naval companions and there was no course left but to obey orders. That night a thorough job was instituted; all her guns were wrecked or spiked and the vessel itself blown up; even the two field guns were dumped into the river. This was the second night after the battle.

By this time the true character and "strength" of the Northern monster had been observed and detected. Hurry-up telegrams were sent down the river to countermand the orders to destroy the *Indianola*. Not long afterwards the "Terror" was "captured." Also the Confederates decided that the *Indianola* was not irretrievably destroyed and they attempted to raise her. They were not successful, however. Later in the year the Federals recaptured her, got her afloat, and towed her up to Mound City, Illinois; but she was never put back in service.

The *Queen of the West*, the *Webb*, and the others never paused in the order of their going till they got back up the Red River. After lengthy refitting at Shreveport, Louisiana, the *Webb* seems to have gone into semiretirement until several days after Appomattox. Under the command of Charles W. Read, formerly of the famous *Arkansas*, she then made a dash for the sea. Just below New Orleans she came face to face with the powerful U. S. S. *Richmond*. Read ran his ship aground and blew her up.

And what of the *Queen?* A month after she helped conquer the *Indianola* she was back looking for trouble. On April 14, she found a good deal of it on Grand Lake, part of the Atchafalaya network between the Red River and the Gulf of Mexico. Together with a boatload of soldiers on the river steamer *Minna Simma* (not two other boats as quoted below) she was on her way down to Berwick Bay. There she hoped to surprise, board, and capture one or two Union gunboats. It so happened that there were three rather capable Yankee side-wheelers lying at anchor in Grand Lake, directly in her path; they were the *Estrella* (flag), the *Arizona*, and the *Calhoun*. During the afternoon of April 13 Lieutenant Commander

Augustus P. Cooke, who was in command of this little squadron, sighted enemy smoke above him on Lake Chicot, apparently coming his way. It was the *Queen of the West* and the *Simma*, the *Queen* sporting a new black coat of paint. They did not appear before dark but the Federal vessels were made ready.

Here is an extract from the diary of Acting Third Assistant Engineer George W. Baird of the *Calhoun* (quoted in *Official Records of the Union and Confederate Navies in the War of the Rebellion,* Series I, Volume 20, pp. 137–38). He describes what happened, and his account is perhaps as authentic as anything we have on this affair. However, it would be well for the reader to discount somewhat the writer's normal propensity to claim that "his ship won the war."

"April 14, 1863.—I had the midwatch; the fires were banked. I was on deck now and then. About 2 o'clock I saw two lights as if on boats, up the lake, and they were moving. Somehow I thought they were on vessels and told the officer of the deck (Sargeant), but he was a phlegmatic old fellow and was not enthused. He noted it and later he reported it. The light came nearer and nearer, but very slowly. At 4 I was relieved and I turned in, thinking I had overrated the importance of those lights. At 5 the lookout reported the lights as on two steamers. At 5:10 I was awakened by 'All hands to quarters!' for we had no drum, nor fife, nor bugle; it was the call by the boatswain's mate. I was so sleepy I waited a moment to see if there was any excitement; I heard the cable slipped and then a gun fired; then I got out in a hurry. The engine was going ahead slowly; day was breaking. There were three vessels, and one of them had opened fire on us. They were the rebel ram *Queen of the West* and the transports *Grand Duke* and *Mary T*. The latter was laden with troops. I did not go to the engine room, but joined Jordan, Bostwick, Brown, and Dr. Whitehead, who stood together on the hurricane deck. We were steaming away from the enemy. The *Arizona* and *Estrella* were headed toward the enemy, and I could see the *Arizona's* beam working. Brown and Dr. Whitehead began to remark about our leaving; then one of them said, 'Why, even the *Estrella* is headed toward the enemy.' Jordan then put the helm down and we headed up. . . . This was a remarkable battle. The captain of the *Queen* was named Fuller; he had commanded the *J. A. Cotton* in all of her fights against us. He was quoted as saying: 'There is that d—— *Calhoun*. I would rather see the devil than that boat.' . . . as soon as the 30-pounder Parrott would bear, it was fired at extreme elevation, for the vessels were nearly 3 miles away. Brown and Dr. Whitehead who stood over the gun, both said they saw the shot as it left the gun and traced its trajectory and saw it strike the *Queen*. I did not see the shot, but I heard it fired, heard its flight, and its landing on the *Queen,* its explosion and the rush of steam that followed. The *Queen* had been cotton-clad above, just as Jordan was hay-cladding the *Calhoun*. The *Queen* was armored like the *Diana* around her machinery, and being much larger, afforded room in the casemate for her larger guns, but she had no armor on her upper deck. So the shell we fired, being a percussion shell, had struck on her roof, exploded, cut a steam pipe, and set fire to the cotton. The engineers were driven from the casemate and no pump could be started; in a few moments the *Queen of the West* was in a blaze; 26 of her people were scalded or burned to death. The boats of our fleet took off her crew, and in about two hours (7:40) her magazine exploded and she was no more."

CHAPTER XIV

DEWEY AT PORT HUDSON

WHEN THE *Queen of the West* and the *Webb* captured the *Indianola* the Confederates definitely regained control of the waters between Port Hudson and Vicksburg; and these waters included the whole Red River system. Even though the *Indianola* was out of commission, and the *Queen* and *Webb* both in need of overhaul, these latter vessels had no opponents to challenge them. As has been mentioned, Porter had nothing immediately available to send down from above to regain supremacy. Farragut decided to come up from below—to run the Port Hudson batteries himself with his fleet of steam sloops and gunboats. The entire topographical and defensive setup was startlingly similar to that at Vicksburg, and no other description of the Port Hudson scene will be given at this point. The *Indianola* was lost on the night of February 24–25. Farragut's ships were below Port Hudson on March 14 ready for the ordeal of running past the cannon on the bluffs. Such an operation was not thought to be as formidable a task as it had been considered back in the days when Foote's fleet lay above Island No. 10. Nevertheless, every preparation was made, every precaution taken.

There were four big ships, the fine, new, screw sloops-of-war *Hartford* (flag), *Richmond* and *Monongahela,* and the old side-wheeler *Mississippi* which had carried Perry to Japan in 1852. Each of the first three had a wooden gunboat lashed to her unengaged side. This was to serve the dual purpose of protecting the smaller vessel and increasing the maneuverability of the larger one; and especially to assist her in case she grounded or suffered any damage to her propelling machinery. George Dewey was executive officer of the *Mississippi*. He is the same Dewey who was later to become the hero of Manila Bay; also he attained the rank of Admiral of the Navy, the only man in all U. S. naval annals ever to rise so high. There was a boy among the Port Hudson defense forces whom

Dewey was to know in later life as Chief Justice Edward Douglass White of the U. S. Supreme Court. On board the *Richmond* at this time there was a civilian minister named Thomas Scott Bacon. Both he and Dewey have left splendid accounts of the stirring engagement. This will be portrayed by presenting the first part of Bacon's "The Fight at Port Hudson," and the last part of Dewey's account from his *Autobiography* published by Charles Scribner's Sons. Dewey himself considered Bacon's story "the best account I have ever read of the battle as I remember it." It appeared in *The Independent* of March 14, 1901.

The words of the first few pages quoted below are those of Bacon. Dewey's name will appear at the beginning of his part of the story. Four of the ships, not all seven as quoted, were with Farragut when he forced his way up the river to New Orleans in 1862.

"The squadron of Admiral Farragut lay at anchor all day, March 14th, 1863, about five miles below Port Hudson, La. It had left New Orleans some days before under orders to ascend the Mississippi far enough to communicate with the army and the fleet of gunboats investing Vicksburg, some four hundred miles above New Orleans by the river. I was the guest of the Admiral and the other chief officers, especially of Captain (afterward Rear Admiral) James Alden, on the 'Richmond,' chaplain *pro tempore* of the squadron in case of need of any such services as I could render. My position was not an official one. In fact, altho often urged to do so, I had never consented to accept such an appointment on either side of the great conflict. My residence, worldly interest and almost all my associations were on the Southern side. My deepest convictions of truth and duty made me inflexibly loyal to the other. This unusual condition, I believe, gave me a power to understand the merits of the whole controversy which few have had.

"I was attracted to this arrangement with my naval friends, whom I had learned to admire and love in quite a long intimacy with them in New Orleans, where we were all far from our homes, by a half laughing promise of theirs to escort me to my own home near Alexandria, La., on Red River, where my wife was living alone with her servants on a plantation; and we had not even heard from one another for eight months—so strictly was the guard kept against correspondence on both sides.

"The eight vessels of Admiral Farragut's fleet were waiting for an opportunity to slip by the dangerous batteries which lined the curved eastern bank of the river for some two or three miles at Port Hudson and which were in full view from our decks, watched as they were by powerful glasses. The river makes one of its great curves there, bending into the eastern bank against the high hills, while the river bed, and for miles the western shore, lay level under the concentric fire of the batteries. This and the mighty current of the river, reducing by some four or five miles an hour the utmost speed of steaming for that heavy ocean craft, as also increasing the danger of running ashore or aground—all this required great daring and patience for the enterprise.

"We must remember that the 'Hartford,' 'Richmond,' 'Mononga-hela' and 'Mississippi,' while they were among the best ships of the old navy, were not at all iron or steel clad, except that a very doubtful attempt that way was made by arranging their chain cables on the fighting side to ward off the fire of the great guns. To the off side of each was lashed a small gunboat (such as the 'Albatross,' 'Genesee,' etc. ['Kineo']) which might furnish some motive power in case their own steam were disabled in action. . . .

"The *personnel* was indeed magnificent, from the Admiral down through all the ranks to the powder-boys. They were quiet, pleasant, even gentle people, among whom one heard no loud, boastful or ferocious talk. All the leading officers were religious men, and this seemed to be the rule among the rest, altho doubtless there were some who in their various ways were not unready for a spree or a row when the opportunity offered.

"Yet there was not among them the slightest suggestion of shrinking from their grim business when the occasion for that came. On the other hand they were all evidently looking that directly in the face as probably a matter of a few hours only away. Much of that 14th of March, 1863, was spent in careful preparation on deck which all understood. Less than a year before these same ships with the same officers and crews had gone through a terrific experience and instruction of the kind. They had accomplished what the equally well trained and fearless Confederate army and navy people at New Orleans had just before in my own hearing quietly declared could not by any possibility be done; they had broken through the great doors of the Mississippi nearly a hundred miles below New Orleans, passed powerful forts, great guns, booms, batteries, fireships and iron-clad rams—all planned by the accomplished Beauregard and completed at leisure by all the wealth and labor of the Queen City of the South.

"The men on the 'Richmond's' deck knew how that was done, and they also knew what it cost the victors. Now, with less force, they were about to rush into new dangers of which they must guess and venture what they could. They must for perhaps two hours slowly creep up past frowning hills from which might suddenly pour storms of destruction, to which they could reply only at great disadvantage. Meanwhile exploding boilers, disabled machinery, dismounted guns, the drowning inrush of the greatest river current in the world in midnight darkness—all these might reinforce shot and shell and the blinding smoke and blaze of their own ships.

"Yet they went about all the preparations for this very quietly and diligently. I could only look on with natural curiosity and sometimes ask questions. I saw them place little square, shallow, wooden boxes filled with sawdust, like the spittoons one used to see in country barrooms, behind the great guns and asked what that meant. I was told that it was to have an absorbent ready to be thrown upon any blood splashed upon the deck. All the brass railings and other such ornaments were unscrewed and stowed below to remove everything which might possibly be struck by the enemy's shot and shell and driven across the deck as deadly missiles. The bulwarks, the timber side walls about the upper deck and the deck floor were whitewashed to supply some light at night when no lights could be allowed as furnishing targets for the batteries. This was a very useful suggestion of Captain Alden.

"I asked a group of officers who, if any, would be with the Captain on the bridge in the expected action. Lieut. Commander A. Boyd Cummings, second in command as executive officer, pointed with a grave smile to his own breast. One of the younger men said to me, 'We have all been pitying you, because if you are hurt tonight, you will get no pension.' I laughed and replied that I was not there for a pension. So passed that short afternoon in which, unlike the two or three preceding days, clouds had begun to gather in the horizon and the very dark night which we were all hoping for to end the waiting was at hand.

"No doubt strong field glasses had been turned upon us all that day from the nearer batteries to find out if possible 'what the Yankees were after now.' Their attention had in fact been summoned in the afternoon by the, of course, ineffective fire of some mortar schooners anchored below us out of sight behind Prophet Island and sending 13-inch shells at intervals and at very long range until dark. Probably the experienced Confederate officers did not take this very seriously. They hardly dared to hope that it meant the desperate and, as they were sure, the disastrous attempt to pass the 'smothering fire' of the batteries. They were perhaps lulled into greater security, as was perhaps the intention, that we would not dare venture within range.

"It was pitch dark at last. In the afternoon the flagship 'Hartford,' which had been anchored below us, got under way and passed near us, mooring just above. As she went by the Admiral hailed and gave this order: 'You come next after me.' And the cheery answer of our Captain was 'Ay, ay, sir.' So it was well understood that we were awaiting orders to make the attempt that night. I now asked Captain Alden what the signal would be. He said, 'Two red lights under the stern of the flagship.' I was asked what choice I had of a place during the action. The excellent surgeon, Dr. Henderson, said that he had a place to offer me, as one of the safest, in his operating room. It was, I think, the chief engineer who offered me another in the gangway through which the great shaft of the propeller worked. Then I appealed to the Captain for a personal favor. I had thought over all the possible chances and mischances, and had decided that one place was just as safe as another. But I certainly did not wish to be drowned like a rat in a hole and not know what had been going on. On the contrary, I wished to see all I could and to share the terror and the courage of my shipmates; and with hope I submitted myself to the Captain's orders. He replied that I should be on the bridge with him.

"The time sped on when at last (9.30 p. m.) an orderly tapped on the door with a message from the officer of the deck. 'What is it?' 'A signal from the Admiral—two red lights under the stern of the flagship.' I looked at the Captain, hardly believing my own ears. He rose quietly but promptly and said, 'Gentlemen, you hear the message; each one will go to his place of duty and the ship will be got under way as soon as possible.' All left the pleasant cabin at once and went into the darkness outside.

"I was careful to say but very little to my companions on the bridge. They had their very solemn duties and were intent upon them with all their eyes, ears and thoughts. And I, also, having committed my soul anew to the merciful love of God, felt like awaiting in silent patience whatever was to happen, but at the same time with an intense interest which printed everything most distinctly and indelibly in my memory. At first, with the most careful peering toward either bank of the river, or looking up-stream toward the high bluffs which I had been used to pass several times in each of the ten years precedent, I could make out nothing but a sense of shadow and darkness. Some faint glimmerings of ships' lights I could still catch looking down stream for a little while and just above us two distinct red spots like burning coals which hung there yet for the information of those in the secret. There seemed at first no sound except the strong steady swish of the muddy Northwestern water rushing down to the Gulf. Yet the careful listener could at first hear low and faint sounds of command and responding 'Ay, ay, sir,' from the other ships, and more distinctly from our own ship, as the anchors were drawn up and made fast, and the engines slowly began their mighty task.

"It was wonderful how softly all this was done. Even I, with all the eagerness of curiosity then, and the awe of such suspense and probable nearness to death, have now no recollection of how slowly moved the minutes of that hour or hour and a half of silence and darkness in which we crept up to the batteries. It was the understanding on our ship that Farragut's wish and hope was to push on without returning the enemies' fire, if possible; and with this in view to steer close into that bank of the river so that they could not depress their guns enough to do much damage. The intense darkness and the strong current, as well as our ignorance of what devices they might have in store, made it necessary to use prompt discretion in varying from this as occasion might demand. As we were getting under way, Commander Cummings, who was to be in change of the broadside firing, stood at the end of the bridge and gave the guns' crews general instructions as to deliberation, precision, accuracy of aim and firing the guns in rapid succession from bow to stern (as, if fired simultaneously, it would give too great shock to the vessel)—all in a very firm and distinct but low and quiet tone.

"At last I whispered to him that we must be well up with the bluffs as well as I remembered the place, and he replied as quietly that we were already 'under fire,'—that is, as I understood him, that we were already in range of the great guns on shore. This meant a great deal, for probably every foot which a hostile vessel would need to travel in passing those batteries had been carefully considered by the skillful military engineers who planned the works and sighted by the practical marksmen who manned them. Just after this a beacon fire suddenly blazed up in the semicircle of low ground on the west side of the river. A few Confederates concealed there with combustibles had at last discovered 'what the Yankees were after,' and had given the fatal signal to the batteries. So I found out at once what to be 'under fire' meant. The flashes and thunders of great guns through which we were rushing with all the power of steam which could be safely used, but in profound silence and darkness on our part; this of itself was something awful.

"But all that was at once forgotten when, as I was peering into the darkness ahead, I saw a great burst of red light and rolling clouds of white smoke in which the flagship appeared distinctly against the black sky with every spar and bit of cordage draped in those white clouds from keel to trucks, while dazzling fires flashed from her fighting side and quick repeating sounds of crashing thunder filled all the air with echoes. Then as suddenly all was dark and still. This was the most terrible and sublime display of human power that I had then ever or have ever since seen. In fact, amazement and admiration overpowered the terror. To this moment I recall it with a thrill that cannot find the proper words for expression.

"On the 'Richmond' and all the other ships this was considered a general order to begin firing. I looked and listened with breathless admiration as the officers in their various details gave the commands. All was calm, firm and careful, and each man, from Captain to 'ordinary seaman,' seemed ready to 'do his duty,' without nervousness or alarm, but with eager readiness. Already for some minutes splinters and ravelings of sails and ropes were falling around us in quite a shower. This made it certain that our ship was already the target of a powerful and accurate fire. In less time than I have written these words of description I had heard the clear, strong and steady voice of Cummings giving his last orders, to this effect: 'You will fire the whole starboard battery, one gun at a time, from the bow-gun aft. Don't fire too fast. Aim carefully at the flashes of the enemy's guns. *Fire!*'

"What followed these words had not to me the glorious beauty of the flagship's opening fire. But it was even more sublimely terrible. The thunder of cannon from the river banks was loud. The 'Hartford's' broadside was very much nearer and more startling. But the crash and roar of the 'Richmond's' own guns under our very feet, with every timber of the strong ship quivering with each discharge, and making her 'stagger like a drunken man,' was more than on land to be in the midst of 'battle's magnificently stern array' and action. To see the earnestness of devotion to duty, supressing all thoughts of each one's own danger, and sobering even the insane excitement of fear, was a great instance of the power of discipline and of the habitual sense of duty."

(Dewey) "The air was heavy and misty. Almost immediately after we were engaged, a pall of smoke settled over the river and hung there, thickening with the progress of the cannonading. This was more dangerous than the enemy's fire, which was pounding us with good effect, while we could see nothing but the flashes of their guns as a target. The *Hartford*, however, had good luck as well as advantage of position. She was at least pushing ahead of her own smoke, while every other ship was taking the smoke of those in front of her. The *Mississippi* had the smoke of all three.

"At the bend, the current caught the *Hartford* and swept her around with her head toward the batteries, her stem touching ground. But the *Albatross*, her gun-boat consort, helped her off. Then, applying the twin-screw method, with the *Hartford* going ahead strong with her engines while the *Albatross* backed, the *Hartford* got her head pointed up-stream again and steamed out of the range of the batteries with the loss of only one killed and two wounded [slightly]. The Confederate gunners had not depressed their guns enough for the *Hartford*, but they did not make this error as the other ships came in range.

"When the *Richmond*, the second ship in line, was in front of the last battery, a shot tore into her engine-room. Such was its chance effect that it twisted the safety-valve lever, displacing the weight and quickly filling the engine-room, fire-room, and berth deck with steam. In short order the steam pressure fell so low that she could not go ahead under her own motive power. The *Genesee*, her gun-boat, was not able with her own power to make any headway for the two vessels against the strong current. There was nothing to do but for the pair to make an expeditious retreat downstream to safety.

"The *Richmond's* gunners, working in furious haste, intent on delivering the heaviest possible fire, did not know that their ship had turned around. Therefore they were firing toward the bank opposite that from the batteries. Mistaking the flashes of the *Mississippi's* guns for the flashes of the enemy's, they fired at her. On our part we did not know in the obscurity of the smoke and darkness that our ships had been disabled. The *Richmond's* casualties included her executive officer, Lieutenant A. Boyd Cummings, who was mortally wounded.

"As the *Monongahela* came along she found herself in the range of musketry from the low bank on the port side, which was silenced by her gun-boat, the *Kineo*. But the *Kineo* received a shot which jammed her rudder-post and rendered the rudder useless. As a result the *Monongahela* had to do all the steering. She ran aground, and the *Kineo*, carried on by her momentum as the *Monongahela* suddenly stopped, tore away all of her fasts by which she was bound to the *Monongahela* except one. Then the *Kineo* got a hawser to the *Monongahela*, and, laboring desperately, under fire, succeeded after twenty-five minutes' effort in getting the *Monongahela* free of the bottom.

"Meanwhile, Captain McKinistry, of the *Monongahela*, had had the bridge shot away from under his feet, and had received such a fall in consequence that he was incapacitated. Lieutenant-Commander N. W. Thomas took command in his place. The *Kineo* drifted on downstream, while the *Monongahela* proceeded on her way until a heated crank-pin stopped her engines, when she had to drift back downstream under the fire of the batteries. She sustained a heavy loss in killed and wounded. [Six and twenty-one.]

"I refer to the experiences of the three ships which had preceded the *Mississippi* in order to show the hazardous nature of Farragut's undertaking. . . .

"The *Mississippi*, bringing up the rear, was soon enveloped in the pall of smoke. We went by the *Monongahela* when she was aground without, so far as I know, either seeing or being seen by her. Both Captain Smith and myself felt that our destiny that night was in the hands of the pilot. There was nothing to do but to fire back at the flashes on the bluffs and trust to his expert knowledge. It was a new experience for him, guiding a heavy-draught ocean-going ship in the midst of battle smoke, with the shells shrieking in his ears. By the time that the *Mississippi* came within range of the batteries they were making excellent practice. Our mortar flotilla posted below the bend was adding to the uproar. When there was a cry of 'Torpedoes!' it might have been alarming had we not seen that bombs striking close to the ship had splashed the water upon the deck. None actually struck us. Some one else shouted, 'They're firing chain-shot at us!' an error of observation due to the sight of two bombs which passed by in company, their lighted fuses giving the effect of being part of the same projectile.

"We were going very slowly, feeling our way as we approached the shoal point. Finally, when the pilot thought that we were past it, he called out: 'Starboard the helm! Full speed ahead!' As it turned out, we were anything but past the point. We starboarded the helm straight into it and struck just as we developed a powerful momentum. We were hard aground and listing, and backed with all the capacity of the engines immediately. In order to bring the ship on an even keel, we ran in the port battery, which, as it faced away from the bluffs, was not engaged. Every precaution to meet the emergency was taken promptly; and there was remarkably little confusion, thanks to the long drills which we had had off New Orleans, and to the fact that all but a few of the crew had already been under fire in passing Forts Jackson and St. Philip.

"But no amount of training could altogether prepare men for such a situation as we were in. With our guns barking, and the engines pounding, and the paddle-wheels making more noise than usual, because we were aground, it was difficult to make commands heard. In half an hour the engines never budged us, while steadfastly and even unconcernedly the engine-room force stuck to their duties. We were being more frequently hit; the toll of our dead and wounded was increasing. Naturally, too, gunners of the enemy, who could see the ship outlined by the bonfires on the bank on the opposite side of us from the batteries, had not failed to note that we were aground. The advantages of training on a stationary target allowed them to make the most of our distress, while the flashes of our own guns and the bursting of the enemy's shells only made the intervals of darkness the more baffling to the eyes. I remember hunting about the deck for Captain Smith and finding him lighting another cigar with a flint quite as cooly as if he were doing it when we lay anchored off New Orleans.

" 'Well, it doesn't look as if we could get her off,' he said.

" 'No, it does not!' I had to tell him.

"Then came the report that we were on fire forward in the store-room. Investigation proved that this was true. The store-room was filled with all sorts of inflammable material and was below the water-line, supposedly out of reach of any shot.

"It was not until forty years afterward that I learned how the fire had started, and this from a gentleman whom I met at Palm Beach, Florida. He had served in what was called the 'hot-shot' battery. This battery had a furnace in which they heated their round shot red-hot before firing them. When I asked him how they kept the shot from igniting the powder, he said: 'We put wads of wet hay or hemp between the shot and the powder.' Our bow in grounding had risen so that the store-room was above the water-line, and one of these hot shot having a plunging trajectory had entered. While we were fighting the fire in the store-room, Captain Smith had given the order to throw the guns of the port battery overboard in the hope that this would lighten the ship enough to float her. But the order was never carried out. He had to face the heartbreaking fact, to any captain of his indomitable courage, of giving up his ship. He had opposed fighting in the night and in the night he had come to grief.

" 'Can we save the crew?' he asked me.

" 'Yes, sir!' I told him.

"But there was no time to lose. Delay only meant still more wounded to move, with the danger of the fire in the store-room reaching the magazine before they were away. Not once had our starboard battery ceased firing. The gunners had kept to their work as if they were sure of victory, gaps caused by casualties among the guns' crews being filled in a fashion that was a credit to our *morale;* For it is in such a crisis as this that you may know whether all your labor in organization and drills has had a vital or a superficial effect.

"And the battery must continue to fire up to the very minute of abandoning the ship, the gunners being the last of the enlisted men to go. Down on the spar-deck I found everybody full of fight. I remember as I passed along seeing Ensign Barker, now Rear-Admiral Albert S. Barker (retired), sighting a gun. To show what a small detail, even in a time of such tension as that was, may impress itself on the mind, I recollect that Barker was wearing eye-glasses. I had never seen him with them on before.

" 'What are we leaving her for?' Barker asked. He was thinking only of his part, without knowing that there was a fire forward. When I explained, he comprehended the situation. . . .

"The three boats on the starboard side toward the enemy's batteries had all been smashed by shells. The three on the port side were still seaworthy.

"We got all of the wounded in the first boat, and started that down the river, with directions to go on board one of our ships. The second and the third, which had some of the slightly wounded, as well as members of the crew who were unhurt, were told to make a landing near by on the bank and to send the boats back immediately. They were slow in returning. As soon as they were against the ship's side the crew began crowding and the officers had difficulty in keeping order. For the moment the bonds of discipline had been broken. The men were just human beings obeying the law of self-preservation.

"I apprehended the reason why the boats had been slow in returning. There was disinclination on the part of the oarsmen who had reached safety to make the trip back. What if the next time the boats did not return at all? They were our only hope of safety. To swim in that swift river-current was impossible. To expect rescue in the midst of battle, when no one could be signalled in the darkness and pandemonium, was out of the question. It would be a choice of drowning or burning for those who were caught on board the *Mississippi*.

"I determined to make sure of the boats' return, and in the impulse, just as they were going to push off, I swung myself down by the boat-falls into one of the boats. Not until we were free of the ship did I have a second thought in realization of what I had done. I had left my ship in distress, when it is the rule that the last man to leave her should be the captain, and I as executive officer should be next to last.

"That was the most anxious moment of my career. What if a shot should sink the boat? What if a rifle bullet should get me? All the world would say that I had been guilty of about as craven an act as can be placed at the door of any officer. This would not be pleasant reading for my father up in Vermont. He would no longer think that I had done the 'rest' reasonably well. If the ship should blow up while I was away and I should appear on the reports as saved, probably people would smile over my explanation.

"We were under fire all the way to the shore, but nobody was hit. As we landed on the beach I said to the men in the boats:

" 'Now, all of you except four get to cover behind the levee. Those four will stay with me to go off to the ship.'

"They obeyed one part of my command with great alacrity. That is, all but one scrambled over the levee in a free-for-all rush. The one who remained standing was a big negro, the ship's cook. He evidently understood that I meant him to be one of the four.

" 'I'm ready to go with you, sir!' he said. And he was perfectly calm about it.

"Each of the others had thought that the order was not personal. But when I called out, shaming them, in the name of their race, for allowing a negro to be the only one who was willing to return to save his shipmates, I did not lack volunteers.

"Then in the dim light I discerned one man standing by the other boat, which had landed some distance up the beach.

"I called:

" 'Who is that standing by the cutter?'

"The answer came: 'It is I, sir, Chase' (one of the acting masters).

" 'Why don't you go off to the ship and get the rest of the officers and men?' I asked.

" 'I can't get the men to man the boat!' he said.

"When I called out asking if they meant to desert their shipmates there was no reply. Then I told Chase to use his revolver and make them go, which he did. It is my firm belief that neither one of the boats would have ever returned to the ship if I had not gone ashore in one of them.

"I was certainly as relieved to reach the ship as the men had been to reach shore. When I say that I lived five years in an hour, I should include about four and a half of the years in the few minutes that I was absent with the boats.

"As soon as I was on deck Captain Smith came to me and said:

" 'I have been looking all over for you. I didn't know but that you had been killed.'

"I explained hastily, and added that we had two empty boats alongside, which we might not have had except for my indiscretion.

" 'We must make sure that none is left aboard alive,' said the captain.

"Then we began a search whose harrowing memory will never fade from my mind. We sent up and down the decks, examining prostrate figures to make sure that no spark of life remained in them, haste impelling us in the grim task on the one hand, and, on the other, the fear that some poor fellow who was still unconscious might know the horror of seeing the flames creep up on him as he lay powerless to move. Meanwhile, we kept calling aloud in the darkness that this was the last chance to escape. As a result of the thorough search, we found one youngster, little more than a boy, who was so faint that he could scarcely speak. We pulled him out from under the body of a dead man, in the midst of a group of dead who had been killed by the bursting of a shell.

"The next step was to make certain that the ship should not fall into the hands of the enemy. Captain Smith gave orders to fire the ship in two places in order to make absolutely sure of her destruction. This was our last service to that old vessel which had known so many cruises, and it was performed while the batteries on the bluff were continuing to improve their practice.

"With Ensign O. A. Batcheller I went below to start a blaze in the wardroom which is both the officers' sitting-room and mess-room and, in a sense, their home afloat, while the rest of the ship is their shop. I had a lantern with me, I remember, and when I got below I looked around at the bare oak table and chairs, wondering what there was that I could ignite. I did not want to delay the boat, and, under the circumstances, as long as we had to go, we did not care to remain in that inferno of shell-fire any longer than necessary. I ran into my state-room, and pulling the mattress off the berth hurried back with it to the wardroom. Then I ripped it open and put it under the dining-table.

"When I had piled the chairs and any other combustibles around the table, I took the oil lamp out of the lantern and plunged it into the mattress, with the result that I had a blaze which required immediate evacuation of the wardroom by Batcheller and myself. My mattress was all that I had tried to remove from my state-room. But just as we were going Batcheller cried: 'I'll save that anyway!' and seized a uniform frock-coat before he ran up the ladder ahead of me.

"In the last boat, besides the captain, were one of the engineers, Batcheller, myself, and four men. I waited on my juniors to precede me, and then the captain waited for me, so that he was the last man ever to press his foot on the *Mississippi's* deck. This order of our going was carried out as regularly in keeping with naval custom as if it had been some formal occasion in a peaceful port.

"As soon as we were free of the ship's side the powerful current caught us and swung us downstream. At the same time, the fire we had started in the wardroom broke through the skylight in a great burst of flame, illuminating the whole after part of the ship. It must have revealed our boat clearly on the bosom of the river, and it was a signal to those on the bluffs along the banks to break into that rebel yell which I then heard in full chorus of victory for the first and only time in my life. It was not pleasant to the ear. The Confederates were gloating over what was the most triumphant of sights to them and the most distressing of sights to us. I remember thinking: 'How they must hate us!'

"Meanwhile, there was no cessation in the fire, and our boat was a target for the batteries. Not one of the officers and crew, except Ensign Batcheller, had saved any of his personal belongings. All the clothes we had were those in which we were clad. Captain Smith had on his sword, and also buckled to his belt a pair of fine revolvers. He still had a cigar in his mouth, and was as calm as ever. But suddenly he unbuckled his belt and threw both sword and revolvers overboard.

" 'Why did you do that?' I asked.

"He was a man of few words, who made up his mind decisively, and his answers were always prompt.

" 'I'm not going to surrender them to any rebel,' he said. This illustrated very well the strong feelings of the time, which now, happily, have no interest for us except in the psychology of history.

" 'We need not land, but go to one of our ships downstream,' I answered.

"At all events, I concluded to keep my sword. Every one in the boat, except Captain Smith and myself, was at the oars, rowing as energetically as if we were in a race. I had the tiller. We were moving so rapidly that we were not hit, and when we were safe around the bend and in sight of the *Richmond* of our fleet, which we were to board in safety, it was evident that the captain had been a little precipitate. A few days afterward, when he was still without a sword, Captain Smith gave my sword a glance and remarked:

" 'You would not have had that if you had followed your captain's example.'

"This was said without a smile, very much in the manner of a bishop. The captain would have made a most dignified bishop and of the church militant.

"I recollect, too, Ensign Batcheller holding up the uniform coat he had saved, after we had reached the *Richmond*, as a token of the advantage he had over the rest of us. Ensign E. M. Shepard examined the coat and said:

" 'Thanks, very much, Batcheller, but that's my coat!'

"So it was.

"Besides setting her on fire in two places, as an additional precaution before abandoning her, we had cut the *Mississippi's* outboard delivery pipes. Thus she filled with water astern, just as the wreck of the ram *Manassas* had in the battle of New Orleans, and with the same result. Her bow was lifted sufficiently for her to float free of the bottom, and she swung around with the current. Her port guns were loaded, and now, as they faced the Confederate batteries, the heat reached the primers and she came downstream, a dying ship manned by dead men, firing on the enemy; and some of the shots, I am told, took effect.

"As she drifted toward us a mass of flame, she had the whole river to herself, lighting its breadth and throwing the banks of the levee in relief. The *Richmond* slipped her chain in order to make sure of not being run down. Captain Smith and his officers were standing on the deck of the *Richmond* watching her, while, I, with that rebel yell of triumph still echoing in my ears, was thinking of the splendid defiance of the last shots in her guns being sent at the enemy.

" 'She goes out magnificently, anyway!' I said to the captain, glad to find some compensating thought for our disaster in a moment when all of us were overwrought by what we had been through.

" 'I don't think so!' he returned sharply.

"I saw that he had misunderstood the idea that led to my remark. I shall never forget the look on his face as he saw his ship of which he had been so proud drifting to her doom. Farther downstream she went aground and soon after exploded. Such was the end of that brave, sturdily built old side-wheeler."

Captain Smith's official report written the next day states that the storeroom fire was lighted by members of the crew just prior to abandoning ship; that it was extinguished by water admitted through shot holes made immediately afterwards; and that the ship was then fired in four other places.

The *Mississippi* was more than twenty years old, the oldest steamer then in the Service, and had been preceded by only two steam men-of-war in all the Navy. This is not to imply that her age prevented her from being as valuable as almost any newer ship for the services required in this particular war. Her fate was a sad one. One cannot help feeling that Captain Smith could have saved the *Mississippi* if he had indulged in less calm cigar-smoking and had put forth more intense driving effort to get his ship afloat; the crew's casualties were not excessive. He received from his superiors anything but censure for his actions of the night. But it does seem that the foremast and bowsprit, etc., could have been cut away to lighten the bow; that all the guns, anchors, and other heavy articles up forward could have been moved aft without too much difficulty, or at least thrown overboard. Later events indicate that this would probably have allowed the ship to back off easily. The engines were functioning as beautifully as ever before; the engineers force was scarcely even aware that the ship was in any difficulty. Something might have been accomplished by alternately backing first on one wheel and then on the other.

Captain Melancton Smith was an "officer of the old school" in the most unfortunate meaning of the phrase. Back in April, 1862, when the midnight dash past the New Orleans forts was being planned, he wanted the fleet to try it in broad daylight. He said they would never make it in the dark. He expressed the same preference at Port Hudson. When the bad visibility caused the pilot to run his ship aground he seemed only too willing to let it go at that. Further: during the grand melee below New Orleans, when the two fleets engaged each other in semidarkness and utter confusion, an opportunity arose for the *Mississippi* to destroy the ram *Manassas.* Whereupon Smith ranged the waters for an appreciable time looking for his superior officer from whom he might obtain specific permission to attack the enemy vessel! (He then destroyed her.) Of course, it can justly be considered as "second guessing" to point out that the *Mississippi* drifted clear all by herself an hour or so after her abandonment. It does prove, nevertheless, that she had not been irretrievably stuck.

The fight at Port Hudson was one of those in which each side is victorious in a different way. Only the *Hartford* and her gunboat got past. Enemy gunfire was responsible at least in part for the failure of the *Monongahela* and *Richmond* and their consorts to make it. The lone *Mississippi* went aground through unsuccessful piloting and was destroyed by her own crew. This totals up to an almost complete failure for Farragut. On the other hand, however, he did get two vessels through, and they alone were enough to maintain control of the Mississippi River up to Vicksburg, including at least the mouth of the Red River. And that is what he set out to do. He was reinforced soon afterwards by an Ellet ram, and the South never again reacquired the use of these waters.

It is worth a sentence to enlarge upon the extremely bad luck which halted the *Richmond* when on the very brink of success. It will be recalled that she was just about past the last enemy battery when a shot brought about the loss of practically all her steam. This shot, as Dewey mentions, knocked open the safety valve of one of her two boilers; it then glanced, passed the base of the smoke pipe, and knocked partly open the safety valve of the other boiler! It did little other damage of any sort. This was a bad-luck night for the ships bearing the good old Yankee names of *Mississippi* and *Richmond.*

It is interesting to trace in summary the chain of events described in this chapter and the preceding one. First, young Ellet came down in the *Queen of the West.* He was able to go almost any place he wanted, and take or destroy almost anything he wanted. On the Atchafalaya a musket ball shattered the leg of First Master Thomas.

That was the first important incident *as it turned out*. A couple of days later Ellet made a rash attack on a fortification; and he did it without first transferring his wounded officer to either the *De Soto* or the *Era No. 5*, both unengaged. When the *Queen* ran aground and became doomed, Ellet did not destroy her because he could not get Thomas out of her. Thus, the Confederates captured the *Queen* intact. The addition of the *Queen's* strength to that of the *Webb* made the Southerners strong enough to attack and capture the *Indianola*. This in turn caused Farragut to attempt the push past Port Hudson and there the *Mississippi* was burned.

> "For the want of a nail the shoe was lost,
> For the want of a shoe the horse was lost,
>
> .   .   .   ."

CHAPTER XV

THE BOHEMIAN NAVY

GOING BACK up the river a way we now find at last a turn for the better, considering matters from the standpoint of the Union forces operating against Vicksburg. The water had finally dropped enough so that Grant, with the help of Porter, was able to move. Water or no water, the Confederates' right or upstream flank was too tough a nut to crack directly. Grant had been waiting all these months for the opportunity to move against Vicksburg from below. At last the floods receded, the low west bank of the river became passable, and Grant was able to move his army down. This he did but the problem was not yet solved. He was still on the wrong side of the river with no vessels to carry his troops across, and with no way of getting flimsy transports past either Vicksburg or Port Hudson. One of two Ellet rams had been lost a short time before in an attempted run past the Vicksburg cannon. Porter felt that he could run his ironclad gunboats past without too much trouble but they would not serve to ferry a large army across the river. He took the bull by the horns and decided to run his entire fleet past Vicksburg all at once—gunboats, transports, a ram, a tug, and finally barges loaded with coal, ammunition, and supplies. The big show came off on the night of April 16–17. The fleet got past with the loss of a single transport! The river steamers used for troop carriers had cotton bales for their sole protection, so the successful accomplishment of the venture was rightly considered a great achievement. It inspired an order for six more transports to try it by themselves a week later, and five arrived safely.

Grant was now successfully below Vicksburg and with boats to ferry his army to the east bank. Nevertheless, although the high waters had receded, he was still forced to go a goodly distance below his objective before he could find a suitable dry place on the left bank where he might land. He decided that it would be best to go all the way down to Grand Gulf where the Big Black River enters the Mississippi from the east—just across from Hard Times (Louisiana) incidentally. The Confederates had erected batteries at Grand Gulf; although not comparable to those at Vicksburg or Port Hudson, these were nevertheless moderately strong and located on good eminences. The ironclads were not able to hammer them into submission so it was decided to ferry the army across still farther down, at Bruinsburg, Mississippi. There was no difficulty at least in getting the transports past Grand Gulf, thanks to the fire of the gunboats before and during the passage. So at Bruinsburg, Grant at long last got his army to the east bank of the Mississippi, even though thirty miles from his objective. The movement forced the evacuation of Grand Gulf, of which Grant quickly took possession after encountering some opposition en route.

The foregoing operations not only eliminated Grand Gulf as a threat to river traffic. In addition, the move of Porter's ships past the Vicksburg batteries brought an overwhelming Union naval force to the Red River sector of the Mississippi. Great strength between Vicksburg and Port Hudson, in conjunction with that already existing above and below, tied up the whole river tightly.

At the end of the first week of May, General Grant struck inland from Grand Gulf and commenced what was probably the most brilliant campaign of the entire war. Cutting loose from his base of supplies, operating deep in the enemy's country, he faced forces numbering double his own, defeated them piecemeal in a series of battles, and finally bottled up the greater part of the remnants within the environs of Vicksburg.

About the time the Union army was occupying Grand Gulf, several newspaper correspondents who had been left behind above Vicksburg decided that they were missing something. Sherman had carried out a diversion against Haines Bluff while the operations were beginning down river, and now his force was following after the rest. The reporters wanted to follow too. They did not deign to hike all that distance with the troops. They had seen how scathelessly the majority of even the fragile transports had passed the Vicksburg batteries. They decided they would proceed to Grand Gulf by river. Their adventures are related by Junius Henri Browne of the *New-York Tribune,* the same correspondent who has already described to us the picture of Commodore Foote's detachment from the gunboat flotilla. The following extracts also are taken from Browne's *Four Years in Secessia*.

"An age ago it seems, and yet the almanac tells me it was on the night of May 3d, 1863, since my confrère, Mr. Albert D. Richardson, and Mr. Richard T. Colburn of the *World* newspaper, with some thirty-two others, left the head-quarters of General Grant at Milliken's Bend, Louisiana, to run the batteries of Vicksburg, Warrenton, and Grand Gulf, where hostilities had already begun.

"I had tried to run the batteries of Vicksburg before; but circumstances interfered; and, as the Calvinists would say, I was preordained.

"The expedition,—consisting of a steam-tug, the Sturges, and two barges loaded with provisions and bales of hay,—was very badly fitted out; the hay lying loosely about, where any bursting shell might ignite it, and neither buckets, in the very probable event of a conflagration, nor small boats as a means of escape, having been provided.

"In addition to this, the moon was at its full, whereas the other battery-running expeditions had gone down on dark nights; and, about the time we reached the point of danger, was in the zenith of the heavens. The night was as light as day.

"As we sat smoking our cigars on the barges, we could see every tree on the banks of the mighty river; and as we neared the peninsula opposite Vicksburg, we could observe the different streets and buildings of the city that had so long defied the combined power of our army and navy.

"An officer with us had a bottle of Catawba, and as there was some probability that, in the storm of shot and shell which awaited us, its flavor might be damaged, we quaffed its contents to the speedy downfall of the hostile stronghold, and the early suppression of the Rebellion; to the women we loved—dwellers in the region of the Infinite—and to the consolation of the unfortunately married—surely a generous sentiment in favor of an ample class.

"Ours was indeed a merry party; and long shall I remember the agreeableness of the occasion before Rebel gunpowder interfered with its harmony.

"We smoked, and laughed, and jested, and chatted, saying if that was to be our last appearance on any (earthly) stage, that we would remember it with pleasure when we obtained a new engagement—on some celestial newspaper.

"There seemed no anxiety among our little band.

"They had all volunteered, and were desirous of an adventure, which they had in extenso.

"As we neared the hostile stronghold, we lighted fresh cigars; destroyed our private correspondence; settled our affairs, in the event of accident, after the Bohemian fashion; and would have commended our souls to our creditors, if we had known we had any—i. e., either the one or the other—and our bodies to the classic process of incremation.

"The incremation process was a flight of romance. We knew, if lost in the Mississippi, we would furnish cold collations for catfish.

"About midnight, or a little after, we were within a mile and a half of Vicksburg by the bend of the river, but not more than a quarter of that distance in a direct line, and directly in range of the heavy batteries planted for several miles above, below, and in front of the town.

"We were moving very little faster than the current of the stream; and as we began to round the peninsula, the trees on which had all been cut down, to give the enemy an open space for the operation of his guns against approaching vessels, the Rebel pickets, who had most needlessly and very unwisely been permitted to cross the river and take possession on the Louisiana shore, gave the alarm by discharging their muskets at us—without detriment, however—followed by a signal-rocket from the city, and the opening of the fiery entertainment to which we had invited ourselves on that bright, soft, delicious night of May.

"Now the heavy guns opened with their thunderous roar, and the first struck one of the barges, as we knew from the jar of the boat. 'Well done for the Rebels,' said we, admiring accuracy of aim even in our foes.

"The truth was, the insurgents had, from various causes, never had a fair opportunity on the previous expeditions. The night had been dark; the artillerymen had not been on the alert; the guns had not been well trained; the fuses had been defective.

"That time, as we subsequently learned, the Rebels were well prepared. They had, from past experience, obtained the exact range, and felt confident of blowing any craft that made the venture out of the water. Certainly they had made a good beginning. . . .

"The round-shot howled, and the shells shrieked over our heads, and sometimes cut the straw of the hay-bales in a manner calculated to give any one not entirely *blasé* something of a sensation.

"We tried to count the shots, but they were so rapid as to defy our power of enumeration. I had witnessed a number of heavy bombardments during the War, but had hardly known more gunpowder to be burnt in the same space of time.

"All along the shore we saw the flashes of the guns.

"The fire seemed to leap out of the strong earthworks for at least a mile, and the bright and quiet stars appeared to tremble before the bellowing of the scores of batteries.

"Clouds of smoke arose along the river like a dense fog, and the water and the atmosphere shook with reverberations.

"Opposite Vicksburg the Mississippi is narrow and deep, and at the same time was rather low, so that at times we were not more than three or four hundred yards from the ten-inch guns.

"It did seem strange our frail vessels, which were struck again and again, were not blown to pieces. But the little tug—semi-occasionally we heard its quick, sharp puff—passed on and we were yet unharmed.

"We had now passed the bend of the river just above the city, where a sand-bar, on which we had been told we would probably strike and ground, was plainly visible, and the greatest danger was over.

"Still we moved on, and the Rebels, as if disappointed and enraged, seemed to augment their efforts.

"Faster and heavier the batteries thundered, and louder howled the shot and shrieked the shell above, below, around.

"Again and again the shells burst over head, and the iron fragments fell about the little crew; but no groans nor cries were heard. We seemed fated to run the gantlet in safety,—to go beyond the power of harm.

"For three-quarters of an hour we were under the terrible fire, and were near the lower end of the city.

"Another quarter would put us out of danger, for we had passed the heaviest batteries.

"Still the guns opposite, from above and below, belched forth their iron messengers of death; and the stars blinked, and the waters shook, and the sulphurous mist crept like a troop of phantoms along the turbid river.

"Every moment we thought a shot might wreck our expedition; but in the occasional pause of the artillery, as I have said before, we could detect the rapid puff, puff, puff of the little tug, which was the sure sign that we still floated.

"Suddenly a huge crash by our side, of wood and iron. A deep and heavy and peculiar report. A rush of steam, and a descending shower of cinders and ashes that covered our persons.

"We heard the puff of the tug no more; but in its place went up a wild yell which we had often heard in the front of battle—shrill, exultant, savage; so different from the deep, manly, generous shout of the Union soldiers, that we knew at once it was the triumphant acclamation of our cruel foe.

"The boiler of the tug had been exploded by a plunging shot from one of the upper batteries. The shot was accidental, but extremely effective. It wrecked our expedition at once. After passing through the boiler, the shell exploded in the furnaces, throwing the fires upon the barges and igniting the loose hay immediately.

"'The play is over,' said Richardson; 'Hand in your checks, boys,' exclaimed Colburn; 'A change of base for the Bohemians,' remarked the undersigned; and we glanced around, and heard the groans and sharp cries of the wounded and the scalded.

"We rushed forward to try and trample out the flames, but they rose behind us like fiery serpents, and paled the full-orbed moon, and lit up the dark waters of the Stygian river far and near.

"The Rebels, who had ceased firing for a moment, now bent themselves to their guns once more, and the iron missiles swept over and around us, and several of the soldiers on board were wounded by fragments of bursting shells.

"Every one was now bent on saving himself. A few of the privates and some of tug's crew plunged madly overboard, with fragments of the wreck in their hands, and in three minutes none but the wounded and the journalistic trio remained on the burning barges.

"We threw the bales of hay into the river for the benefit of the wounded and those who could not swim—for we had early learned Leander's art—and then arranged our own programme.

"Richardson went off first on a bale of hay, from which a large round-shot, passing near, and dashing a column of spray into the air just beyond him, soon displaced his corporeality.

"Colburn followed; and I, seeing my field of operations hemmed in by rapidly advancing fire, answered his summons, and dived, after divesting myself of all superfluous clothing, into the aqueous embrace of the Father of Waters.

"Several bales of hay were floating below, but I swam to the one nearest Colburn, and there we concluded to get beyond the town and pickets, and then, striking out for the Louisiana shore, make our way as best we could back to the army.

"The Rebels had then ceased firing—certainly not for humanity's sake, we thought—and the reason was patent when we heard the sound of row-locks across the water.

"The . . . were evidently coming to capture us.

"My companion and myself believed if we kept very quiet, and floated with our faces only out of the water, we would not be discovered.

"A yawl full of armed men passed near us, and we fancied we would escape. Like the so-called 'Confederacy,' we wanted to be let alone.

"Just as we were internally congratulating ourselves, a small boat darted around the corner of the burning barge, and we were hauled in by a couple of stalwart fellows, after the manner of colossal catfish, without even the asking of our leave.

"In fifteen minutes we were under guard on shore, where we found our collaborateur Richardson safe and sound.

"About half our small crew had been killed and wounded, and the rest were prisoners.

"More unlucky than the defenders of Thermopylae—one of them reached Sparta to bear the tidings—not one of us returned to tell the story.

"'We were all reported lost, we learned afterwards; though General Sherman's humorous comment, when apprised that three of the Bohemians had been killed— 'That's good! We'll have dispatches now from hell before breakfast'—did not prove a veracious prediction.

"The gifted General's mistake arose from his confused topography.

"The army correspondents do not usually date their dispatches at his head-quarters.

"The Bohemians lost all their baggage; and I, having prepared myself for Byronic exercise, went ashore with nothing on but shirt and pantaloons.

"Barefooted was I also, and I appeared most forlorn as I walked in company with the others through the moonlit streets of the town.

"A sudden metamorphosis was ours, from freedom to captivity; and we discovered by crossing the river we had reached another phase of civilization.

"We prisoners formed a sad and droll procession, as we moved across the bayou towards the town.

"A number of the captives were either wounded with fragments of shell or scalded by the steam, and groaned and wailed piteously as we walked along; while others, barefooted, bareheaded, coatless, and begrimed with cinders and ashes, looked like Charon's ferrymen on a strike for higher wages.

"The author bore a close resemblance to old Time without his scythe, endeavoring to rejuvenate himself by hydropathic treatment.

"All of us, save the poor fellows who had been wounded and scalded, were in the best of spirits; and we marched merrily through the streets, chatting and laughing at our mishap—which proved a farce, so far as we the unhurt were concerned, for it was an escaped tragedy—and gayly speculating upon what would be the next turn of Fortune.

"The night was exceedingly lovely; and the moon poured down its tranquil radiance, and the soft May breezes kissed our brow and cheek, while we moved through the Rebel town closely guarded, as if they pitied our condition, and would have consoled us for our ill-starred fate."

Despite their noncombatant status the reporters soon found themselves held as prisoners of war in durance vile—very vile according to Browne. Because of the intensely anti-Southern policy of the *New-York Tribune*, its correspondents met with the greatest harshness; they were allowed neither release, exchange, nor parole —nothing but confinement "for duration." Browne spent more than a year and a half in Southern prisons. The first was infamous

Libby, where the captured officers of the U. S. S. *Indianola* put in an appearance while our chronicler was there. Then followed "Castle Thunder," another converted tobacco warehouse in the Confederate capital. Finally the Penitentiary at Salisbury, North Carolina. In December, 1864, Browne and several companions effected their escape after many abortive attempts. They finally reached the Union lines after a thrilling journey through the enemy's country, their hardships greatly increased by the rains and bitter cold of winter. This jaunt of four hundred miles required twenty-six days and, together with their prison life, provided material for as gripping a narrative as any of their war experiences. But that is no part of the story about the fighting on the rivers.

CHAPTER XVI

GUNS ON THE SUWANEE RIVER

Ouise phase of the sea warfare has not yet been touched upon. That was the small-scale, short-range blockade-running and its suppression. The proximity of Cuba and the Bahamas to the Confederate coast offered suitable neutral ports to which goods could be run in and out through the blockade by quite small vessels. Especially did the very lengthy coast line of Florida provide innumerable small rivers and bayous close enough to Havana and Nassau to form particularly suitable termini for blockade-running expeditions. No one of these ventures by itself was of appreciable size or importance; all put together, however, they would have constituted an appreciable factor in the South's wartime economy if they had not been checked. The principal exports from these Florida "ports" were cotton and turpentine.

Of course, the chief means of breaking up this practice of small-scale blockade-running was the same as that used against the larger vessels, i. e., incessant patrol of all parts of the coast not yet in Federal hands. However, there was one spectacular alternative that was often possible, and that consisted of "cutting out" a steamer or sailing vessel known to be moored in harbor or stream not out of reach of the blockaders. One of these cutting-out expeditions will be recounted in the following pages by Edward Shippen, a Union naval officer, who tells his tale in *Thirty Years at Sea,* published by J. B. Lippincott & Co. Contiguous chapters in his book make it virtually certain that the stream described in the story is the "Suwanee River" itself, which empties into the Gulf of Mexico just a short way down the great peninsula of Florida.

As the story opens, the gunboat of which Shippen was executive officer was lying at Key West; she was there for supplies and repairs after a tour of blockade duty. She was ordered to proceed from Key West and relieve another blockading vessel whose station was in the neighborhood of Cedar Keys, just below the mouth of the Suwanee.

"The first thing we heard from the barque we relieved was that a refugee had reported a small paddle-wheel steamer lying about six or seven miles up one of the rivers, loaded with cotton, and waiting a chance to run out.

"The same man had also indicated the position of quite extensive salt-works about thirty miles higher up the coast, where they were boiling, day and night, and making nearly two hundred bushels of this necessary article every twenty-four hours.

"We determined to look after the steamer first, and then to pay attention to the salt-works, and for this purpose we devoted the day to a careful preparation of our boats.

"One of the remarkable things about this wonderful and interesting west coast of Florida is, that there is only one ebb and one flow of tide in the twenty-four hours, and on the night of our intended expedition the flood would not serve us until after midnight.

"In the mean time, to lull suspicion of any boat expedition in case we were watched from the keys, we sent the smaller boats to fish, and kept a few men aloft, pretending to work at overhauling the rigging; but the greater number were busy as bees inboard.

"Our boats returned at dinner-time with more fish than we could use, for this is a paradise for fishermen. Sheep's-head, red-fish, sea-trout and grouper, pompano, cavalli, mullet, and hog-fish, besides many other kinds, filled the bottom of the boats with their beautiful and varied colors. A splendid drum-fish occupied the place of honor in the stern-sheets of the dingey, which boat had also visited an isolated key beyond gun-shot of any over-watchful 'home-guard,' and brought quantities of fine oysters.

"We had two or three large turtle already on board, but a week or two at Key West causes turtle-soup and turtle-steak to pall, and our people much preferred the fish. Having got our launch and first cutter all ready, the crews told off, oars muffled, and arms and ammunition supplied, we got under way just before sunset, and stood slowly down the coast, as if shifting station for the night. But as soon as darkness came on we retraced our course under low steam and with all lights concealed, until we took up our anchorage of the morning. We were about two miles from the mainland; but, as it was now very calm and still, we used all precaution to prevent noise as we lowered and manned our boats, putting the howitzer in the launch. Finally all was ready, and the time having arrived, I shoved off with twenty-two men and officers, some of whom were engineers and firemen. The tide was making, and we pulled cautiously in, grounding lightly two or three times from getting out of the channel, but the rising water soon took us off again.

"When we got across the bar and inside the keys, we could make out the gap in the dense foliage, caused by the creek, or rather river, which we were in search of. Entering this, we pulled steadily but quietly for nearly an hour, when I thought we must be near the spot where we should find the steamer.

"I now ordered the men to lie on their oars, and allowed the boats to drift quietly up with the tide. The river was narrow but deep, and in some places the huge trees seemed almost to meet over the water, the darkness in such places being intense, and our only guide the sky-line above, which looked quite bright in comparison.

"Occasionally an alligator would bellow or slide off the bank into the water, startling us at first and causing locks to be cocked, until we found out what it was. Great horned-owls laughed and hooted as they sailed up the river in advance of us, while night-herons took flight from the shallows at the bends as we disturbed them, the flapping of their huge wings causing a strange, low, mysterious echo from the banks. Occasionally the howl of a wolf would be heard far away, answered nearer by the shriek and wail of a panther or wild-cat. Birds of various kinds, which were roosting in the trees, aware that something strange was passing, chattered and moved upon their perches, rustling the leaves, as though a breeze was stirring. Altogether it was as 'spooky' a time as I ever passed.

"At last the river widened again, and we saw the dim outline of the steamer we were in search of.

"She was lying at a little wharf, around which was a clearing of a few acres. A small barn, or store-house, stood close to the wharf, and we could see the sky through a break in the woods, caused by the clearing for a road, which came in from the east.

"We had been told that there were thirteen people on board the steamer, several of whom were negroes; but that a company of 'home-guards' were at a little settlement about a mile off, some of whom were apt to be at the landing at night. I felt pretty confident, however, that I could manage the surprise with the force I had, even if the militia were there.

"Finding that our approach was unobserved by any sentry, I kept the boats under the bank, holding on by the mangrove-bushes, and then enjoining absolute silence, allowed the men to get something to eat, and look to their arms.

"Just as daylight was beginning to make things visible I gave the order, and we made a dash for the vessel, boarding her on each bow, as she lay with her head down-stream.

"Just before we reached her a man came out of the store-house in his shirt-sleeves and without a hat, apparently just awaking from his night's sleep. Seeing us, he gave a tremendous yell to alarm those on board the vessel, and then broke for the woods with most surprising speed.

"Tumbling on board, some of the men, according to instructions, closed and secured the forecastle-hatch, just in time to prevent the hands from coming up, some of them being actually on the ladder. At the same moment four or five men came out of the deck-cabin and commenced firing at us along the gangways left by piling the cotton-bales on deck.

"I felt my forehead grazed by a ball, which cut the skin and caused the blood to flow into my eyes so profusely that I was blinded by it for a few minutes. I got out my handkerchief, and, binding up the wound, was soon able to see the state of affairs. I found that we had possession of the vessel. One of our opponents, a man with a long black beard, had been shot dead, upon which the four others leaped over the rail and on to the wharf, whence they ran for the woods, at least two of them being badly wounded. Two of our men were hurt by buckshot, but no one was killed on our side.

"I knew very well that there was no time to lose, not only on account of the tide, but because the militia at the settlement would soon be down upon us, being roused by the man who had first discovered us, and who had gone off like a deer. I therefore ordered the dead man to be laid on the wharf, and the howitzer and the slide to be got out of the launch and mounted on the hurricane-deck of the prize.

"The engineers and firemen were directed at once to look to getting steam on the vessel, and I ordered the fasts to be cast off and the boats to go ahead and tow. We had allowed the prisoners to come up from the forecastle one by one, and found that they were all negroes, firemen and deck-hands, much frightened, but docile enough. I set them at work, telling them they would be free as soon as we got out of the river. They told us that the man with the long beard who was killed was the captain, and that the white men who had escaped were the mate and engineers.

"The boilers were found all pumped up, and the furnaces crammed full of pine-wood all ready to light, so there was every probability of having steam within an hour. As I found the tide was still flood, and that the boats could do little in the way of towing, while the crews were much exposed, I called them alongside, and secured them well under the guards, dropping the anchor which was ready at the bows.

"Of course I was very anxious, and kept a bright lookout for any signs of the militia. We hastily arranged some cotton-bales about the pilot-house, leaving chinks to see out of, and placed others along the guards to make bulwarks for our small-arm men.

"This was all arranged, and the men stationed under cover, when I heard sounds of axes, chopping at trees below us, at the narrow part of the river.

"I knew at once what this meant. Our friends were felling trees to obstruct the narrow passage, and if they succeeded in doing this, our capture or death was only a question of time. Meantime, we could not see a soul on shore, and could hear nothing but the sound of the axes.

"The next few minutes seemed to me very long, but in a little time the steam began to blow from the escape-pipe, and I have never heard a more welcome sound. The engineer now reported that he would turn his wheels and then be ready to go ahead, but I restrained my impatience for a few moments longer until the steam had reached a good head, and then gave the order to slip the chain, and for every one to shelter himself.

"I went into the pilot-house with two good men, and away we went down-stream. As we came in sight of the narrow part, I saw that one tall cottonwood was already down on the left bank, its branches reaching much more than half-way across the narrow stream, while two stout fellows were slashing away at another on the opposite side, which appeared already tottering to its fall. If it did fall before we passed, there was a slim chance for us.

"Seizing the pull, I rang four bells, 'go ahead strong!' and then waited breathless with suspense.

"As we got nearer, I hailed our men to fire at the choppers, which they did, causing one of them to throw up his hands and fall, while the other dodged behind another tree. Our fire was answered by a regular volley, every tree seeming to conceal a rifleman, but, thanks to our cotton-bales, no one was hurt, though there were a number of narrow escapes. One ball came through a chink into the pilot-house, and buried itself in the barrel of the wheel, and barely missed stranding the tiller-rope, on which so much depended. On we went, foaming down the river at full speed, keeping well to the right bank, and in a moment the light-draft steamer had passed over the bush of the tree, depressing it sufficiently to escape much damage to the buckets of her wheels. We had hardly got by when the swaying tree fell, amid the yells and curses of our disappointed opponents, who now came out from cover and began to pepper away at us as fast as they could load. As soon as we were somewhat out of reach of their small arms I left the pilot-house, and, training the howitzer upon them, fired into the midst of the group with shrapnel. This caused great commotion and scattering, but I could not tell how much damage, for we now turned a bend in the stream, and, as we had more narrow places to pass, I did not think it prudent to delay.

"We had no more interruptions, however, and within an hour were at the mouth of the river. Bringing one of the negro deck-hands up, I made him pilot us over the bar, and we soon ran out to our ship, when I reported the steamer Suwanee prize to the United States steamer Eagle."

CHAPTER XVII

THE CRACKER LINE

VICKSBURG surrendered on the Fourth of July, 1863. This was twelve months after Farragut's fleet first steamed past the city, six months after the first abortive measures were taken against it, and two months after Grant was really able to start after his prize. Port Hudson surrendered a few days later, as soon as its commander learned of Vicksburg's fall. Thus, complete control of every mile of the Mississippi came into Federal hands and this control was never again challenged.

By a strange coincidence Lee was stopped at Gettysburg on the third of July. Thus within a span of less than twenty-four hours the South's dream of military victory was finally extinguished. Its two remaining hopes for independence now rested respectively upon the possibility of war-weariness in the North, and intervention by some strong European power. The chances of this latter were immeasurably reduced by these very same Federal victories at Vicksburg and Gettysburg.

After Grant captured Vicksburg he sent Sherman against Johnston, and the latter was again defeated at Jackson, Mississippi. This opened the way to Mobile, the next logical objective. Halleck at Washington, however, could not be persuaded. Instead, Grant's splendid veteran army was broken up for various minor operations —exactly the same thing that had happened the year before after the victories at Shiloh and Corinth.

But to go back a little. The southerly advance of the National armies from Tennessee into Alabama and Georgia had been held up more or less awaiting the consummation of the Vicksburg campaign. The Union general, William S. Rosecrans, at Murfreesboro, Tennessee, was faced by Braxton Bragg. When the latter began to detach parts of his army to assist the opponents of Grant, the latter urged Rosecrans with the utmost insistence to take the initiative. He could not be budged. Finally, *after* the fall of Vicksburg, Rosecrans did advance. He pushed on across the Tennessee River to Chattanooga and then beyond, while Bragg was getting his detachments back from Mississippi. Rosecrans finally got himself into a sufficiently unfavorable position, and Bragg finally became sufficiently strong numerically; whereupon the latter attacked at Chickamauga where Rosecrans absorbed a very fancy thrashing and was driven back into Chattanooga. In Rosecrans' army, General George H. Thomas alone came off well. A good defensive fighter, he there achieved the sobriquet of the "Rock of Chickamauga." This battle was fought on September 19 and 20, 1863.

Not only was the Union army driven back a number of miles but it was forced into an almost untenable position. Supplies could be obtained only from Nashville. This in itself would not have been a serious matter except for one very important fact. The Nashville railroad struck the Tennessee River at Bridgeport, Alabama, twenty-six miles by rail below Chattanooga, and from there into the city it was another matter. The Confederates now after their victory dominated this whole area of supply lines consisting of railroad, river, and the shortest and best wagon roads. The supplies for every soldier and civilian in Chattanooga had to be unloaded at Bridgeport and hauled over the mountains to Chattanooga along sixty miles of almost impassable mud roads. The army was simply being starved out. It faced the alternative of surrender or else a retreat which would probably at least destroy the effectiveness of the troops for a long time to come. Nearly ten thousand beasts had starved to death and scarcely a draft animal remained. The men had been on half rations of hard bread and little else for a considerable time. Beef that had been driven cross country from Nashville arrived in such condition that the soldiers called it "beef dried on the hoof." Fuel within the Federal lines was exhausted, even to the stumps of trees. The limited means of supply had to be given over wholly to the transport of food. The army did not have enough ammunition for one day of fighting. It was running short of shoes and clothing, and the weather was becoming severe. Rosecrans was virtually besieged by the force confronting him; he was doing little to improve matters and was giving serious consideration to the idea of retreat.

Into this desperate situation Grant was dragged out of the hospital where he was recuperating from a painful and incapacitating leg injury. In mid-October he was placed in command of a newly formed Military Division of the Mississippi which comprised virtually everything in the West including primarily the Chattanooga mess. The first thing he did was to replace Rosecrans with Thomas; he ordered the latter to hang on at all costs. Thomas replied, "We will hold the town till we starve." It now behooved Grant to see that they did not starve.

The key to the situation was the line of supply from Bridgeport to Chattanooga. Grant undertook to move against the enemy and clear him out of the positions which denied to the Union army the use of the vital stretches of railway, river, and roads. For this purpose Grant at least had strong forces available; these had been forwarded to reinforce Rosecrans but had been kept out of Chattanooga in order not to aggravate the supply problem.

There was not a single steamer in the possession of the Federals for use on this stretch of river. Muscle Shoals prevented the ascent of any gunboats or other craft from below. Early in October, however, a start had been made on the construction of a steamboat. A sawmill was built to supply the planks for that and other projects; her engine was taken from a neighboring factory. It was hoped that the river might later be freed from enemy threat. If worse came to worst, perhaps the enemy's guns might be passed at night; the river was not so completely in his possession or under his fire as were the railway and some of the roads. Kelly's Ferry was the real river objective rather than Chattanooga itself. It was an easy eight-mile land haul from Kelly's to the city. This eliminated double the length of river where the current was so swift that no steamboat engine could prevail against it without the help of ropes hauled upon from the banks.

Lieutenant Colonel William G. Le Duc was among the Union reinforcements from Virginia which reached Bridgeport on October 3, and which for the time being went no farther. In *Battles and Leaders of the Civil War,* Volume III, he tells the story of the little steamboat mentioned above. The title of Le Duc's yarn will not be given until the end of this chapter because it tells "how the story comes out." In reading the following pages it should be borne in mind that Grant's moves to clear the river valley began on October 26.

"At Bridgeport I found Captain Edwards, Assistant Quartermaster, from Detroit, preparing to build a steamboat to navigate the river, by mounting an engine, boiler, and stern-wheel on a flat-bottomed scow, to be used in carrying and towing up supplies. . . .

"I quote from my Diary:

"Oct. 5, 1863.—General Hooker was over yesterday . . . and examined the little scow. He appreciated the probable importance of the boat, and ordered me to take it in hand personally and see that work was crowded on it as fast as possible. . . . I turned my attention to the boat. Captain Edwards has employed a ship-builder from Lake Erie—Turner, an excellent mechanic, who has built lake vessels and steamers, but who is not so familiar with the construction of flat-bottomed, light-draught river steamers. He has a number of ship and other carpenters engaged, with some detailed men from our own troops, making an efficient force. Men who can be serviceable as rough carpenters are abundant; not so with calkers, who will soon be needed, I hope. The frame of the boat is set on blocks, and is only five or six feet above the present water of the river. This mountain stream must be subject to sudden floods, which may make trouble with the boat.

"Oct. 16.— . . . I found Turner, the master mechanic, in trouble with the hull of the little boat. The planking was nearly all on, and he was getting ready to calk and pitch her bottom when I went to Stevenson [Alabama]. The water had risen so rapidly that it was within sixteen or eighteen inches of her bottom planks when I returned, and Turner was loading her decks with pig-iron that the rebels had left near the bridge-head. He thought he would thus keep the hull down on the blocking, and after the waters went down would then go on and finish.

" 'But,' I said, 'Turner, if the planking gets wet, you cannot calk and pitch until it dries.' 'That's true; and it would take two weeks, and may be four, to dry her after she was submerged, and who knows how high it may rise and when it will abate?' 'Then, Turner, what's the use of weighing it down with pig-iron? Rosecrans's army depends on this little boat; he must have supplies before two weeks, or quit Chattanooga. Can't you cross-timber your blocks, and raise the hull faster than the water rises?' 'No; I've thought of that, and believe it would be useless to try it. Captain Edwards and I concluded the only thing we could do was to weigh it down with pig-iron, and try to hold it, but if the water rises very high it will be swept away, pig-iron and all!' . . . I went rapidly over to Edwards's tent . . . and found him in his bunk, overcome by constant work, anxiety, and despair. . . . In answer to my question if nothing better could be done than weigh the hull down with pig-iron he said, 'No; I've done all I can. I don't know what the water wants to rise for here. It never rose this way where I was brought up, and they're expecting this boat to be done inside of two weeks, or they will have to fall back!' I turned from his tent, and stood perplexed, staring vacantly toward the pontoon-bridge. I saw a number of extra pontoons tied to the shore—flat-bottomed boats, 10 to 12 feet wide and 30 feet long, the sides 18 inches high. I counted them, and then started double-quick for the boat-yard, hallooing to Turner, 'Throw off that iron, quick! Detail me three carpenters; one to bore with a two-and-a-half or three-inch auger, and two to make plugs to fill the holes. Send some laborers into all the camps to bring every bucket, and find some careful men who are not afraid to go under the boat and knock out blocks as fast as I bring them down a pontoon.' "

These pontoons presumably were longer than the breadth of the steamboat. It would seem that the proposed procedure was as follows: bore a hole in one end of each pontoon near the bottom; admit water until the top of the pontoon is slightly lower than the bottom of the steamboat; plug the hole; knock out enough blocks from under the boat to make room for the pontoon; run the pontoon under the boat thwartships; bale out the pontoon at the projecting ends until the top of the pontoon rises and meets the bottom of the boat; when all the pontoons are thus placed, bale all the rest of the water out of them; the added buoyancy thus given to the pontoons will cause them to lift the boat off of the remaining blocks upon which she is resting. Thus finally the steamer's hull will be entirely supported on the floating pontoons.

Returning now to Le Duc's diary:

"Turner who had been standing silent and amazed at my excitement and rapid orders, exclaimed, with a sudden burst of conviction, 'That's it! That's it! That'll do! Hurrah! We'll save her yet. Come here with me under the boat, and help knock out a row of blocks.' And he jumped into the water up to his arm-pits, leaving me to execute my own orders. The pontoons were dropped down the river, the holes were bored in the end allowing them partly to fill, and they were then pulled under the boat as fast as the blocks were out. The holes were then plugged, and water was dipped until they began to lift up on the bottom of the hull, and when all were under that were necessary, then rapid work was resumed with the buckets, till by 2 o'clock in the morning she was safely riding on the top of the rising waters. They are now calking and pitching her as rapidly as possible, and fixing beams for wheel and engines; as many men are at work as can get around on her to do anything.

.   .   .   .

"22d.—General Grant and Quartermaster-General Meigs arrived on their way to the front with Hooker and staff. I accompanied them as far as Jasper. During the ride I gave Grant what information I had of the country, the streams, roads, the work being done and required to be done on the Jasper branch [railroad], also on the steamboat. He saw the impossibility of supplying by the dirt road, and approved the building of the Jasper branch, and extending it if practicable to Kelley's; also appreciated the importance of the little steamboat, which will be ready for launching to-morrow or Saturday. General Meigs . . . approved of the Jasper branch scheme and gave me a message ordering the iron forwarded at once.

"23d.—Steamboat ready to launch to-morrow. Railroad work progressing.

"24th.—Steamer launched safely.

"26th.—Work on boat progressing favorably; as many men are at work on her as can be employed.

"Extract from a letter dated Nov. 1st, 1863:

"I had urged forward the construction of the little steamer day and night, and started her with only a skeleton of a pilot-house, without waiting for a boiler-deck, which was put on afterward as she was being loaded. Her cabin is now being covered with canvas. . . . I loaded two . . . barges during the night, and started at 4 o'clock A. M. on the 30th for Kelley's Ferry, forty-five miles distant by river. The day was very stormy, with unfavorable head-winds. We made slow progress against the wind and the rapid current of this tortuous mountain stream. A hog-chain broke, and we floated down the stream while repairing it with help of block and tackle. I ordered the engineer to give only steam enough to overcome the current and keep crawling up, fearful of breaking some steam-pipe connection, or of starting a leak in the limber half-braced boat. Had another break, and again floated helplessly down while repairing; straightened up once more, and moved on again—barely moved up in some places where the current was unusually strong; and so we kept on, trembling and hoping, under the responsibility of landing safely this important cargo of rations. Night fell upon us—the darkest night possible—with a driving rain, in which, like a blind person, the little boat was feeling her way up an unknown river. Captain Edwards brought, as captain, a man named Davis, from Detroit, who used to be a mate on a Lake Erie vessel; but, as he was ignorant of river boats or navigation, could not steer, and knew nothing of wheel-house bells or signals, I could not trust him on this important first trip. The only soldier I could find who claimed any knowledge of the business of a river pilot was a man named Williams, who had steered on a steam-ferry running between Cincinnati and Covington. Him I put into the wheel-house, and as I had once owned a fourth interest in a steamboat, and fooled away considerable money and time with her, I had learned enough of the wheel to know which way to turn it, and of the bell-pulls to signal Stop, Back, and Go ahead. I went with Williams into the wheel-house, and put Davis on the bows, to keep a lookout. As the night grew dark, and finally black, Davis declared he could see nothing, and came back wringing his hands and saying we would 'surely be wrecked if we did not land and tie up.'

" 'There's a light ahead now, Davis, on the north shore.'

" 'Yes, and another on the south, I think.'

" 'One or both must be rebels' camp-fires.'

"We tried to keep the middle of the river, which is less than musket-shot across in any part. After a long struggle against wind and tide we got abreast of the first camp-fire, and saw the sentry pacing back and forward before it, and hailed:

" 'Halloo! there. What troops are those?'

"Back came the answer in unmistakable Southern patois: 'Ninth Tennessee. Run your old teakittle ashore here, and give us some hot whiskey.'

"The answer was not comforting. I knew of no Tennessee regiment in the Union service except one, or part of one, commanded by Colonel Stokes, and where that was I did not know. So we put the boat over to the other shore as fast as possible, and to gain time I called out:

"'Who's in command?'

"'Old Stokes, you bet.'

"'Never mind, Williams, keep her in the middle. We're all right. —How far to Kelley's Ferry?'

"'Rite over thar whar you see that fire. They're sittin' up for ye, I reckon.'

"'Steady, Williams. Keep around the bend and steer for the light.'

"And in due time we tied the steamboat and barges safely to shore, with 40,000 rations and 39,000 pounds of forage, within five miles of General Hooker's men, who had half a breakfast ration left in haversacks; and within eight or ten miles of Chattanooga, where four cakes of hard bread and a quarter pound of pork made a three days' ration. In Chattanooga there were but four boxes of hard bread left in the commissary warehouses on the morning of the 30th. About midnight I started an orderly to report to General Hooker the safe arrival of the rations. The orderly returned about sunrise, and reported that the news went through the camps faster than his horse, and the soldiers were jubilant, and cheering 'The Cracker line open. Full rations, boys! Three cheers for the Cracker line,' as if we had won another victory; and we had."

The title of the above is "The Little Steamboat That Opened the 'Cracker Line,'" and her name was *Chattanooga*. Her first trip to Kelly's was made only a few hours after the riverbanks had been seized by the Federal forces.

Grant proceeded to organize his lines and strengthen his army. A month later he attacked Bragg who had temporarily detached some units from his command, but who was still holding what was believed to be an impregnable position including Lookout Mountain and Missionary Ridge. The Battle of Chattanooga, however, was a smashing victory for the Union armies and opened the way for Sherman's advance to Atlanta the following season, and his march "from Atlanta to the Sea."

CHAPTER XVIII

THE RED RIVER VALLEY

WITH THE Mississippi River clear of the enemy from source to mouth the U. S. naval forces in those waters had no further important objective. One unimportant and very unfortunate objective was provided for them, however. All moves against Mobile Bay and the city of Mobile were still unwisely postponed; whereupon someone (Halleck?) thought of the idea of a very strong joint expedition up the Red River. This was to proceed all the way to Shreveport, Louisiana, and even into Texas. Not that there was anything of any military importance in this region. As has been pointed out earlier, the western part of the Confederacy could help to win the war only in so far as it could aid the eastern part. Since the Union forces had obtained absolute control of the Mississippi, all the aid that the West could now give was little more than zero.

It may as well be pointed out at once that there was a very unsavory odor attached to this Red River expedition. With all the existing evidence there can be little doubt that some prominent party or parties on the opposing sides were in cahoots with each other, the object being to sell Southern cotton through Northern civilian dealers. By such a procedure the Northern armed forces would be collecting Southern cotton for transport and sale; its owners would be reimbursed in due course, and the furtherance of the rebellion would thus be assisted. Ordinarily the Federal forces were not in a position to seize much cotton and carry it off for condemnation. When they did take any privately owned cotton or other valuable property the usual procedure was to give receipts for it payable after the close of hostilities. Confederate government property was of course seized outright or destroyed. Most of the suspicious-looking events which came to pass in connection with the Red River affair certainly appear to be part of the cotton-collecting plan.

Something, at any rate, brought about several moves which seem very peculiar from a military standpoint. Be it said to the credit of practically every rank and file on both sides, however, there was no pulling of punches when any fighting took place.

Having noted the evil-smelling auspices under which the expedition was launched, let us consider the events themselves. The attacking forces were properly given a wide enough margin of superiority over the enemy to ensure success. Porter was in command of the naval end of the affair, and his superiority was overwhelming in that the Confederate forces afloat were negligible and only one weak fort stood in his way. Since the early days of the first nine ironclads the National river flotillas had been augmented to a tremendous extent numerically. There was not a great increase in the total number of heavily armored gunboats; there was no need for a huge fleet of that type. There were all kinds of other armed vessels now in commission, however. The biggest need that had been filled in the past year was that of shallow-draft gunboats. These of necessity, however, could carry no protection heavier than bullet-proof iron sheets. They were the famous "tinclads." Their speed and armament were all right but it was, of course, impossible for them to stand up, for instance, against field guns on the riverbank. The heavier ironclads were still very necessary against fortifications, and in fact against anything heavier than musketry.

Much of the land force was to move by water a good part of the distance up the Red River. Accordingly, there were numerous transports on hand, also supply vessels and other fleet auxiliaries. All the craft that had little or no permanent protection, improvised as well as they could with bales of cotton or hay. Thus the forces afloat ran the whole gamut of light-draft monitors, ironclads, "tinclads," "cotton-clads," and "hay-plated" vessels. Our old friends *Lexington, Carondelet,* and *Essex* were along.

Nathaniel P. Banks, an impressive dresser, was in command of the land force. Perhaps it would be most charitable to dismiss him with the statement that, after studying law, he had spent almost his entire prewar career in politics. If any of his performances on the Red River expedition may seem shady, such was probably not really the case; his mistakes more than likely were due solely to the fact that he was a very poor general. It would be surprising if a general with no previous military experience were anything but a poor general.

It is fairly certain that Porter included Banks in his thoughts when he penned the following poem in his *Incidents and Anecdotes.*

"Now all you old fellows who have studied the laws,
And who make a good living by quibbles and flaws,
Who ne'er had a gun or a sword in your paws,
Deceiving, whose trade is,
Old men and old ladies,
Don't mount heavy boots and a long 'yaller' sash,
Or expose your rich coat, or bright *sabretache,*
In battle or skirmish, or where there's a chance
Of a shot from a pistol or poke from a lance.
Be wise, stay at home, read Blackstone and Wheaton,
And study Coke's tactics, where you can not be beaten."

Fortunately for all concerned, the principal general under Banks this time was Porter's old friend A. J. Smith of Fort Hindman introduction ("be God!"). It was his force of 10,000 ragged but splendid troops that filled the transports which accompanied Porter's gunboats. They all left the Mississippi on March 12, 1864. The heaviest vessels could barely cross the bar at the mouth of the Red, an adequate warning of the low water that might be expected to plague them. However, the wise ones gave assurance that a rise would soon come.

The one obstacle between the Mississippi River and Alexandria was Fort De Russy. However, neither its ordnance nor all the obstacles set in the river below it, were a match for the force moving against it. The fort and its garrison were captured, and the entire flotilla pushed on to Alexandria. All of Smith's troops and all of the gunboats had arrived by March 18, the small Confederate army falling back before them. There was no sign of Banks who was already overdue on his overland march with the main body.

There was a shallow stretch in the river at Alexandria called the "Falls." Here again there was barely enough water to get the ironclads up. And the river was dropping. The worst feature now was the great delay. Finally Banks arrived, settled down, organized, and eventually moved to Grand Ecore and Natchitoches; the enemy again fell back without opposition. The movements were on the right or southwest bank of the river. Banks had 36,000 men including Smith's command, more than twice the number of Confederate troops in the vicinity. Nor does this figure include another Federal army under General Frederick Steele striking toward Shreveport from the northeast. Finally, on April 6, the van of the expedition left Natchitoches for Springfield Landing, *more than three full weeks after the occupation of Alexandria*. Only 2,500 troops were carried up by river, principally as guards for the ships of the train. A prodigious number of supply vessels had assembled by this time. The main body of the troops, instead of following the gunboats for mutual support, marched far from the river by a route diverging widely to the westward.

Porter reached Springfield Landing April 9 on time, exactly when Banks also was due. The gunboats were now within thirty miles of Shreveport. No sign of Banks. The commander of the troops and the Admiral went on a little scout, and they sighted some Confederate soldiers ducking around through the high grass. The two leaders deduced that Banks had been challanged and defeated. If the Confederates had been beaten or were still giving ground without battle, they would still be between the invading army and Shreveport. But if victorious, the next move of at least some of them would be toward the river against the other Federal force. Thus did the Admiral and the General reason, and they decided to move fast. A detachment of troops was landed with artillery. They advanced a distance, made a demonstration, were re-embarked, and the entire aquacade began a retreat downstream looking for the army.

Porter knew he was in for it. He had *nearly fifty vessels* to shepherd back to safety. He guessed that he would be attacked en route by an enemy now victorious and between him and the Union army. He figured that he might have to face captured Union guns among others. The river was tortuous and low. The fleet had not a pilot familiar with the changeable channel and shoals as they now existed. The story of this water-borne *katabasis* deserves a seagoing Xenophon to recount it. There was no chronicler of that caliber with the expedition, but we do have two or three eyewitness recorders of some outstanding incidents that came to pass. For instance, there was Lieutenant Commander Thomas O. Selfridge who was in command of the light-draft, stern-wheel monitor *Osage*. She was one of those queer-looking hybrids designed for special river service in this strange naval war. Like the original U. S. S. *Monitor*, she looked like a raft and mounted a single turret. A large house for the stern paddle also rose above the deck. In battle trim, little in addition was in evidence except the tall, thin smokestack. *She mounted two 11-inch guns and drew less than four feet of water!* Captain Selfridge describes one of the many attacks which the river force had to meet before getting entirely out of the Red more than a month after the start of the retreat. The following is taken from an unofficial letter to Porter, printed in Porter's *Naval History of the Civil War* (Sherman Publishing Company).

". . . You directed me (at that time in command of the light-draft monitor 'Osage') to bring up and protect the rear.

"The river was very low, and the swift current in the bends made the 'Osage' almost unmanageable while descending. For this reason, the next morning, April 12th, I lashed the transport 'Black Hawk' on my starboard quarter, and by her assistance made the descent successfully, till late in the afternoon, when we grounded on the point opposite Blair's plantation. Our bow was therefore pointed down stream, and our starboard broadside opposite the right bank, which was 20 feet high and 100 yards distant. The transports had necessarily passed down, as my position was in the rear. Seeing my situation, Bache, of the 'Lexington,' which had stopped near by, came on board. We had been for some time vainly trying to get the 'Osage' afloat, when the pilot of the 'Black Hawk,' who, from his elevated position, could see over the bank, reported a large force issuing from the woods, some two miles back. I ascended to the pilot-house, and from their being dressed in Federal overcoats thought they were our troops; but soon their movements —dismounting and picketing their horses—convinced me they were enemies. I accordingly descended, made all preparations for battle, and directed Bache to go below with the 'Lexington,' and take up an enfilading position.

"Then commenced one of the most curious fights of the war, 2,500 infantry against a gun-boat aground. The battery unlimbered some hundred yards below and abreast of the 'Lexington,' which opened upon it with her port broadside, while I sent a few raking shells from the 'Osage' in the same direction. Compelled to plant their guns close to the edge of the bank in order to reach us, on account of the low stage of the river, they could not long maintain the situation, and soon retired with the loss of one gun dismounted.

"By this time my attention was wholly directed to the attack upon my own vessel. The rebels came rapidly across the fields in column of regiments, so the pilot of the 'Black Hawk' reported, who alone, from his elevated position, could see beyond the bank. So rapid was the advance that this pilot, intent on watching them, stayed too long, and dared not leave the protection of the iron shields of the pilot-house, and so accurate was the fire, that after the fight no fewer than 60 bullet marks were counted upon the shield, behind which the poor fellow was hiding.

"I loaded our two 11-inch guns with canister, elevated just to clear the top of the right bank, and as the heads of the first line became visible, fired.

"One regiment would come up, deliver its fire, then fall back under cover, and another advance. It was necessary to carefully reserve our fire until the rebels were about to fire, or our shots would have gone over them to the rear, a condition of affairs which made gun-boat firing very inaccurate at a low stage of water.

"The fire of 2,500 rifles at point-blank range, mingled with the slow, sullen roar of our two great guns, was something indescribable. No transports of wood could have stood such a terrible fire; the few soldiers on the 'Black Hawk' sought refuge on the 'Osage,' while the frightened crew of the steamer stowed themselves in her hold. During the three-quarters of an hour that this singular combat lasted, I had expended every round of grape and canister, and was using shrapnel with fuses cut to 1", when the firing suddenly ceased, and the enemy drew off. During the latter part of the engagement I noticed an officer on a white horse, some 200 yards below the troops, and aiming one of our guns at him, when the smoke cleared away saw him no longer. I learned after, that the officer killed was their General Green. The rebel loss was reported at 700, while ours was only seven wounded. The destructiveness of the 'Osage's' fire, delivered at point-blank range, was much increased by an ingenious device by which I could personally aim the guns from the outside of the turret, and thus have a clear view of the field, which would have been impossible had I remained inside. The wood-work of the 'Black Hawk' and 'Osage' was so pitted with bullet holes, that

". . . we blew her up with fifty barrels of powder, after removing from her everything of value.

"So careful were the two pyrotechnists in charge of the explosion (Captain Phelps and myself) to see that the powder all exploded, that we came very near going up with the vessel. Phelps was in a boat near the bow, and I was in a boat but a very short distance off, and great pieces of the hull fell all around us.

"The Confederates, who had been constantly watching our movements and waiting their chance, had now assembled near this point some twelve hundred men, and took the opportunity to pay their compliments to us.

"The other small gun-boats were lying at the bank near by, not suspecting an attack, but still prepared for one, as was always the rule.

"The Confederates discharged their rifles and made a rush to carry the vessels by boarding, but met with such a warm reception that they were glad to retreat. The sailors followed them into the woods and succeeded in capturing a noncommissioned officer, who gave us all the information we wanted for a good mess of pork and beans.

"This information quickened our movements down the river, and we lost all appreciation of the scenery, so intent were we upon getting to Alexandria.

"It seems that the Confederates, having failed to make any impression on the troops under Franklin, had determined to fall back on the river and, if possible, capture *us;* and that a force of three thousand men with three companies of artillery was already posted at a point on the river below us, and, as our prisoner expressed it, would give us 'Glory, Hallelujah!' when we got there.

"The rebs in this quarter were a saucy and independent set of fellows, and the prospect of punishment didn't seem to make them a bit more respectful. I rather admired them for their independent spirit; they were foemen worthy of our steel, and can be relied on now to defend our country, if necessary, against the world combined.

"Their valor was equal to that of the Northern soldiers, and their endurance, I think, greater. Had they been the people of any other nation, our troops would have walked over them without much difficulty.

"When we left Grand Ecore, about five hundred negroes of both sexes and all ages took passage with us, anxious to reach 'the land of freedom.' When the Eastport was blown up I put them on board the two pump-boats, thinking that would be the safest place for them in case we were attacked, for I presumed the Confederate gunners would devote themselves to sinking the 'tinclads,' for so our light-draught gun-boats were called, having but one eighth of an inch of iron over their thin wooden sides. . . .

"I got the two pump-boats right astern of my vessel, with another 'tinclad' astern of the pump-boats, and the other two vessels bringing up the rear. My little flag-ship, the Cricket, had six twelve-pound boat-howitzers (smooth bores), and carried forty-eight officers and men. The other 'tinclads' had each about the same number, except the Juliet, which carried the Eastport's crew.

"One of the Cricket's guns was mounted on the upper deck forward to command the banks, and a crew of six men were kept stationed at it, ready to fire at anything hostile.

"We went along at a moderate pace to keep within supporting distance of each other. I was sitting on the upper deck reading, with one eye on the book and the other on the bushes, when I saw men's heads and sang out to the commanding officer, Gorringe, 'Give those fellows in the bushes a two-second shell!' A moment after the shell burst in the midst of the people on the bank.

" 'Give them another dose,' I said, when, to my astonishment, there came on board a shower of projectiles that fairly made the little Cricket stagger. Nineteen shells burst on board our vessel at the first volley. It was the gun battery of which our prisoner had told us. We were going along at this time about six knots an hour, and before we could fire another gun we were right under the battery and turning the point, presenting the Cricket's stern to the enemy. They gave us nine shells when we were not more than twenty yards distant from the bank, all of which burst inside of us, and as the vessel's stern was presented they poured in ten more shots, which raked us fore and aft.

"Then came the roar of three thousand muskets, which seemed to strike every spot in the vessel. Fortunately, her sides were musket-proof.

"The Cricket stopped. I had been expecting it. How, thought I, could all these shells go through a vessel without disabling the how badly we had defeated General Green's division, covering the ground with killed and wounded, and determined to get even with us; but they had not the satisfaction of stopping a single gun-boat, or even one of the transports which were so unwisely tacked on to the squadron.

"The Cricket had thirty-eight shells explode on her decks in less than four minutes; the Juliet almost as many. The other two 'tinclads' did not fare so badly.

"Most of the white men on board the pump-boats escaped.

"I had a relative on board the Cricket who had gone on the expedition 'to see sheol.' He was satisfied that what he had seen was next door to it, and he was willing to return to his post.

"As I came out of the engine-room I saw a contraband holding on to Mrs. Holmes's horse. 'Why, Bob,' I said, 'you are a bigger coward than that horse; you are frightened to death, and ought to be ashamed of yourself.'

" 'No, Massa,' answered Bob, 'I ain't no coward. Dis nigger stan's by his colors to de las'. If you was half as frightened as dis chile you'd swim fo' de sho'. I've got what you call de moral courage, sar.'

"And so he had, and that sort of courage is better than physical bravery. I took Bob home with me after the war and made him my coachman."

(N. H.) "General Taylor told the Admiral, after the war, that he was present and in command on this occasion, and, besides three batteries of artillery, he had three thousand infantry pouring their fire into the vessels all the time. The Admiral reproached the General for his want of courtesy in shooting at him as he passed along the upper deck, but Taylor assured him that he ordered the firing to cease the moment he recognized the Admiral.

"If this was so, and amid all the noise and confusion, no one could pretend to recollect the exact circumstances of the case, the Admiral must attribute it to the chivalric feeling in General Taylor's breast towards one with whom he had been intimate in the days when the South did not dream of shedding Northern blood."

. . . .

"In August, 1884, I received a letter from Pilot Drening, whose cool bravery on this occasion deserves remembrance, yet a grateful country has so far withheld a pension to which he is clearly entitled. He must be upward of eighty years of age.

"GALENA, ILLINOIS, August 27, 1884.

"ADMIRAL PORTER, Washington, D. C.

"DEAR SIR: Your very kind letter is received, and with many thanks I wish you long life and happiness. Twenty years have passed since the battle, yet I remember each name of the killed, wounded, and living, and how by a miracle we were saved from such terrible firing to see the greatness of the country that our comrades died to save.

"Yours respectfully,
"T. G. DRENING.

.   .   .   .

"I do not mention our little incident as a battle, but simply to show the kind of experience to which the navy in the West was subjected, and the courage which the officers and men exhibited. It is one thing to be on the open ocean, able to see your enemy and know that you can give gun for gun in manly fashion, instead of being shot at from behind bushes and banks. Think of being pursued day after day by a party of bushwhackers watching from behind trees a chance to pick you off!

"One can hardly realize the danger to which the pilots and engineers of the squadron were exposed. I have seen a pilot receive a ball in his brain just as his hand touched the wheel. The pilots were targets for the enemy to shoot at, and he who could boast that he had killed one was a popular man.

"The pilots were mostly Western men by birth, but passing their lives on the Mississippi brought them into intimate relations with the Southern people, who looked upon all that were loyal to the Union as traitors to the Southern cause.

"I never knew one of these men to quail in the presence of danger, and when I have beheld them passing a battery with balls flying all about them, I have been struck with the coolness they displayed.

"I think there is a magnetism in a ship's wheel in time of action which is communicated to the helmsman. He feels that the lives of all are in his hands, and I never knew a pilot faithless to his trust."

reach the waters of the Mississippi in safety." He received the thanks of Congress; and by the officers of the Mississippi Squadron he was presented with a splendid sword and a purse of $3,000. Before he resigned at the end of the war he was made major general "for gallant and meritorious services in the campaign of Mobile, Ala." Later as sheriff of Newton County, Missouri, he became a nemesis to border ruffians. In 1867, while arresting two desperadoes, he was shot dead by one of them with a concealed pistol.

The gunboats suffered one unfortunate disaster during the period of construction of the dam. A steamer was loaded with soldiers and army-seized cotton, and dispatched to New Orleans. Porter furnished as escort the best gunboats available—two tinclads. About this time some Confederate forces had succeeded in slipping around and below the army at Alexandria. Some of them took station with field guns at a suitable bend of the river and attacked the Federal convoy as it descended. The steering gear of the cotton boat was damaged and she ran aground. The gunboats halted in an attempt to save her. In the ensuing fight all three vessels were lost, and the personnel casualties were heavy.

A very sad and appropriately shameful climax marked the end of the Red River expedition, When all the land and naval forces were ready to take their departure from Alexandria, the town caught fire from undetermined causes and burned to the ground. Little if any attempt was made to check the conflagration. The inhabitants who were either loyal, or at least friendly to the Union forces, were in an appreciable majority. All or them lost their homes and some of them lost everything. The departure of the Union fleet left this forlorn multitude on the riverbank; and in the crowd were many poor blacks who had been in expectation of sailing away from Alexandria in the Yankee steamers when they left.

Banks was shortly relieved of his command, whereupon he resigned from the Army and went back into politics.

CHAPTER XIX

THE ENCOMPASSMENT

THE ILL-FATED Red River venture was the last affair in the West of any consequence from a naval standpoint. At this juncture, therefore, it might be well to repeat in outline the grand strategy in this area as it developed, whether consciously or unconsciously; and to make it clearer, it should be remembered that the Red River expedition was a side show only. Finally, we shall view briefly the later episodes of the naval war which took place elsewhere.

The early activities of the Union gunboats on the Tennessee and Cumberland rivers against Forts Henry and Donelson were undertaken to provide assistance to the army which at that time was penetrating southward from the Ohio River into Kentucky and Tennessee. The National forces held both sides of these rivers; so, after the fall of Henry and Donelson, the chief mission of the Navy on the Tennessee and Cumberland consisted of patrol duties in limited force. The Mississippi River was another matter, however. As was pointed out on an earlier page the "opening of the Mississippi" was not for the purpose of enabling commerce to flow again from Northern states to the sea. The clearing of the enemy from its banks opened it as a highway over which might be carried troops and supplies for armies operating near it. Even this, however, was a secondary accomplishment. The most important result of the "opening" of the Mississippi was in fact the *closing* of its entire length to Confederate traffic *across* it; this prevented supplies from reaching the important eastern part of the Confederacy from its great western areas. Thus the Union gunboats *blockaded* the whole east bank of the Mississippi, and the water ring was completed from the Ohio River all the way around to the Potomac. Most of this last-completed link consisted of the hundreds of miles of river which bound the State of Mississippi on the west. Union armies were in general control of the territory east of the river, but well as submerged, but had all the necessary arrangements and apparatus required for submerged operation as we know it even today. However, since the boat lacked refinements in design, and her personnel lacked operating skill, she was a suicidal affair, to put it mildly. No less than five different times during early experiments or on practice runs, she went to the bottom; and there was a total of only three survivors of all five disasters. One of these three escaped twice. New volunteers were never wanting, however. Her scheme of torpedo attack was well conceived. She was to tow a floating mine (or "torpedo") astern of her on a long line, dive under the target ship, and then come to the surface on the other side; this procedure would cause the torpedo to be pulled against the side of the target and explode.

Crew No. 6 was enrolled and the latest commander proposed to attack the new screw sloop-of-war *Housatonic*. Because of the previous failures while operating submerged, permission was granted to make the attack only if carried out in *David* fashion, i. e., running on the surface with a torpedo projecting ahead of her on a spar. Accordingly, she operated this time not as a submarine but as a low-freeboard surface vessel. She ran her spar torpedo into the *Housatonic* and sank her all right, but the explosion sank the *Hunley* too, again with the loss of all hands. This time, owing to the location, she could not be raised again till after the war. The original scheme of submerged attack probably offered to her crew a better chance of survival than the method used. The *David* attack was made on the night of October 5, 1863, and the *Housatonic* was sunk by the *Hunley* on February 17, 1864.

After the "sub scare," most of the excitement on the East Coast for 1864 was furnished by the Confederate ironclad ram *Albemarle*. There were no Federal ironclads available that could navigate the waters of the North Carolina sounds. The inner blockade in that area had to be maintained by wooden gunboats. Consequently, when the *Albemarle* issued from the Roanoke River she created considerable consternation on the Sound whose name she bore. She and her wooden opponents engaged in two slashing battles, in April and in May, 1864. One Union gunboat was sunk in the first fight, but the *Albemarle* seems to have suffered enough injury in the second set-to to lay her up for a considerable period. The main point in the situation, however, was the great threat to the blockaders which the powerful Rebel vessel embodied. What counted was the damage she *might* do at any time. Her constant menace existed for months; it had begun before she was launched. Now she was awaiting the completion of a consort before venturing out again. Finally, one night late in October, the immortal Cushing attacked her at her moorings at Plymouth, North Carolina. Stealing up the river in a spar-torpedo boat, he rode over her protecting log boom and sank her. The explosion swamped his boat, but he and one other escaped capture by swimming and hiding, tramping and rowing. Only two lost their lives.

The three *Albemarle* episodes provide an epic saga all by themselves. It is unfortunate that space forbids their inclusion in this volume at greater length. The *Albemarle* was the only Confederate ironclad ram to go down fighting, except the little *Manassas* back in '62. And there were 28 of them altogether. Strangely enough—or maybe it was not just a coincidence—the same officer, Alexander F. Warley, was in command of both the *Albemarle* and *Manassas*. As for all the others—three or four not completed—anyone who has read the preceding chapters knows that, in the Confederate navy, there was no cowardice to which any ship losses can be charged. Nevertheless, it is a very noteworthy fact that 18 rams were destroyed by their own crews, 5 surrendered, 3 were lost by shipwreck, etc., while only the *Manassas* and *Albemarle* were destroyed by the enemy. Consideration of the several reasons for this peculiar fact makes an interesting study which, however, cannot be included here.

On August 5, 1864, Farragut took his battle fleet past the forts and mine fields at the entrance of Mobile Bay, and destroyed the small Confederate squadron inside—"Damn the torpedoes! Go ahead!" Two days later the fort on the west side of the entrance surrendered to the fleet. On the twenty-third the fort on the other side, the principal defense, surrendered after a joint land and sea attack. As soon as Farragut succeeded in obtaining possession of the Bay, the city of Mobile ceased to exist as a blockade-running port. The monitor *Tecumseh* was mined and sunk during the passage of the forts.

The war picked up momentum as 1864 drew to a close. Sherman was moving east after his capture of Atlanta. He took Savannah on